THE CATHOLIC CATECHISM

Bishop Donald W. Wuerl
Thomas Comerford Lawler
Ronald Lawler, O.F.M. Cap.

Our Sunday Visitor Publishing Division
Our Sunday Visitor, Inc.
Huntington, Indiana 46750

Nihil Obstat:
Rev. William M. Ogrodowski, STL
Censor Deputatus

Imprimatur:
✠Anthony J. Bevilacqua
September 27, 1985

International Standard Book Number: 0-87973-802-2
Library of Congress Catalog Card Number: 85-63061

Cover design by James E. McIlrath

PRINTED IN THE UNITED STATES OF AMERICA

Table of Contents

PART FOUR
IN CHRIST: FULFILLMENT OF ALL

APPENDIXES

ACKNOWLEDGMENTS

The Scripture quotations in this publication are from the *Revised Standard Version Bible, Catholic Edition,* © 1965 and 1966 by the Division of Christian Education of the National Council of the Churches of Christ in the U.S.A., and used by permission. Special permission has been received to use the you-your-yours forms of the personal pronouns in address to God, and to capitalize personal pronouns referring to God.

Quotations from the Constitutions, Decrees, and Declarations of the Second Vatican Council used in this book are from the translation, with some amendments, appearing in *The Documents of Vatican II,* Walter M. Abbott, S.J., General Editor. Reprinted with permission of America Press, Inc., 106 West 56th Street, New York, NY 10019. © 1966. All rights reserved.

Excerpts from the English translation of *Rite of Baptism for Children* © 1969, International Committee on English in the Liturgy, Inc. (ICEL); excerpts from the English translation of *Rite of Marriage* © 1969, ICEL; excerpts from the English translation of *The Roman Missal* © 1973, ICEL; excerpts from the English translation of *Rite of Penance* © 1974, ICEL; excerpts from the English translation of *Rite of Confirmation* (Second Edition) © 1975, ICEL; excerpts from the English translation of *Pastoral Care of the Sick: Rites of Anointing and Viaticum* © 1982, ICEL. All rights reserved.

Preface

Jesus once said to his disciples and through them to us, "If you live according to My teaching, you are truly My disciples; then you will know the truth, and the truth will set you free" (John 8.32).

Gradually those disciples who heard those words and looked on the face of Jesus died. But the truth of Jesus lives on. It lives on in His Church, which continues the work of Jesus and is the surviving witness to the truth that will make us free.

Generation to generation the saving message of Christ is passed on so that an increasing number of people can enter into the mystery of Christ's revelation and find in His light the life that will never end. But this light is available to us only because we have seen the truth. As St. Paul reminds us, "everyone who calls on the Name of the Lord will be saved" (Rom. 10.13). As he continues, "But how shall they call on Him in whom they have not believed? And how can they believe unless they have heard of Him?" (Rom. 11.14).

Catechesis is the effort of the Church to preach the Word of God to those who wish to grow more fully in their acceptance and understanding of the Word. *The Catholic Catechism* is a serious effort to provide those involved in the teaching of the faith with a useful, exact, faithful, contemporary yet perennial presentation of the Catholic faith.

The Catholic Catechism is a balanced account of the message of the faith, since catechesis "must take diligent care faithfully to present the entire treasure of the Christian message" (General Catholic Directory, No. 38). The completeness of *The Catholic Catechism* is of two kinds. There is a certain material completeness in that it covers each of the many points that a catechism should discuss. Completeness is found also in the way that each Mystery of the Faith is treated.

Its style is readable. It presents the ancient faith in today's terms and shows an awareness of the current problems facing the Church while attempting to respond with confident, clear answers. Perhaps its most telling characteristic is the style in which it is written that provides an inspiring overall view of the Catholic faith.

Nor does *The Catholic Catechism* hedge when it comes to issues that are not particularly popular today. The Catholic Church has always followed the Lord's injunction not to conform itself with this world. It is also true that the Church has experienced as did its founder the phenomenon of those who would no longer walk with us because the teaching was too

7

"hard." While neither acerbic nor harsh, *The Catholic Catechism* does not hesitate to present the full teaching of Christ.

Challenges abound today in the world of catechetics, yet the overriding norm for the transmission of the faith should be the desire to communicate the truth that will make all of us free. As an instrument that contributes to this effort, *The Catholic Catechism* can only be praised. It is a fine and insightful presentation of the Catholic Church's profession of faith in Christ, the light of the world.

Bernard Cardinal Law
Archbishop of Boston

Introduction

This is a Catholic catechism. In question-and-answer form it provides a brief but comprehensive account of Catholic faith and life.

This catechism is based on a longer account of Catholic faith which appears in *The Teaching of Christ, A Catholic Catechism for Adults*. That catechism, the cooperative work of many theologians and pastoral leaders, has been translated into many languages, and has been widely celebrated as a thoroughly reliable and balanced account of Catholic teachings, richly documented, entirely up-to-date, a warm and attractive presentation of the whole message of faith.

This small catechism seeks to guard all the essential merits of *The Teaching of Christ*. The smaller size and the question-and-answer format may make it more useful to many in giving instructions to inquirers, in catechizing those preparing for baptism, and in classes and study clubs.

In presenting the Catholic faith, a catechism recalls also the words of many witnesses to faith. In this book we cite often the words of Scripture, and those of the Second Vatican Council, in which the Church has spoken her faith forcefully to the present age. Many other witnesses to faith are recalled: the words of Church fathers and saints, the voices of the Councils of the Church, and the prayers of the Church at worship.

The brevity of this work requires that quotations from such witnesses to faith must be limited in it. However, this book follows carefully the order of *The Teaching of Christ*, and those who seek more references to Scripture and other sources of faith can find them easily in that book, together with more complete bibliography information.

A catechism is a book of faith. The Church has always believed that faith is a gift of God. But it is a gift offered to free and intelligent persons. When Jesus invited men to faith, He clearly respected their intelligence. His words were accompanied by signs of their truth, in the wisdom of His teaching, in the goodness of His life, in the power of the deeds He performed.

Today too the faith must be presented in ways that assist hearers to come intelligently and freely to a strong personal faith in Christ and His message. But Catholic faith has a rich community context as well. To find Catholic faith is to find the Lord teaching, shepherding, and sanctifying in the midst of His people.

The whole message of faith itself is a sign of its own truth. For when the words of faith are heard, and reflected on thoughtfully, they are grasped as an astonishingly profound answer to the deepest questions that the human heart asks.

Scripture speaks in many ways of the gift of faith. Faith brings one to a new life with a new way of knowing (cf. John 1). It gives vision: faith opens the eyes of one born blind (cf. John 9). God Himself opens the eyes of the heart (cf. Eph. 1.18) and brings one into the freedom of faith. No one can come to faith unless the Father draws him or her (cf. John 6.44). But those who are called by God draw near to faith and grow in it only freely.

Faith is so profound a gift that those who seek to receive it or grow in it would be wise to pursue it in a spirit of prayer and with hearts generously open to the voice of God. St. Paul rejoiced to see how those who heard the Good News he proclaimed came to faith, not in Paul, but in the Lord. "And we thank God constantly for this, that when you received the word of God which you heard from us, you accepted it not as the word of men but as what it really is, the word of God, which is at work in you believers" (1 Thess. 2.13).

"Make me know Your ways, O Lord; teach me Your paths. Lead me in Your truth, and teach me, for You are the God of my salvation; for You I wait all the day long" (Ps. 25.4-5).

Documents of the Second Vatican Council

AA   Decree on the Apostolate of the Laity *(Apostolicam Actuositatem)*

AG   Decree on the Missionary Activity of the Church *(Ad Gentes)*

CD   Decree on the Bishops' Pastoral Office in the Church *(Christus Dominus)*

DH   Declaration on Religious Freedom *(Dignitatis Humanae)*

DV   Dogmatic Constitution on Divine Revelation *(Dei Verbum)*

GE   Declaration on Christian Education *(Gravissimum Educationis)*

GS   Pastoral Constitution on the Church in the Modern World *(Gaudium et Spes)*

IM   Decree on the Instruments of Social Communication *(Inter Mirifica)*

LG   Dogmatic Constitution on the Church *(Lumen Gentium)*

NA   Declaration on the Relationship of the Church to Non-Christian Religions *(Nostra Aetate)*

OE   Decree on Eastern Catholic Churches *(Orientalium Ecclesiarum)*

OT   Decree on Priestly Formation *(Optatam Totius)*

PC   Decree on the Appropriate Renewal of Religious Life *(Perfectae Caritatis)*

PO   Decree on the Ministry and Life of Priests *(Presbyterorum Ordinis)*

SC   Constitution on the Sacred Liturgy *(Sacrosanctum Concilium)*

UR   Decree on Ecumenism *(Unitatis Redintegratio)*

Part One

The Invitation to Faith

CHAPTER 1

The Hope of Our Calling

Christ is our Teacher. "You call me Teacher and Lord; and you are right, for so I am" (John 13,13).

All that the Catholic faith teaches is Christ's answer to us in our search for the meaning of life and in our desire to lay hold of what the heart longs for. The message of Christ is a message of joy to a world in need of hope.

This chapter speaks of the goodness of the life to which Christ invites us. It shows how Christian hope is realized already in part in this world. Already Christ enables us to live a new life, a life supported by divine gifts, that we may care in love to make this world a presence of God's kingdom. It shows how the Christian life is essentially a life of hope, pointing confidently toward perfect fulfillment of the gifts God has already planted in our hearts. Finally, the chapter speaks of the central role of Christ in our hope and in our life.

1. Why is life so puzzling to us?

This life is mysterious because it contains so much that is excellent and stirs up hope in our hearts and also confronts us with profound tragedies. We find here much that is true and good and beautiful and much that proves radically disappointing. "Hope and joy, grief and anxiety" (GS 1) are strangely intermingled in this world, and we cannot help asking ourselves: Why do we exist? Who are we, and why do we live in a world like this?

2. Why is it important to learn what our life means?

We need to understand the meaning of our lives because the span of our years is limited. To live intelligently and well we must grasp in time what life is for and what it means.

Clearly it is not easy to come to intelligent confidence about matters that have puzzled even the most intelligent of people. Yet we need understanding to live our lives wisely and well.

3. Who teaches us the meaning of life?

Catholic faith teaches that God Himself, the Lord who created us and all things, has become for us a Teacher of life. In and through Jesus Christ, God is our Teacher, and we are set free from doubts and anxieties by the light of His word.

4. How could one know that Catholic faith is true?

One receives faith, with the certainty faith brings, only as a gift of God. Yet God gives this gift to us in ways that respect our humanity and all the needs of our intelligence and heart.

When Jesus invited people to faith in Himself, He clearly respected their intelligence. The good news He taught was accompanied by many signs of its truth: the words He spoke rang true and appealed to their intelligence; His own life and the life He called them to shone as very good; and the power of His deeds convinced them of God's powerful presence. Still, the intelligence and goodness and power of His message was not enough to quiet human anxiety. They longed for a certainty only God could give. He touched their hearts from within, and enabled them to share by God's grace in the light of God's own wisdom.

Thus Christ taught His disciples to pray for faith, and taught them that the certainty of faith was not merely the fruit of human insight into the signs that He gave, but the gift of the Father. When St. Peter came to faith in Christ, Jesus told him: "Blessed are you, Simon Bar-Jona! For flesh and blood has not revealed this to you, but My Father who is in heaven" (Matt. 16.17).

5. Are intelligence and freedom both important in coming to faith?

Yes. Faith is concerned with what is really true and really good. It answers questions that spring spontaneously to the minds of thoughtful people. The intelligent God wishes us to come to faith intelligently and responsibly. But we must come to faith freely as well. God by the free gift of His grace makes it possible to realize that it is He who speaks to us in Christ His Son; and we are invited to respond freely to the invitation of grace.

Catechetical instruction points out many of the signs by which God invites us to faith. It presents the message of Jesus Christ, urging us to experience how it rings true when we reflect thoughtfully upon all of what He has taught us. It urges us to taste how good is the life to which Christ calls us. It invites us to consider how mighty the word of Christ has been in human history: how even now it shapes a family of faith sealed with exceptional marks of its authenticity and goodness. It speaks to us of the ways God calls us to share in His own life by faith, hope, and love; it teaches us how we should respond if we wish to experience ourselves the richness of the life to which faith calls us.

6. What is faith?

Faith is a gift of God, enabling us to recognize His voice and to believe Him. In giving us faith, God gives us the light and the power to assent willingly and intelligently to what He teaches us.

16

7. Does coming to Catholic faith mean giving up the ordinary joys of human life?

No. The invitation to faith is a call to an excellent life now, and to an eternal hope. Crowds flocked after Christ, because they saw that He lived a perfect life, and that He enabled those who came to Him to live more richly. He invited those who heard Him to grasp more intensely what all persons desire: knowledge of the truth, confident hope that they would have what their hearts longed for, and an experience of divine love that transforms everything. He taught them how to love and enjoy basic human goods in the most human ways.

If Christ invited us to the generosity which bears crosses gladly, it was not because He wanted us to despise the good things God has made, but to guard the most fruitful pursuit of good as intelligent love calls us to. "The kingdom of heaven is like a treasure hidden in a field, which a man has found and covered up; then in his joy he goes and sells all that he has and buys that field" (Matt. 13.44).

8. Does faith seek a happiness greater than that which we can find in this life?

Yes. The life that God calls us to now in time is very good. The light of faith, the warmth of hope, and the peace of God's love transform the ordinary joys of life for those who have come to share the life Christ calls us to. But all these are incomplete forms of happiness, and of their nature call for a more perfect fulfillment. Faith longs for vision, hope hungers for satisfaction, and love that in this life patiently bears a multitude of frustrations, longs for the perfection it will have in eternal life when we shall love God and one another perfectly.

The eternal life we long for is not a life alien to this life, but it is the fulfillment of longings that we now experience.

9. Why were we not created in heaven?

In His mercy God made us not only to have happiness, but to have the overwhelming happiness of sharing His own joy and life forever. Moreover, He wills that we should come to this blessed life freely, of our own choice. God freely chose not to create us in heaven, but in the circumstances of a life of trial, that we might love Him more freely, and that He might graciously give us the dignity of even meriting to have life forever with Him.

10. Does hope for eternal life lead to contempt for this life and its problems?

No. The hope for eternal life leads to a greater love of this world, and to a more intense concern to make every good flourish in this world. God

17

calls us to live excellently in this life and to make this world as much as possible an image of His eternal kingdom. By living well in this life and by making this world flower in every kind of goodness, we are to become worthy of eternal life with Him.

11. Does faith offer simple answers to human questions?

The answers that faith gives to life are both complex and profoundly simple. Faith in no way denies the reality of evil in this world, nor the reality of complex problems that often hinder people from coming to faith. To come to God we must have both integrity of intellect and that simplicity and purity of heart that are always needed in the pursuit of truth.

12. Can eternal life be shared now in this life?

The gifts that Christ offers us to make this life on earth more rich and human are themselves the beginning of eternal life in us. He calls us to become more fully human by becoming children of God, sharing in His wisdom by faith, finding strength through hope in Him, and living generously by the experience of His love. But these divine gifts which transform life now are the beginnings of that life which we shall enjoy fully only in heaven.

13. Why is Christ central to a life of faith and of hope?

Christ is central to the life of faith because He is our God, and because He entered into human history by becoming a man like us. He chose to share the poverty and weakness of our lives that we might share the richness of His life. He became our Teacher and our Savior, to instruct us in the ways of life and to give us power to walk in them. He taught us God's love most of all by dying for us. In the power of His resurrection He has made it possible for us to live now in ways that promise eternal life. He Himself remains intimately present to us in His Church, teaching in all those who teach in the family of faith, touching us by His sacraments, shepherding us in the care He yet gives us to all His flock.

"I am the Way, and the Truth, and the Life; no one comes to the Father, but by Me" (John 14.6). Christ alone is sufficient. All that the Catholic Church teaches is Christ, who is the Way we must walk, the Truth that enlightens our path, and the Life for which we hunger.

Part Two

Through Christ:
Coming to Knowledge of God

CHAPTER 2

The Father of Our Lord Jesus Christ

God is. "Before the mountains were brought forth, or ever You had formed the earth and the world, from everlasting to everlasting You are God" (Ps. 90.2). All of creation gives testimony to God; all has reality only from Him.

"No one has ever seen God; the only Son, who is in the bosom of the Father, He has made Him known" (John 1.18). Christ reveals the Father in many ways. Christ is the "image of the invisible God" (Col. 1.15), and He makes the Father known by what He Himself is. In His words Christ declares the mystery of God, and by His saving works He makes it possible for men and women to have a living faith.

This chapter speaks of the mystery of God our Father, of God revealing Himself, and of the ways we come to know God. It points out how human reason can come to a knowledge of the existence of God, and how faith supplies for the limitations of reason. It then discusses the attributes of God, recalling what the infinite and infinitely perfect God has revealed Himself to be.

1. How do we come to know God?

God can be known in many ways, but most securely by His own revelation of Himself. For God wishes to be known by the creatures He has made, and He is able to make Himself known. "In His goodness and wisdom God chose to reveal Himself. . ." (DV 2).

Reason and the world bear witness to God, but the chief witness to God is God Himself.

2. How does God reveal Himself?

In the course of salvation history God has revealed Himself in many ways. In the days before Christ He caused prophets to speak of Himself and of His saving will, and He made it possible for His people to recognize that it was He who spoke in them. But most of all God revealed Himself when the eternal Son, truly God, became man and lived among us, that He Himself might teach us and lead us to faith in Himself.

3. What does it mean to know God by faith?

Faith is a gift of God that enables us to recognize that it is indeed He who has revealed Himself to us and has made known the saving plan that is taught in the family of faith. Through faith we come to believe God and to assent firmly to all that He has revealed.

The gentle assistance of grace is necessary for us to come to faith. But this faith is not an irrational leap. The Lord Himself gives outward signs and inner graces that we may intelligently and freely come to Him. God forces no one to acknowledge and believe in Him. But He makes an intelligent and responsible faith possible for those who seek the truth with earnest hearts. "For it is the God who said, 'Let light shine out of darkness,' who has shone in our hearts" (2 Cor. 4.6).

4. Do we naturally seek to know God?

Yes. In fact, our whole being was made in such a way that it needs the richness of God to fulfill it. "You have made us for Yourself, and our heart is restless until it rests in You" (St. Augustine).

5. Why do so many people fail to believe in God?

Atheism, a refusal or inability to believe in God, is an obvious reality today. The Church is deeply sensitive to the fact of atheism, and is aware that there are many different reasons for unbelief.

Some people reject faith in God because they do not want to admit the reality of One far superior to man. Others deny the reality of a good God by expressing "violent protest against the evil in the world" (GS 19), though not in the healing way in which Christ taught the saints to fight against evil. Others abandon all hope of knowing God because philosophical prejudices convince them that no absolute truth can be known or that human knowledge is limited to grasping material things. Many put their hearts elsewhere and never seriously consider the question of God; they are "choked by the cares and riches and pleasures of life, and their fruit does not mature" (Luke 8.14). Many are also pushed toward atheism by governments committed to atheism or by the unbelieving molders of cultures who in greed and lust have turned away from God.

6. Is it sinful to refuse to believe in God?

"Undoubtedly, those who willfully try to shut out God from their hearts and to avoid religious questions are not following the dictates of their consciences and hence they are not free of fault" (GS 19). But the extent of their willfulness is hard to assess. Those who do not know God are often victims of the sins of others as well, and "believers themselves often bear responsibility for this situation" (GS 19). Atheism can be a reaction to the base words, actions, and behavior of those who should be signs of the reality of God.

22

7. Can human reason of itself know that God is?

Yes. "God, the beginning and end of all things, can by the natural light of human reason be known with certainty from created things, 'for since the beginning of the world the invisible things of Him are perceived, being understood through the things which have been made' (Rom. 1.20)" (First Vatican Council).

One path that philosophers and others took toward finding God was a reflection on the causes of order and beauty in the universe. "For from the greatness and beauty of created things comes a corresponding perception of their Creator" (Wisd. 13.5).

The moral order of the universe led others to realize God's reality. Aware of their human duties to be just and truthful and temperate, many come to realize that the insistent call to goodness, which they hear in their conscience, in fact manifests the reality of One who rightfully demands goodness of them.

8. Have many come to know God's existence by reason?

Philosophers pointed out various paths by which one may come to know Him who is the source of all. The greatest thinkers have been able to demonstrate that this world, which bears clear marks of its own transiency and borrowed reality, must be caused to be by One who is the Author of time and of all passing things.

There is no reason to suppose that God did not assist with His grace those who sought Him with sincere hearts but who did not have any clear voices to bring them the gift of supernatural revelation.

9. Is knowledge of God by reason alone often obscure?

Yes. In everyday life emotions, pleasures and problems, the demands of work, and so on, tend to obscure the way to God by reason alone. It would be especially difficult to achieve a purely rational knowledge of God that is certain and devoid of errors, and to do so early in life, so that all of one's living could be illumined by the knowledge of God.

It is only by the gift of God's revelation that even "those religious truths which are by their nature accessible to human reason can, even in the present state of the human race, be known by all men with ease, with solid certitude, and with no trace of error" (DV 6).

10. Is faith free?

God acts with entire freedom in revealing Himself and in calling us to faith. And God wishes us to respond freely to His invitation to faith, and to believe freely in the One who calls us to life.

23

11. How do people ordinarily come to faith?

God Himself initiates the process of coming to faith. He makes present in the world visible signs that can incline the heart to long for faith. By His grace He moves us to hunger to find Him, and even to pray for faith: "Increase our faith" (Luke 17.5). He who made us affects our intelligences directly by His grace, helping us to see the reasonableness of belief. At the same time He moves us to prayer, to a burning desire for faith, and to an openness to God that changes everything. Then God gives the transforming gift of faith in which one realizes, in the light God provides, that it is God Himself who is present and calling to faith. Only then can one responsibly, joyfully, wholeheartedly respond with the free act of faith.

12. What is meant by salvation?

Eternal salvation is the gift of God which enables us to share richly the life and joy of God forever, in friendship with Him and one another. Salvation begins in this world: the grace of Christ is able to save us from the darkness of uncertainty, from despair, from the weakness that keeps us from lives of love.

13. Is faith necessary for salvation?

Yes. Faith is the beginning of human salvation. It is the foundation and root of all justification. "Without faith it is impossible to please God" (Heb. 11.6).

Moreover, knowledge growing out of faith is far stronger and more secure than any other knowledge we have. God gives the believer's faith such certainty that he or she can wisely build a whole life on that foundation.

14. Does God surpass human understanding?

God reveals Himself as a tremendous mystery whose greatness exceeds our understanding, but also as a Father who is near to us and truly loves us.

In His splendor God is utterly beyond us, but in His bountiful mercy He has willed to be "God with us" (Matt.1.23), so that we may have friendship with Him.

15. Does God reveal Himself as a personal God?

In the Old Testament God revealed that He is a personal God through the wisdom He communicated in prophetic words, and by the tender mercy with which He cared for His people. But most of all it is in Jesus that God is revealed to us as a personal God, as a Father whose wisdom and goodness surpass all understanding. Thus God reveals Himself as a personal God, not as an impersonal source of things.

16. Does God know all things?

Yes. God's knowledge encompasses all that is. Not even the most trivial things escape Him: "Even the hairs of your head are all numbered" (Matt. 10.30). The future and the most hidden secrets of our hearts are open to Him.

17. Does God love us?

Yes. To know the true God is to know One who loves His people and wishes them to come freely to salvation. "I have loved you with an ever-lasting love" (Jer. 31.3). In a sinful and wounded world the love of God is revealed above all in His mercy. "It is 'God, who is rich in mercy' (Eph. 2.4), whom Jesus Christ has revealed to us as Father" (Pope John Paul II).

18. Is God all-powerful? ALL POWERFUL

Yes. In the creeds of the Church we profess our belief in "God the Father almighty." To say that God is almighty is to say that He can do all things. God never lacks the power to keep His promises; His will is never frustrated by those who seek to oppose Him.

19. What is meant by saying that God is eternal and changeless?

In a restless and changing world, God reveals His own unchanging constancy. "For I the LORD do not change" (Mal. 3.6). In His very being God is unchanging. Material things are dependent on one another and constantly change; but God is utterly independent and suffers no alteration. To say God is eternal is to say that He is without beginning and without end. He is above all the currents of time; every moment of all time is always present to Him.

> God's eternal changelessness is not like that of a rock which cannot of itself change, but is that of the utter fullness of life and love that is always totally present to us who depend on Him that we may be.

20. Is God a spirit and present everywhere?

Yes. God is a spirit. This means that God is not a material body, restricted to this place or that, with the limitations that are inseparable from matter. He has no body, but is a living Spirit who is His own knowing and loving and rejoicing in all that is good. God is present everywhere because He has created and sustains all things. Nothing could be unless God were present to it by His power, keeping it in being. But God is present in a richer way to those who love Him, dwelling in them as a Giver of many graces and with a presence of infinite concern.

21. What is meant by calling God transcendent?

To say that God is transcendent is to say that He is distinct from and

25

greater than all other realities. Though He is ever with us and always present to the world, He is utterly distinct from the world. He is the Maker of all things, radically different from the changing things He has made. "Behold, heaven and the highest heaven cannot contain you" (2 Chron. 6.18).

22. Why is God called holy? ALL HOLY

Scripture frequently expresses God's otherness by proclaiming that He is perfectly holy. His holiness is far more than freedom from any touch of moral evil, for God cannot sin. References to His holiness also express more than His hostility to the moral evil that wounds and bruises creation and calls for punishment from Him. Primarily God's holiness signifies His absolute perfection. The holiness of God attracts the human heart because of the goodness it implies, a goodness of such intensity that it touches sinful man with awe and reverential fear.

23. Is there only one God?

Yes. There is only one God. In Him alone is our hope; and anyone who fears the Lord should fear no one else. He is the one mighty wisdom, the one infinite goodness and beauty for which all hearts long.

Everything that is learned in the study of faith speaks of Him: "Hear, O Israel: The LORD our God is one LORD; and you shall love the LORD your God with all your heart, and with all your soul, and with all your might" (Deut. 6.4-5).

26

CHAPTER • 3

God the Lord and Creator of All

"O LORD, our Lord, how majestic is Your name in all the earth!" (Ps. 8.1). Everything that God has made is a voice that speaks His glory and goodness. "The heavens are telling the glory of God; and the firmament proclaims His handiwork. Day to day pours forth speech, and night to night declares knowledge. There is no speech, nor are there words; their voice is not heard; yet their voice goes out through all the earth, and their words to the end of the world" (Ps. 19.1-4).

The Lord God who created all things created all of us. "Have we not all one Father? Has not one God created us?" (Mal. 2.10). "The rich and the poor meet together; the LORD is the Maker of them all" (Prov. 22.2).

This chapter speaks of God the Creator. It treats of the meaning of creation, and of the account of creation given us in Scripture; and it shows how there can be no real conflict between Christian faith and human reason, or between the truths of the faith and genuine scientific truth. It notes how the Creator God continues to sustain all things in being, and guides them by His providential care. Finally, the chapter speaks of God's invisible creation and of the reality of angels.

1. Did God create all things?

Yes. "In the beginning God created heaven and earth" (Gen. 1.1). That is, He created all things and persons other than Himself.

2. What does creation mean?

To create is to make a reality out of nothing. This does not mean that "nothing" is a kind of existing stuff out of which God made things. Rather it means that all things other than God, and all the elements that enter into their constitution, have been made by Him and are utterly dependent upon Him. All things "in their whole substance have been produced by God" (First Vatican Council).

3. Did God reveal to us that He is Creator of all?

Yes. When He brought the Israelites out of slavery "with a mighty hand and an outstretched arm" (Deut. 5.15), they knew he was a mighty God. When He won their battles, manifested His glory at Sinai, and led them to the promised land, they knew that His power passed all understanding. But only gradually did He reveal to them that He is the Creator of all. For to know that all things have their very being from God alone is to know that nothing whatever could resist Him. To know the creative might of the good God is to know that He "can do all things" (Job 9.3); it is to know that no one is ever in a position to "contend with Him" (Job 9.3).

Christian philosophers often argue from the very nature of a finite being that all beings other than God had to be created by Him. But the philosophers of antiquity, though they knew God to be of surpassing power, never knew His glory as Creator. Awareness of this came from divine revelation.

4. Did God create the world freely?

Yes. In His generosity God freely willed that what had not been should be, to enjoy the blessing of existence. God is a personal God, a blessed Trinity rich in interpersonal love, possessing the fullness of all that is good. He had no need to create; but He freely chose to do so.

5. What essential truths are taught in the Genesis account of creation?

Many important religious truths are taught in the Genesis account of creation. It teaches that a good God is the source of all things that are; that the world was made "very good" (Gen. 1.31). There was a beginning to time and to finite realities; until He created, nothing existed save God Himself. The special dignity of the human person, made in the image of God, is stressed. The bitter myths of paganism about the origin of the world are corrected: no evil forces or elements are involved in the work of creation. There are no primitive evil beings that can rival God. Evil has come into the world only by the free choice of created persons who were made good, and were called to serve God freely, but chose instead to reject Him.

6. Is there any poetic or figurative language in Genesis?

Yes. Scripture always speaks the truth, but it sometimes uses figurative language. The Fathers of the Church interpreted details of the Genesis narrative of creation in a rich variety of ways. But they agreed in teaching the literal truth of the essential features of the Genesis account that we have mentioned above.

For example, the sacred writer portrays the work of creation as extending over a period of six "days," and says that on the seventh day God "rested from all His work which He had done in creation" (Gen. 2.4). As early Christian writers noted, the six "days" of creation could hardly be solar days such as we now know, for according to the Genesis account the sun was not made until the fourth day. Nonetheless, the structure and literary form of the creation narrative serve the memory, and provide a suitable framework for expressing the central truths about creation.

7. Is the Genesis account of creation in conflict with scientific studies?

No. For example, though the Bible certainly does not teach evolution, neither does it say anything that is opposed to genuinely scientific theories about bodily evolution. It simply is not concerned with the kinds of questions the scientist deals with.

Sometimes, however, the philosophical presuppositions of scholars contradict teachings of faith. They may, for example, assume that strict creation is impossible or that the things of space and time could not possibly have had a beginning. Such opinions, however, do not imply a conflict between faith and science, but between faith and certain dogmatic philosophical assumptions.

8. Why can there be no real conflict between faith and science?

There can never be any real disagreement between faith and science "since the same God who reveals mysteries and infuses faith has put the light of reason in the human mind, and God cannot deny Himself, nor can truth ever contradict truth" (First Vatican Council).

In disagreements that in fact occur among men and women on these matters, it is never the faith and human wisdom that are opposed. Differences develop rather among people who either have not grasped the true meaning of what the faith teaches or have gone astray in the human sciences, usually because of false philosophical presuppositions.

9. Do the teachings of Catholic faith differ from age to age?

No. Doctrine can, however, be said to develop and to be more fully comprehended through the assistance of the Holy Spirit over the ages. But that which has been once proclaimed definitively and recognized as the word of God is enduringly true. What the Church has once infallibly proclaimed as the content of God's message will never be found false.

10. What is meant by "pluralism"?

To speak of pluralism in the Catholic faith is to speak of proclaiming the one message of faith in diverse ways suited to varied circumstances. For the message of faith can be expressed in more than one way. Even the Gospels speak the same truth in ways that are often distinctively different; indeed, the same message may receive a variety of expressions suited to various cultures. There is one other kind of diversity in the Church that can be called "pluralism." In addition to the insistent teachings of the Church, which are proclaimed in the name of Christ, the Church clearly permits a wide variety of positions on matters in which the Church has not taken a firm stand.

In Catholic faith, however, there is never room for a doctrinal pluralism that rejects some teachings that the Church proclaims in the name of Christ, or doctrines that she proposes as essential for safeguarding the faith. Catholic faith involves a common acceptance of the teaching of Christ as it is insistently proclaimed, with the assistance of His Spirit, by the authentic teachers of the Church. This acceptance is not merely of a set of words, but it means confessing the truth Christ causes to be proclaimed in His Church, in the sense in which it is proclaimed there.

11. Does faith encourage the development of the human sciences?

Cultivation of the sciences is part of our proper service to God as His creatures. Through the arts and sciences we can contribute to the human duty to "elevate the human family to a more sublime understanding of the true, the good, and the beautiful" (GS 57).

Each of the sciences is free in its own sphere to use its own principles and its own method. The Church "affirms the legitimate autonomy of human culture and especially of the sciences" (GS 59). Still it is true that some modes of fostering science can encourage "a certain phenomenalism and agnosticism, when the research methods which those disciplines use is wrongly regarded as the supreme rule for discovering the whole truth" (GS 57). This abuse, however, flows from a philosophical error, not from the nature of science itself.

12. Does God continue to rule the world He has made?

Yes. Faith believes in divine providence, that is, she knows that God cares for the world with great love, ever directing it toward the goal for the sake of which He made all things. He does not will any evil for the world, but permits some evil to occur because He loves freedom, and wishes the free service of those He has called to be His friends. He is able to guide the world toward the end He chose despite the evils our sins bring into the world. His providence extends to all His creatures, but in a special way to the persons He has made.

13. Does God predestine some to eternal life and some to damnation?

No. God invites all to eternal life with Himself. Some persons are predestined in the sense that God's merciful gift precedes and makes possible every mercy, especially that of the eternal salvation to which they finally come. There is no predestination in the sense that God would select certain persons who were not to attain eternal life and withhold from them gifts that could lead to salvation.

God's providence and predestination do not imply that at some time in the past God decided all that would happen, and that the future unfolds mechanically, like scenes from a motion picture already entirely determined. For God does not live in the past, but in an eternity which is always present to all time. His eternal care for His people always takes into account their free responses to His gifts and graces.

14. Is creation limited to the material things that can be seen?

No. God is the Creator of "all things, visible and invisible" (Nicene Creed). God created angels, and Scripture, in both the Old and New Testaments, portrays them as having important roles in salvation history.

15. What are angels?

Angels are persons, spiritual beings of surpassing intelligence and power. To say they are spiritual beings is to say that, like God, they have no bodies and no material components, though they are very real.

Angels are not impersonal forces, nor is the word "angel" used merely figuratively in Catholic teaching. They are creatures more like God than we human persons are. But they are mere creatures. They are instruments of God's providence for us in mighty but hidden ways. The liturgy frequently celebrates them: "Countless hosts of angels stand before you to do your will; they look upon your splendor and praise you, night and day" (Roman Missal). The liturgical celebration of angels recalls the Catholic teaching that angels guard us; they watch over each human person as agents of God's love. For this reason Catholics are encouraged to invoke the intercession of angels as they do that of the saints.

CHAPTER 4

Living Man — The Glory of God

"What is man that You are mindful of him, and the son of man, that You care for him?" (Ps. 8.4). Human life is mysterious. "He often exalts himself as the absolute measure of all things, or debases himself to the point of despair" (GS 12). By art and industry humanity has worked wonders that delight the imagination; at the same time, human history is also a record of sin and of sorrow, a series of relentless waves eroding human self-respect. Grandeur and misery, holiness and sin, hopes and fears mark the mystery of human reality. But Catholic faith proclaims that "all things on earth should be related to man as their center and crown" (GS 12). Even more, we are touched by the love of God Himself. "You have made him little less than God, and crowned him with glory and honor. You have given him dominion over the works of Your hands; You have put all things under his feet" (Ps. 8.5-6).

In this chapter we speak of the human person as the image of God, wonderful in body and soul, and of God's design in creating and in giving profound unity to the whole human race. We speak also of the social nature and the dignity of each person, of how Christ Himself reveals the meaning of our being, and of the tasks to which God calls us.

1. What was the crowning work of God's creation?

God, who created all things out of generous love, created man and woman as the crown and glory of all that He had made. "Then God said, 'Let us make man in our image, after our likeness; and let him have dominion'" (Gen. 1.26). Much of Scripture is an elucidation of what we are and of the purpose of our life.

> Both in having individual personal dignity and in possessing a social nature the human person mirrors the one God who is the Trinity.

2. Does the human person have both spiritual and material dimensions?

Yes. Spiritual and physical dimensions are intimately joined in each human being. Our soul gives us spiritual depths, the power to understand and love and live in freedom. But we are just as truly material beings: our flesh and blood are an essential part of what we are.

> We are not simply souls dwelling in bodies. Neither are we purely material things. In the human person body and soul make up a single living being; and man is "not allowed to despise his bodily life" (GS 14). In-

deed, "through his bodily composition he gathers to himself the elements of the material world. Thus these elements reach their crown through him, and through him raise their voice in free praise of God" (GS 14).

3. Does the soul exist before the body?

No. The whole living person comes to be at the moment the soul is created by God, and begins to give structure and life to the body. God immediately creates each human soul at the moment that the whole person comes to be.

4. Is each human being an image of God?

Yes. Each of us is like God especially in the traits that we have as persons. A person mirrors God in the possession of intelligence and freedom, in caring about good and evil, and in having an immortal destiny.

5. How does our freedom make us like God?

God is supremely free, and fully master of all He chooses to do. In having freedom we are like God in having a certain autonomy, a self-possession, and mastery over our own actions and being. Human persons are not simply driven by blind forces or instincts. We have responsibility and freedom. Even in our fallen state we retain this freedom to make our own choices, to act or not to act, to do this or to do that.

Human freedom is of course not as full and perfect as God's is. The pressure of circumstances can limit greatly a person's freedom and responsibility. Yet as long as one retains the power to live in a human way, he or she will retain a measure of this freedom.

More sublime than this freedom of choice is the freedom which gives us power to live in God's friendship, to do the good things one's heart longs for, and to fulfill one's divinely implanted longings. This freedom comes not simply from our nature, but comes from the gift of grace.

6. Would God have enabled us to escape death if our first parents had not sinned?

Yes. We human beings are material persons who by nature are subject to the dissolution of death. Yet by His special mercy God would have kept us "immune from bodily death" (GS 16) if our first parents had not sinned.

7. At death does our life end absolutely?

No. At death our bodies, which are part of our very being, die and are dissolved. But we do not totally die. What we call death is not a complete ceasing to be, but is a transition to another state of living. "Lord, for your faithful people life is changed, not ended" (Roman Missal).

33

Each person is like God in being destined to live forever. This is one reason why every human being is to be treated with great reverence.

"The Church affirms that a spiritual element survives and subsists after death, an element endowed with consciousness and will, so that the 'human self' subsists. To designate this element, the Church uses the word 'soul,' the accepted term in the usage of Scripture and Tradition" (Sacred Congregation for the Doctrine of the Faith).

8. What does "saving one's soul" mean?

"Saving one's soul" means saving one's total self for eternal life. Catholic pastoral ministry speaks often of care for souls. This does not mean nurturing some inner part of a person, but rather care for one's whole being through nurturing love of God and neighbor, and through responding to the graces that enable one to have that friendship with God that blossoms into eternal life.

One reaches full salvation only when body and soul together are joined in the joy of the resurrection, when the family of God rejoices before Him in eternal life.

9. Are men and women equal?

Yes. Scripture stresses the equality and complementarity of men and women. While they may have diverse roles their essential vocation is the same: to come to love God and their brothers and sisters with free and generous hearts.

In the divine institution of marriage men and women are called to complete one another, relieving the loneliness of the human condition. They are to see each other as equals: for only in the equal respect that they give each other can they become fully one in marriage.

To honor the equality of man and woman, marriage ought to be monogamous, as it should endure as long as both spouses live. Such was the vision of Genesis. Christ appealed to this when He declared that divorce is wrong, contrary to the will expressed by the Creator from the beginning.

10. Are we by nature social beings?

Yes. "Social life is not something added on to man" (GS 25). By our very nature we are called to and need to share life with others. "Through his dealings with others, through reciprocal duties, and through fraternal dialogue he develops all his gifts and is able to rise to his destiny" (GS 25).

Individuals must make sacrifices for the common welfare. This enhances rather than diminishes their personal dignity. Yet society does not have the right to assail or violate the personal dignity of any person for any reason whatever. For societies exist to ennoble and enrich persons; and persons are not mere means by which societies may reach their desired ends.

11. Does Scripture speak much of the condition of life of our first parents?
No. Scripture tells us little indeed about the condition of human beings in the springtime of their creation. Genesis does not seek to answer the questions that challenge modern sciences of early man. But Scripture does tell us important truths about the human condition that are important for an intelligent faith.

For example, revelation teaches us that the evils that we experience in this world were certainly not all inevitable, and human misery was not part of God's original plan. Rather, much of the discord and pain we experience is the fruit of the deliberate sins human beings committed in the beginning, and that we still commit.

12. Were our first parents created in holiness?
Yes. There is much about our first parents that we do not know. But faith teaches that they were created in that grace that made them children of God. They were created possessing a certain universal harmony. Grace and divinely given virtues bound them in peaceful friendship with God. They did not suffer from that inner turmoil we know, which is called concupiscence, an inner disorder which inclines us toward acting unreasonably and doing evil. Rather they had inner peace and peace with the world and possessed special gifts of God that were appropriate to their grace and innocence. *Concupiscence*

13. Was Christ in any way present to the beginnings of human history?
Yes. Christ was foreshadowed in many ways at the beginning of human history.

Our first parents were created in grace, which related them to Christ, as sharers in His sonship. But Christ the eternal Son is "the first-born among many brethren" (Rom. 8.29). Christ is called by Scripture the "first-born of all creation" (Col. 1.15), obviously not because His human nature was created first in time, but because Christ has absolutely first place in the divine plan. He is the first in dignity, and all things that were made were created with Him in mind: "He is before all things, and in Him all things hold together" (Col. 1.17). The world was made not simply for the random satisfaction it gives to scattered individuals, but that it might come to a full completion in the unity and fullness of life that Christ brings.

14. What tasks does God give us here on earth?
We were created to know God and to live in friendship with Him. We

35

were created to love one another and to share life in peace and unity. Moreover we were created to "have dominion" (Gen. 1.26) over the earth and to "subdue it" (Gen. 1.28). We were created to serve God freely in these ways and so to merit eternal life with Him.

Clearly it is part of our vocation to take responsibility for this world and to seek to make it a presence of God's kingdom. It is important that we seek to make this world just and merciful, to mirror God not only in being good but also in generously causing good. It is through living an excellent life and serving one another in this world that we glorify God and prepare ourselves to enter the blessed vision of God.

God wishes us to seek His glory not for His own sake, but for ours. For this is His glory: that His children grow in love and in every precious gift before Him.

Some wonder why God did not create us from the first in heaven rather than call us to endure the burdens of this time of trial. But this indeed seems to flow from His mercy and His reverence for our freedom. God wished us not simply to have the joys of eternal life, but also to possess them because we freely chose to. He honored us by giving us, by His grace and mercy, power to do freely excellent deeds that merit eternal life.

CHAPTER • 5

Fallen Man and the Faithfulness of God

"And God saw everything that He had made, and behold, it was very good" (Gen. 1.31). Revelation teaches us that God created all things well, but that we sinful people have brought upon ourselves a multitude of evils. Seeing so many evils that flourish in our sinful world, some have grown weary and bitter and have criticized God and complained of His ways, or have even denied Him.

In this chapter we speak first of the mystery of evil, and of how our personal sins and those of the fallen angels touch upon it. We then speak of how God promised a Redeemer, and of how in the old covenant God sustained the hope for redemption, the redemption which Christ came to achieve. For it is "through Christ and in Christ" that "the riddle of sorrow and death is illumined" (GS 22).

1. What is the mystery of evil?

The mystery of evil is this: that in a world created by God and ruled by Him there is found an immense amount of moral and physical evil, and that the innocent as well as the wicked suffer many evils.

Faith certainly recognizes that the world is heavily marked with suffering and grief. Much of Sacred Scripture is a record of human sorrow. We cannot understand clearly why there is so much evil, or why evils in the world are distributed as they are. But Scripture does teach us much about evil. It tells us that God does not love human suffering. He does not will any evil as such or for its own sake. In giving His creatures freedom He endowed them with sublime dignity; but in doing this He also permitted evil to be done. God also inflicts just punishments, but He does so in the service of the great good of justice.

Scripture speaks of the complex problem of evil in various ways. When it teaches us that "good things and bad, life and death, poverty and wealth, are from the Lord" (Sir. 11.14), it is reminding us that all things are subject to the providence of God. When Scripture tells us that "God did not make death, and He does not delight in the death of the living" (Wisd. 1.13), it is pointing out that the infinitely good God does not take pleasure in the sorrows that He in His wisdom and mercy permits. Never does God will or cause any moral evil or sin.

2. How have people reacted to the mystery of evil?

People have reacted to the mystery of evil in a great variety of ways.

Some, with the saints, have shared Christ's response to evil in the world. They have had great compassion on those who suffer, and have wept over the sins and folly of the world. They have been tireless in imitating Jesus, who "went about doing good" (Acts 10.38), and found many ways to comfort those bearing trials, as they sustained hope in God's healing mercy. Others have reacted very differently: some cite the existence of evil in the world as their reason for denying the very existence of God; some, pressed by sorrows, have felt tragically driven toward rebellion against the Lord; some use the pain they experience or observe as a facile pretext for unbelief.

3. Did the Old Testament explore the problem of evil?

Yes. The problem of evil was frequently explored in the Old Testament, notably in the book of Job. This book teaches that in this world the innocent sometimes suffer, and that human understanding often cannot grasp why goods and evils are distributed as they are; yet God is almighty and just. While we often cannot understand His ways, we can be certain that He is able finally to vindicate the just and assure the triumph of justice.

In this book Job is portrayed as basically a very good man who suffered terrible reverses and sufferings. He loses all his possessions, his health and his peace, and even all his loved ones. Though friends come to console him, their words are shallow and useless. Job complains that the evils he bears are not the fruit of his sins, but are a stark mystery, while his friends give easy, moralistic answers. And the divine response at the end is that it is Job who is right. Or, rather, more nearly right, for Job in his sorrow did not sufficiently reverence God's mysterious ways. He spoke as if there were some edge of unfairness in God. So God asks Job questions in response to the complaining questions Job had put to Him. Job, fundamentally good, sees God's concern and recalls that he really knows that God is altogether righteous, though God dwells in mystery. "Behold, I am of small account; what shall I answer You?. . . I have uttered that which I did not understand, things too wonderful for me, which I did not know" (Job 40.4, 42.3).

Those who complain of God's ways with none of Job's patience, or blaspheme God because of the evils they experience, may also be called to account by God's questioning. Often they give easy rationalizations. They argue that if God were almighty, He would be able to remove all evil from the world; if God were good, He would wish to do so. But there is very much evil; hence there cannot exist an almighty and good God. But in this they oversimplify everything, and miss the mystery of God's ways. "For who can learn the counsel of God? Or who can discern what the Lord wills?" (Wisd. 9.13).

Doubtless God could have made a world in which no evil whatever were permitted. But would a world absolutely guarded from every kind of evil serve the good purposes this world was made for? Could there be a world of persons, freedom, love, generosity, forgiveness, hope, courage, if an almighty force made it impossible for anyone to suffer any harm whatever? Could this world be a suitable place of trial in which men and women could serve God willingly and come to deserve eternal life if they had no freedom to choose to do good or do evil? We do not really have light to see the nature of the whole world and all its workings; but God does give us light enough to know His reality, and the wisdom of seeking to serve Him, even in the midst of trials.

4. Does the life of Christ shed light on the mystery of evil?

Yes. When the Son of God became our Brother He cast a bright light on the mystery of evil. His will to share our poverty and pain, and to suffer for our salvation, made it clear that God has compassion with us in all our sorrows. In the mystery of the Incarnation God found ways to share personally in all our suffering, that we might understand that He yet loves us, and that He hates the evil that torments our lives. In His teaching on God's holiness and mercy, on freedom, on the malice of sin, and on the divine plan of redemption, Jesus helped us understand more fully the mystery of evil. But even more His redemptive work saved us. He gave us the power to turn from sin and begin to live as God's children, and He taught us to hope for the day there would be no more death nor "mourning nor crying nor pain any more, for the former things have passed away" (Rev. 21.4).

Yet Jesus did not seek to make us understand precisely why this or that suffering occurred in a particular life. When His friends Mary and Martha sought to understand why He had not saved Lazarus their brother from death, Jesus did not provide detailed explanations. But He wept with them. By His tears, and much more by dying for us, the Son of God revealed how deeply God understands our suffering and loves us.

The New Testament teaches us that God does not cause any moral evil; it is our free and deliberate will that brings the worst evil into the world. God does not will or permit any physical evils for their own sake. He made the world good, but free and vulnerable, and vulnerable only that it might have glorious possibilities. When evil entered this world against His commandment, He showed Himself to be the saving God, and revealed that for those who love Him He is able to draw overwhelming good out of the evil that is done against His command.

5. Why does this world suffer so many evils?

The created world is finite; unlike God, it is essentially limited and imperfect. Yet God created man and woman in the beginning in a state of holiness, freedom, and peace. But our first parents sinned deliberately, and brought great sorrows upon themselves and all their descendants.

"Although he was made by God in a state of holiness, from the dawn of history man abused his liberty, at the urging of the Evil One. Man set himself against God, and sought to find his fulfillment apart from God" (GS 13).

6. What was the nature of the first sin?

The account of the first sin in the book of Genesis is given in language somewhat figurative in its details. Scripture suggests that the malice of that sin lay chiefly in its elements of pride and disobedience.

7. Did the sin of the first man affect all his descendants?

Yes. Basing its teaching firmly on Scripture, the Church teaches that from Adam sin has been transmitted to all his descendants. "Therefore as sin came into the world through one man and death through sin, and so death spread to all men because all men sinned" (Rom. 5.12). Each individual is born in a condition of sin, and can be freed from that condition only by the merits of Jesus Christ.

The first sin was for Adam an actual sin for which he was personally responsible. The original sin which we inherit is not an actual sin in us. Yet it is a sinful condition and it harms us in many ways; because it deprives us of grace, it separates us from friendship with God. "It is human nature so fallen, stripped of the grace that clothed it, injured in its own natural powers and subjected to the dominion of death, that is transmitted to all men, and it is in this sense that every man is born in sin" (Pope Paul VI).

Universal human experience confirms the teaching that we are born in a sinful state. "Examining his heart, man finds that he has inclinations toward evil too, and is engulfed by manifold ills which cannot come from his good Creator. Often refusing to acknowledge God as his beginning, man has disrupted also his proper relation to his own ultimate goal, as well as his whole orientation toward himself, toward others, and toward all created things" (GS 13).

The most tragic and central aspect of original sin is the loss of grace and with it of friendship with God. By baptism this grace is restored. But concupiscence remains even after baptism, and we still experience disorder within us.

8. Is God unjust in permitting the sin of the first man to affect all his descendants?

No. The losses that we have incurred as a result of original sin are not

40

losses of anything due to us by right. Our solidarity as members of one human family requires that, as we would have been blessed in Adam's faithfulness, we rightly lose the exceptional gifts that we would have had because of his unfaithfulness. The gift of intimate friendship with the Lord, a gift of grace, is more than human nature could rightly claim. Freedom from death and from the sufferings that flow from our creaturely state is no native right of ours. God is both just and merciful; He punishes sin rightly, yet in His love He keeps us in being and still calls us to great hope.

Moreover, God does not count original sin as actual sin in the descendants of Adam. Those who would die in original sin, without having committed any personal grave sins, would not suffer the pain of damnation for that.

Even more, God's permission of original sin involved a merciful plan in which the latter state of man would be better than the first. Christ's redemptive love on the cross was to be a gift of such overflowing richness that it would more than lighten the whole burden of sin. The Church in its liturgy for the vigil of Easter does not hesitate to sing of the first human sin: "O happy fault, O necessary sin of Adam, which gained for us so great a Redeemer."

9. Are all the evils we suffer the fruit of original sin?

No. The many sorrows of human life are by no means the fruit of original sin alone. In fact, the most severe and unbearable of human evils are the fruit of our continued deliberate sins.

Our sins are not predetermined and inevitable. God gave us not only free will, but also grace sufficient to enable us to resist temptation. God "will not let you be tempted beyond your strength, but with the temptation will provide the way of escape, that you may be able to endure it" (1 Cor. 10.13). "If you will, you can keep the commandments. . . . Before a man are life and death, and whichever he chooses will be given to him" (Sir. 15.15, 17).

10. Does the Church teach terror of Satan?

No. The Church does not teach terror of Satan. It commends only a holy fear of God, which implies a fear of deliberately doing evil. For the influence of Satan is decisively subordinated to the power of God. The Second Vatican Council reminds us time and again that Christ "has freed us from the power of Satan" (SC 6). Because of Christ's redeeming work, the devil can genuinely harm only those who freely permit him to do so.

Catholic faith teaches, as Scripture does, that devils or fallen spirits really exist. They were not evil from the beginning, but became evil through their own free sinful acts. That human history is often marked by

41

sad and irrational currents is partly due to their influence. Yet God remains the Lord of all, and by His providence severely limits their power.

The Gospels speak of diabolical possession, and they show Christ casting out demons and instructing His apostles to do the same. Scripture portrays Satan also as a source of temptation. He is "the treacherous and cunning enchanter, who finds his way into us by way of the senses, the imagination, lust, utopian logic, and disorderly social contacts in the give and take of life, to introduce deviations. . ." (Pope Paul VI).

World history itself is influenced by the devil. Indeed, "a difficult struggle against the powers of darkness pervades the whole history of man; the battle was joined from the very origins of the world and will continue until the last day, as the Lord has attested" (GS 37).

11. Does God remain faithful in spite of our sin?

Yes. "If we are faithless, He remains faithful — for He cannot deny Himself" (2 Tim. 2.13). The first man sinned, and his descendants have followed him, but God remains faithful. "Again and again You offered a covenant to man, and through the prophets taught him to hope for salvation" (Roman Missal).

The account in Genesis of the first human sin concludes with a foretelling of a divine redemption. God is portrayed there addressing the tempter. "I will put enmity between you and the woman, and between your seed and her seed; he shall bruise your head, and you shall bruise his heel" (Gen. 3.15). Jesus is the "seed" or "offspring" of the woman, and "the reason why the Son of God appeared was to destroy the works of the devil" (1 John 3.9). Through the ages of salvation history preceding Christ, God repeatedly called man to repentance, to renewed greatness, and to salvation. He never forgets that it was He who made man, and called him to share His own life and friendship.

God made a covenant with Abraham, and, through Moses, with the people of Israel. "If you will obey My voice and keep My covenant, you shall be My own possession among all peoples" (Exod. 19.4-5). "All the people answered together and said, 'All that the Lord has spoken we will do' " (Exod. 19.7-8). Repeatedly, however, they fell into sin, and experienced the sorrows and the punishment sin entails. But God's constant mercy made repentance possible, and God renewed the covenant again and again.

12. How did the prophets sustain the hope for redemption?

Through the prophets He sent, God taught His people to hope for the decisive salvation that the Messiah would bring. Through them also God taught the people how to live as they awaited His redeeming mercy. The prophets were God's spokesmen; their task was both to teach His people the ways of life and to foretell His saving works. God Himself had called the prophets to their tasks, and He could make others recognize them as prophets.

There is, to be sure, a certain obscurity in prophecy. Still, the Church teaches that the Old Testament prophecies of Christ, like Jesus' own prophecies in the New Testament, are "most certain signs of divine revelation" (First Vatican Council).

13. Did the pagan nations too retain hope for salvation?

Yes. Among the pagan nations too God kept alive the hope for salvation in various ways. Through the natural gifts of the various cultures, as through the philosophy by which some of the Greeks came to speak sublime truths about God, God was preparing the world for the advent of His Son.

This divine work of preparation continues even today, for there are many who do not know Christ and His message, and some who have not yet arrived at an explicit knowledge of God. But God can save them also if, moved by His grace, they seek to lead upright lives. No one can be saved except by Christ, but not all whom He saves have known Him clearly.

14. Is the Old Testament still instructive for us?

Yes. The Church encourages us to read and meditate on the books of the Old Testament, for these books "give expression to a lively sense of God, contain a store of sublime teachings about God, sound wisdom about human life, and wonderful treasures of prayer, and in them the mystery of our salvation is present in a hidden way" (DV 15).

These books are always to be read in the light of Christ, who is their fulfillment. "God, the Inspirer and Author of both Testaments, wisely arranged that the New Testament be hidden in the Old and the Old be made manifest in the New. . . . The books of the Old Testament . . . acquire and show forth their full meaning in the New Testament and in turn shed light on it and explain it" (DV 16).

15. Is our fallen world both very good and marred by much evil?

Yes. Faith teaches that God cares for all, and constantly blesses us with many gifts; He wishes all to be saved, and He wishes His kingdom and His peace to be in our midst in many ways. Yet this world clearly is deeply wounded by our sins.

The world, then, has a twofold aspect. In its sin and its sorrow it mirrors the frailty and malice of creatures who resist their Creator God. In its grandeur and in the grace that yet penetrates it, the world continues to show the boundless goodness of God. This goodness we often see too dimly. To grasp reality in truth, we need most of all to see in the light of Christ.

CHAPTER • 6

The Son of God Becomes Our Brother

"You know the grace of our Lord Jesus Christ, that though He was rich, yet for your sake He became poor, so that by His poverty you might become rich" (2 Cor. 8.9). Through the centuries humanity in its sin and sorrow needed desperately the Savior God had promised through the prophets. When God's gift of a Savior came, it was a far richer fulfillment of the promises than anyone could have hoped for: "But when the time had fully come, God sent His Son, born of a woman" (Gal. 4.4).

This chapter speaks of the good news of Jesus, of how He who was born on earth as our Savior is as fully human as we are, our Brother, but is also our God. He is nonetheless but one Person, the eternal Son of God. He suffered the humiliations and limitations of humanity; but in His humanity He bore the saving gifts that were needed to heal our infirmities.

1. Who is Jesus Christ?

Jesus Christ is the Savior of the world. He is the eternal Son of the Father, who in time became truly a man, that in our humanity He might save us from sin and from the bitter effects of sin, and might enable us to share His divine nature.

> This central teaching of Christianity, that in Jesus Christ the true God
> really became man, is called the mystery of the Incarnation.

2. What does it mean to say that Jesus is the eternal Son of God?

To say that Jesus is the eternal Son of God is to say that He has from eternity the same nature as the Father. He is literally "one in being" with the Father. He is what the Father is: "Light from Light, true God from true God" (Nicene Creed). With the Father, He is the wisdom and love that made the world and keeps it in being. Yet He is a person distinct from the person of the Father; He proceeds from the Father eternally, perfectly mirroring the splendor of the Father.

3. Do the Scriptures teach that Jesus is true God?

Yes. In some places in the Scriptures Jesus is called God. Even more frequently the divine title LORD is given to Him. Moreover the Scriptures portray Him as doing the deeds of God, acting as one with the dignity, status, and power of God; and it presents Him as one to be believed, trusted, prayed to, and regularly reverenced as God by those who come to have faith in Him.

The prologue of John's Gospel portrays Jesus as the Word of God who became a man for our sake and lived among us. Of Him the Gospel declared: "In the beginning the Word was, and the Word was with God, and the Word was God" (John 1.1). In some other places the New Testament calls Jesus simply God.

Regularly Jesus is called the Lord. "At the name of Jesus every knee should bow, . . . and every tongue confess that Jesus Christ is Lord, to the glory of God the Father" (Phil. 2.10-11). The most sacred divine names are attributed to Him.

Divine revelation attributes creation only to God; but of Jesus it declares: "All things were made through Him" (John 1.2). In God alone is salvation; only He can forgive sins and restore life to the dead. But Jesus, whose very name means "Savior," is portrayed as personally forgiving sin on His own authority, and as the one who restores life to the dead. Only God is to be glorified as God; but Scripture teaches that the glory given to the Father is to be given to the Son as well, and we are to love Him above all, just as we are to love the Father above all. And Jesus is presented in the Gospels as declaring: "The Father and I are one" (John 10.30).

Many are called "sons of God" because God gives them His grace and friendship, and enables them even to share to some measure in His own nature. But only Jesus is by nature the true Son of God, being by His nature all that the Father is.

4. How did people come to believe that Jesus was literally God?

Only gradually did Jesus lead His followers to realize the tremendous mystery of His divinity. They first saw the glory of His humanity; they experienced His power and His wisdom and His goodness. Gently the Lord led them to recognize that He was the Messiah, the long-awaited Savior, and finally that He was indeed truly God.

5. Did the Son of God really become a man?

Yes. Catholic faith believes that the eternal Son, literally and truly our God, truly became one of us, our Brother. He did not merely appear to be a man. He became fully a man, with human feelings, human intelligence, human freedom. All that we are by nature He took upon Himself, sharing our life that He might enable us to share in His divine life.

In His human nature He became able to grow "in wisdom and in stature, and in favor with God and man" (Luke 2.52). He experienced what it was to be weary, thirsty, hungry, and homeless. In His passion the reality of His humanity was made clearly evident in the distress, sorrow, and anguish He felt and in the physical pain and death He endured. He never abandoned the humanity which for our sake He took on and made His own. After the resurrection He took care to show Himself in His fleshly human reality: "See My hands and My feet, that it is I Myself; handle Me and see, for a spirit has not flesh and bones as you see that I have" (Luke 24.39).

Of no other historical person is it so important to insist that He is truly man. The humanity of Jesus is important because in Him human nature is most ennobled, and He is the perfect pattern for human living, because through His humanity He redeemed us, and because He is the man who is our God.

6. Did Jesus remain God when He became man?

Yes. Had the Son of God ceased to have the glory of God when He became man, it would not have been the Son of God who shared our sorrows and poverty, and who redeemed us by His saving death.

"Let no one therefore believe that the Son of God was changed or transformed into the Son of man; but rather let us believe that He, remaining the Son of God, was made the Son of man, without loss of His divine substance and by a perfect assumption of the human substance" (St. Augustine).

Since Jesus has two natures, He has also both human intelligence and divine intelligence, divine freedom and human freedom.

7. Is Jesus only one Person?

Yes. Though He possesses fully the divine nature and fully our human nature, Jesus is one Person, and that a divine Person, the Person of the Son of God. The One who was born of Mary and became our Brother is also God. The Jesus whom the apostles saw, who walked this earth, is the Lord who created all things.

Though God in His own nature dwells in eternal blessedness, He wished to experience personally and immediately all our trials, and to redeem us by suffering death for us. He created in the womb of the virgin Mary a human nature which was created as His own, in which He could experience human feelings and human pain. "One and the same Christ, Son, Lord, Only-begotten, must be acknowledged in two natures unconfused, unchangeable, undivided, inseparable" (Council of Chalcedon).

Jesus is not a human person. He is a Person who is human, a Person with the richest and most sensitive humanity. But to be a person in the sense in which the Church teaches that Jesus is only one Person, is to be "a distinct intelligent being." Now when the humanity of Jesus was created, a new person was not created. The humanity of Jesus was not a person distinct and separate from the Person who is the Son of God. Rather

47

the Person who dwelt always with the Father began to exist also in a new way, as man. But Jesus in His humanity is not a person other than the Son of God; He is undivided, a single Person. That is the good news of the Gospel: that the One who died on the cross for us is the very Son of God. It is not a distinct human person other than the Son of God who did the works of Jesus.

Devotion to the Sacred Heart grows out of this sound faith in the unity of Jesus' Person. The eternal love with which this one Person, Jesus, has loved and understood us as God is inseparably united to the tender human love He has for us in His humanity. We can have exceptionally close personal relationships with this man Jesus, precisely because He is not merely a human person, but a true man who is the Son of God.

8. Did the Son of God humble Himself in the Incarnation?

Yes. He who as God is Ruler of all came to share the natural frailties and humiliation of our human estate. In becoming man He "humbled Himself and became obedient unto death, even death on a cross" (Phil. 2.8).

9. Is humanity exalted by the Incarnation?

Yes. Our human nature was raised to the highest possible state when the Son of God took a human nature as His own.

Jesus took upon Himself a true human nature, capable of growth, of suffering, of death. But because His human nature was that of the Son of God, His knowledge had a wealth appropriate to His role as Savior of all, and His human soul, heart, mind, and will are enriched with all virtues and holiness.

10. Is the human knowledge of Jesus surpassingly rich?

Yes. In his risen glory His human wisdom is indescribably great. In Him "are hid all the treasures of wisdom and knowledge" (Col. 2.3). He knows us with a thorough and loving knowledge. Even in His earthly days He had surpassing human wisdom and understanding. Yet His wisdom did nothing to make Him less human and less near to us; for it was a compassionate and loving wisdom.

Thus Christ had intimate and immediate knowledge of the Father. He knew Himself and the mystery of His Person, His Messianic dignity, and the tasks the Father had given Him. His human knowledge extended to all that was appropriate for His mission as Savior and Shepherd of all. He knew the hearts of those He spoke with, and knew even what was to happen to them.

Yet His human knowledge was not infinite. As man He grew in wisdom. The Gospels speak of Him as knowing wonder about things that He came to experience humanly, and even as professing Himself unaware of the time of the last things. The precise meaning of this unawareness is not clear. Many Fathers and Doctors have judged that this meant that He had no knowledge about such matters to communicate to us; that whatever knowledge He had of this was not proper to Him as man. Others today say that such texts may reveal to us more fully the depths of Jesus' self-humiliation. Theologians must explore these questions more deeply. But no new knowledge will ever contradict what the Church has taught and teaches authoritatively about the rich human wisdom of Jesus.

11. Was Jesus entirely sinless?
Yes. Jesus was entirely without sin. Because He is the Son of God He was incapable of sinning. The Gospels indeed portray Him as undergoing temptation. In His agony He felt sorrow and fear, and a natural human longing to escape the bitter passion. Yet there was no inclination of His heart toward evil, such as we might experience. His human heart was steadfastly fixed on doing the Father's will.

12. In what way is Jesus holy?
The divine nature of Jesus has the very holiness of God. His human nature shared most richly in that holiness from the moment of the Incarnation. His human nature was holy not only because it is the humanity of the Son of God, but also because He in His human nature is the crown of creation, and the source of holiness for all who are called to life. In Him there was the fullness of grace and all the gifts of the Holy Spirit.

13. Did Jesus as man live in freedom?
Yes. The gracious and saving deeds Jesus performed in His human nature were done in full divine and human freedom. His humanity had all the traits essential to man, and precious among these is freedom. When in obedience to the Father He endured the cross, He acted in perfect freedom. "For this reason the Father loves Me, because I lay down My life, that I may take it up again. No one takes it from Me, but I lay it down of My own accord" (John 10.17-18).

14. To what did the power of Jesus extend?
As God, Jesus had infinite power. His humanity was created and finite in its native power. Because of the personal union of His humanity with His divinity, however, Jesus exercised divine power also through His humanity. For His human nature served instrumentally the mercy and

strength of His own divine nature. Hence Jesus in His visible humanity performed personally and authoritatively works that are proper to God. Thus He who is both God and man spoke in human language the saving truth to us, and by His own power performed miracles in the service of faith and love.

CHAPTER • 7

The Mother of Jesus

Everything faith teaches us about Mary is intended to draw us nearer to Jesus. He is the Son of God who has become our Brother. She is His mother; no created person is closer to Him. God surrounded her life with a variety of graces and privileges. But every special gift God gave her centered on this essential grace: that she, though but a creature and "handmaid of the Lord" (Luke 1.38), was to be the mother of the eternal Son.

In a later chapter we shall speak of Mary's association with Jesus in the mystery of our redemption, and of her maternal relationship to the Church and the faithful. Here we treat the first gifts of God that bound her so closely to Jesus: the gift by which she was made the Mother of God; the grace of her faithful and fruitful virginity; and the holiness that God gave her for the glory of her Son.

1. Who is Mary?

Mary is the mother of Jesus. She is celebrated by Catholic faith as the virgin Mother of God, as eminent in holiness, as the closest associate of Jesus in His poverty and in His trials, as a sharer in the glory of His resurrection, as our spiritual mother, and as the mother and model of the Church.

2. Why does Catholic faith praise Mary so highly?

Catholic faith praises Mary because of her central role in Christ's saving mysteries. She is contemplated not so much for her own sake as for the light she casts upon Jesus.

Thus Cardinal Newman observes that the glories of Mary were always for the sake of her Son. To insist on the sublimity of Mary's role was a way of glorifying Jesus. Efforts to minimize Mary's role seemed to flow from lack of faith in Jesus. Thus the Nestorian denial of the teaching on Mary's motherhood of God seemed to flow from the Arian denial that Jesus, her Son, was the eternal Son of God.

3. Does the New Testament say much of Mary?

The New Testament does not speak at length about Mary, but the essential truths concerning her place in the mystery of Christ are rooted there.

The earliest New Testament references to Mary identify her as the human way by which the Son of God entered history, stressing that she is truly His mother and He is really her Son, and suggest that her greatness flows even more from her faith and love than from her physical motherhood of Jesus.

The fullest treatment of Mary in the New Testament is found in St. Luke's Gospel and in his Acts of the Apostles. Mary appears as a central figure at the outset of his Gospel in the infancy narrative; we also behold her persevering in prayer with the disciples in the upper room at the beginning of the Acts of the Apostles. St. John opens and closes his account of the public life of Jesus with two scenes in which Mary figures very prominently, Cana and Calvary.

4. What do the "infancy narratives" reveal about Mary?

The so-called infancy narratives are in the opening chapters of St. Matthew and St. Luke. Each is distinctive. For the two evangelists drew upon separate streams of tradition and each had a distinct and different theological purpose. Each tells us in its own way of Mary's divine motherhood, her virginity, her faith, and her holiness.

St. Matthew reflects on the history of Jesus' origins in the light of the Mosaic tradition and promises. His account is largely a collation of quotations from the Old Testament whose promises are fulfilled in Jesus. He gives prominence to St. Joseph as the legal father. At the same time he wishes to make clear that Jesus was not Joseph's natural son, but that Mary His mother conceived Him virginally by the power of the Holy Spirit. In this virginal conception St. Matthew recognized the fulfillment of the prophecy: "The Virgin shall be with child, and bear a Son, and shall name Him Immanuel" (Isa. 7.14 NAB). The substance of St. Matthew's message is that Jesus is the promised Messiah.

St. Luke's account provides further insight into the meaning of Mary's motherhood of Jesus. His infancy narrative may be divided into two parts, that covering the period before the births of John the Baptist and Jesus, and that recounting their births. He intends to parallel and to contrast Jesus and John, as well as Mary and Zechariah. His theological purpose is to portray Jesus as divine Messiah and Lord. He also lets a special ray of Christ's splendor shine on His mother, Mary, who is the true daughter of Zion.

5. What scriptural passage tells us most about Mary?

St. Luke's account of the angel Gabriel's message to Mary is most rich in what it tells us of Mary.

In this passage the heavenly messenger greets Mary: "Hail, full of grace, the Lord is with you!" (Luke 1.28). Gabriel announces to her the advent of a new age, the fulfillment of the ancient promises in the divine Messiah to be born of her. She is called "full of grace" because she is to be the mother of the Savior. She is "blessed among women" because she is so highly favored by the Lord's presence in her.

Mary's words "How can this be, since I have no husband?" (Luke 1.34) recall her commitment to serve the Lord with the undivided love of a virginal heart. But a human father was not necessary: "The Holy Spirit will come upon you, and the power of the Most High will overshadow you" (Luke 1.35). Once God's plan was made clear to her, Mary freely gave her consent in an act of humble faith and loving obedience: "Behold, I am the handmaid of the Lord; let it be to me according to your word" (Luke 1.38).

6. What do the Gospel accounts of the Visitation, the birth of Jesus, and the Presentation tell us of Mary?

The Gospel account of the Visitation praises Mary's great faith through the lips of Elizabeth, the mother of John the Baptist: "And blessed is she who believed that there would be a fulfillment of what was spoken to her from the Lord" (Luke 1.45). Mary replied with her magnificent canticle of praise of God, the *Magnificat*.

The birth of Jesus occurs in a setting of poverty which, by divine design, seems to call attention to the reality of the Child's humanity. And at the Presentation His parents observe the law of the Lord; they offer the least expensive of sacrifices, the offering of the poor. In the temple, Simeon's prophecy links Mary with the sufferings of the Messiah.

7. What does the Gospel of St. John say of Mary?

Although the fourth Gospel speaks of Mary only twice, once at the beginning of the Lord's public life and again at the foot of the cross, the author reveals much about Mary.

First of all, the use of the title "Woman" when Christ addresses His mother at Cana and from the cross on Calvary suggests her unique association with His redemptive mission. We may view this title, as did many of the Fathers of the Church, as a symbolic designation of her as the "woman" of Genesis 3.15, the "New Eve," the mother of all who are called to live by the "new creation" of her divine Son.

At Cana, Christ chose to anticipate the "hour" in which His glory would be manifested by working a miracle (or "sign") at her bidding. The circumstances indicate that her faith was unparalleled among His associates. Furthermore, it was as a result of her intercession that the others "believed in Him" (John 2.11).

So also on Calvary, where the words of Jesus, "Woman, behold your son!" (John 19.26), point to Mary's spiritual motherhood of all the faithful. Now that the hour of His saving death had been accomplished, Mary is definitively designated as the "Woman," the "New Eve" associated with the "New Adam" in bringing to new life the adopted children of God, the brothers and sisters of her divine Son.

8. What did the early Church believe about Mary?

The earliest Fathers of the Church guarded what the Gospels themselves said of Mary. The principal expression of Christian faith concerning Mary was the simple teaching of the creeds: Christ was truly in Mary's womb and was really born of the Holy Spirit and the Virgin.

During the early patristic period, the Church's primary need was to safeguard the reality of the Lord's humanity against the heresies of docetism and gnosticism, heresies which denied that Jesus was really a man or that He truly had a human birth from Mary.

9. Why is Mary called the "Mother of God"?

Mary is called the Mother of God because she really conceived Jesus, who is the Son of God, and really gave birth to Him. The woman who conceives and gives birth to a person is that person's mother. Although the divine nature of Christ is eternally begotten by the Father, He who is the Son of God was conceived and born in time of Mary. She is, therefore, truly the Mother of God.

The heretic Nestorius wished Mary to be called only "mother of Christ," not "mother of God." The reason for his denial seems to have been this: that he shared the Arian denial that Jesus was really the Son of God. The entire Eastern Church arose to proclaim its faith that Mary is the Mother of God. In 431 the Council of Ephesus proclaimed the faith of the earlier Fathers who "have not hesitated to call the holy Virgin 'Mother of God' (Theotokos). . . ."

10. Is it fitting that the Mother of God should be a virgin?

Yes. It is fitting that the Mother of God should be a virgin. The virginal conception of Jesus is a fitting witness to the divine transcendence of her Child who has no human father, since God alone is His Father.

Mary's virginity has also an ecclesial significance. For, metaphorically speaking, the Church too is a virgin mother, who brings forth the adopted brothers and sisters of Christ through her ministry of the Word and the sacraments. Moreover, Mary is the model for those who choose chastity as priests or religious; she inspires them to bear witness to the ultimate meaning and final goal of salvation history, the heavenly city where there will be no marriage.

11. Did Mary conceive as a virgin?

Yes. It is a dogma of Catholic faith that Mary conceived Jesus virginally through the power of the Holy Spirit.

True, this teaching has never been solemnly defined by an ecumenical council or by a pope. But it is a dogma, founded on the clear teaching of Scripture, as understood and constantly taught by the universal and ordinary teaching authority of the Church.

12. Did Mary give birth as a virgin?

Yes. The Church also proclaims that Mary gave birth as a virgin.

"She brought Him forth without the loss of virginity, even as she conceived Him without the loss of virginity . . . it was a miraculous birth" (Pope St. Leo I). "A virgin who conceives, a virgin who gives birth, a virgin with Child, a virgin delivered of Child — a virgin ever virgin! Why do you marvel at these things, O man? When God vouchsafed to become man, it was fitting that He be born in this way" (St. Augustine).

13. Did Mary remain always a virgin?

Yes. It is a dogma of Catholic faith, taught firmly from early centuries, that Mary remained a virgin throughout her entire life.

This teaching is implicit in Scripture, and it became explicit and clear in the faith-consciousness of the Church in early centuries. The Church has steadfastly believed and taught that Mary remained true to God in the intense fervor of her virginal love. By the miracle of the virginal conception He had enabled her to be both virgin and mother. The constant use in the Church of the title "virgin" for Mary gave testimony to the firm faith that she guarded this gift always. By the fourth century "ever-virgin" became a popular title for Mary. This faith remains firm in the Church; the Second Vatican Council also proclaims her a "perpetual virgin" (LG 52).

14. Was Mary eminently holy?

Yes. Mary was blessed by God with outstanding gifts of grace, because she was to be the Mother of God and to play a central role in her Son's work of redemption.

In the *Magnificat*, Mary acknowledges that God is the source of all the blessings she has received, and in it she was moved to acknowledge prophetically: "Henceforth all generations will call me blessed" (Luke 1.48) precisely because almighty God freely chose to do great things in her.

15. What is the Immaculate Conception?

The Immaculate Conception is a singular grace and privilege in virtue of which Mary was created by God in holiness from the first moment of her existence. She was kept free from original sin, and enjoyed the grace of God from the moment of her conception.

Only gradually did the faith of the Church come to realize fully the reality of Mary's Immaculate Conception. From early days of the Church it seemed entirely inappropriate that she who was "Mother of God" and "full of grace" should ever have been touched by sin. But how could she be said to be redeemed by Christ if she had never experienced even original sin? The Holy Spirit at length led the Church to a solution of this difficulty by helping the faithful to realize that Mary was redeemed in a singular way. As a member of a sinful race Mary would naturally have incurred original sin; but a special divine mercy kept her free from sin precisely because of the foreseen or anticipated merits of Jesus Christ. Mary's holiness from the first moment of her existence, therefore, was the first fruit of her divine Son's redeeming work.

CHAPTER 8

The Public Life of Jesus

The Church's love for Jesus, flowing from faith in Him as the divine Savior, has always led it to have a special appreciation of eyewitness testimony about the Messiah. The memory of His words and deeds was guarded with great affection. The most esteemed material is found in the inspired texts of the New Testament.

Here, then, we speak of the words and deeds of Jesus in His public life, that is, in the years between His baptism and His passion. The chapter treats of the truth of the Gospels, Jesus' public life, His miracles, His preaching, His self-revelation, and His first planting the seeds of His Church.

1. Do the Gospels give us a true account of the words and works of Jesus in His public life?

Yes. The Gospels are inspired and true accounts of the things that Jesus said and did. The authors of the Gospels took great care to gather information from many who had seen and heard Jesus. They wrote both with personal care and with the assistance of the Holy Spirit so that their readers would "know the truth concerning the things of which you have been informed" (Luke 1.4).

This does not mean that the Gospels are simply chronicles giving in every case the precise words of Jesus, or histories written in a modern form. But it does mean that the inspired accounts are thoroughly reliable, and the evangelists "told us the honest truth about Jesus" (DV 19).

2. What role did John the Baptist play in preparing for Jesus?

John the Baptist, the cousin of Jesus, prepared the people for the coming of Jesus by leading them toward conversion of life and repentance for their sins, and by stirring up expectation in the coming of the Messiah by preaching that "the kingdom of heaven is at hand" (Matt. 3.2).

Through his heroic and courageous life John won the trust of the multitudes, so that when he pointed out Jesus as the "Lamb of God" (John 1.29) and as one far greater than himself, the people were able to turn to Jesus with expectation and hope.

3. Was the baptism John conferred the same as the baptism instituted by Jesus?

No. John's baptism was simply a symbolic act, calling people to express sincere repentance for their sins. But the baptism instituted by Jesus is sacramental: through it Jesus entirely takes away sin, confers grace, and makes one a child of God.

> John said: "I baptize you with water for repentance, but He who is coming after me is mightier than I, whose sandals I am not worthy to carry; He will baptize you with the Holy Spirit and with fire" (Matt. 3.11).

4. How did Jesus begin His public life?

Jesus began His public life by receiving the baptism of John. Jesus then went into the desert region for a period of prayer and fasting, and allowed Himself to be tempted by the devil. Jesus was utterly unmoved by these temptations, and showed Himself aware of the meaning and mission of His life. He was then about thirty years old.

> At His baptism Jesus received not only the testimony of John the Baptist; divine signs at the time of His baptism showed also the seal of the Father's approval on the work He was about to begin.

5. Did Jesus choose apostles to assist Him in His mission?

Yes. When Jesus began His preaching, He gathered around Himself a small band of close followers or disciples who accepted Him as their Teacher and who followed Him wherever He preached. From among these Jesus chose a select group, the Twelve, who were also called apostles, to whose instruction and formation Jesus gave special care.

> "The names of the twelve apostles are these: first, Simon, who is called Peter, and Andrew his brother; James the son of Zebedee, and John his brother; Philip and Bartholomew; Thomas and Matthew the tax collector; James the son of Alphaeus, and Thaddaeus; Simon the Cananaean, and Judas Iscariot, who betrayed him" (Matt.10.2-4).

6. Did Jesus prepare the apostles to be leaders in His Church?

Yes. To His apostles He gave more intense instruction in the message He was teaching, and more careful formation in prayer and in the spirit of their mission.

> Gradually He led them to realize more fully the mystery of His mission and His Person. He promised to give them a share in His own authority in the service of the saving mission He gave them. To the leader among them, Simon, He gave a new name, Peter (which means "rock"), after Simon had professed faith in Jesus in the name of all the apostles. "You are Peter, and on this rock I will build My church, and the powers of death shall not prevail against it. I will give you the keys of the kingdom of heaven, and whatever you bind on earth shall be bound in heaven, and

58

whatever you loose on earth shall be loosed in heaven" (Matt. 16.18-19).

Jesus had made clear to them the purpose of their teaching and pastoral authority. They were not to lord it over others, but to serve them, as Christ Himself came to serve. Yet this was to be a faithful and courageous service, firmly helping all to be able to come to faith and loyal service to the Lord.

7. Why were crowds of people attracted to follow Jesus?

The witness of John the Baptist first called the attention of the multitudes to Jesus. But the crowds were drawn to Him more by the beauty and strength of His words, by the goodness and power of His merciful works, and by the immense attraction of His personality.

8. Why did many of the leaders of the Jews become hostile to Jesus?

Some, devoted to the teachings of Moses and the prophets, and not understanding that Jesus came to fulfill the law rather than abolish it, seem to have judged that His new teachings were unfaithful to the word of God long handed down. But jealousy was also evident. Moreover, Jesus' teachings made great demands on those who heard them; and those not prepared for the profound conversion of heart He called for became resentful and hostile.

Early rejection turned gradually into hostility so great that some began plotting to take Jesus' life, persuading themselves that this would be a service to God and His law. But their plots were hampered by their fear that people would side with and protect the Galilean Preacher.

9. Did Jesus work miracles in His public life?

Yes. Catholic faith acknowledges that Christ the Lord "wrought many obvious miracles" and that these miracles are "signs of revelation that are most certain and suited to the intelligence of all" (First Vatican Council). Christ's miracles were not simply wonderful or astonishing works. They are, above all, signs of God's presence and care, ministering to the faith and love of those who saw or heard of them.

Clearly Jesus did not want His followers to develop a taste for "signs and wonders" (John 4.48). It was both in compassion for human sorrows, and to signify the presence of God's love and power, that He cured the lame, the lepers, and the deaf and dumb, and that He raised the dead to life. One of Jesus' more frequent signs was a demonstration of His superiority over the powers of darkness by driving out devils from the possessed.

10. Was Jesus' preaching a sign of His divine mission?

Yes. Jesus preached with such wisdom and understanding that even hearers inclined to be hostile reported: "No man ever spoke like this man!" (John 7.46). "He taught them as one who had authority" (Mark 1.22), with a confidence and strength based on the certainty of His knowledge and the resolute goodness of His heart.

Jesus preached in attractive parables that enabled each hearer to grasp as much as he or she was capable of receiving. The message He taught was the Good News of salvation, the truth that we were made to know and love; and He preached this with a power and grace that won the hearts of multitudes. Yet He also preached difficult and demanding truths, and did not cease to do so when those who refused to "repent and believe in the Gospel" (Mark 1.15) rejected His saving message.

11. Did Jesus reject the moral teachings of the Old Testament?

No. He confirmed the heart of the Old Law, the ten commandments, and the traditional precepts of love. Frequently He insisted that He had come not to abolish the law, but to fulfill it.

Jesus in fact taught more excellent and more demanding precepts than the Old Law had. The law, for example, forbade adultery; but Jesus taught that "everyone who looks at a woman lustfully has already committed adultery with her in his heart" (Matt. 5.28). General practice in first-century Palestine condoned divorce in certain cases, but Jesus explained that this was a deviation from the original divine plan, and that there should be no divorce at all. He taught that love of God should have absolutely first place in our lives, that we should forgive even those who have hurt us deeply, and that we should love our enemies. Yet Jesus taught that those who came to Him with all their heart would not find His precepts burdensome: "Come to Me all you who labor and are heavy laden, and I will give you rest. . . . For My yoke is easy, and My burden is light" (Matt. 11.28-30).

12. Was Jesus Himself a sign of His own mission?

Yes. Though many were attracted to Jesus by His words and by His powerful deeds, it was His very being and personality that most attracted attention. His deeds of mercy flowed from a heart that was infinitely loving and entirely devoted to doing the will of the Father. He was concerned with the good of His brothers and sisters whose humanity He shared. His great goodness led Him to forgive the repentant, as it led Him to rebuke those who needed correction. In fact His personal wisdom and goodness were so great that they led to a crisis: His contemporaries began to become slowly aware that Jesus was far more than just an exemplary human being. His identity became the key issue in their dealings with Him.

When some sought to kill Jesus, He asked them: "I have shown you many good works from the Father; for which of these do you stone Me?" And the mob retorted: "We stone You for no good work but for blasphemy; because You, being a man, make Yourself God" (John 10.32-33).

13. Do the Gospels portray Christ as establishing a new covenant?

Yes. As Jesus taught and defended His doctrine, it became more and more evident that He was inviting people to a new form of life, to a new relationship with God that could not be contained within the institutions of Judaism. Those who followed Him were to be a new people, to be subjects for God's new kingdom, which was at hand.

There were very demanding requirements for entrance into this kingdom: conversion of heart, faith in the teachings of Jesus about the Father and the kind of response the Father wishes from those who are called to the kingdom, and personal faith in Jesus as the Cornerstone of all. Through the sacred signs that Jesus gave, such as baptism, they were to be gathered together. Jesus Himself was to be the new Bread from heaven, nourishing them in their journey to the truer Promised Land; it was not the blood of lambs but His own blood that was to be the sanctification of the new and everlasting covenant.

CHAPTER 9

By Dying He Destroyed Our Death

"We believe in our Lord Jesus Christ, who is the Son of God. . . . Under Pontius Pilate He suffered, the Lamb of God bearing the sins of the world, and He died for us on the cross, saving us by His redeeming blood. . . . We believe that our Lord Jesus Christ by the sacrifice of the cross redeemed us from original sin and all the personal sins committed by each one of us, so that, in accordance with the word of the apostle, 'where sin abounded, grace did more abound' (Rom. 5.20)" (Pope Paul VI).

In this chapter we speak of Jesus Christ the Redeemer, of His passion and death for us, and of the meaning of our redemption. The follower of Christ glories in the cross of Christ, the cross "which is a stumbling block to the unbelievers (cf. 1 Cor. 1.23), but to us is salvation and eternal life" (St. Ignatius of Antioch).

1. Did Jesus Christ intend to suffer and die for us?

Yes. Jesus Christ, the Son of God, came into this world to save us by dying for us and rising again. "For us men and for our salvation he came down from heaven" (Roman Missal).

> The Gospels portray Christ foretelling His passion, death, and resurrection; but they indicate also that His disciples could not begin to understand this saving mystery until it had been accomplished.

2. Was the death of Christ necessary for our salvation?

The death of Jesus was not absolutely necessary for our salvation. God could have saved us in other ways. He could have accepted inadequate expressions of human repentance and atonement as satisfaction for human sin, or indeed He could have simply forgiven the sin gratuitously. But it was God's will that redemption be achieved in the most perfect and fitting way. For this it was necessary that He who is God should become man and suffer for us. In this sense we can say that Jesus' passion was necessary for our salvation.

> The prophets had foretold that the Savior would suffer to bring salvation to His people. The passion was necessary also in the sense that prophetic words, inspired by God, must be fulfilled. Recalling these prophecies, Jesus asked the disciples on Easter day: "Was it not necessary that the Christ should suffer these things and enter into His glory?" (Luke 24.26).

3. Why is Jesus a perfect Redeemer?

Jesus is a perfect Redeemer because He is truly God and truly man. Jesus, as the man who is the Son of God, is the new Adam and Head of the Mystical Body. He has profound solidarity with all of us; He enables us to be united with Him as closely as the branches are with the vine. Since we are so united with Him, His saving acts can count as ours. Because His humanity is the humanity of One who is the Son of God, His saving acts have infinite value, and are more than sufficient to atone fully for all our sins against the infinite God.

> Through the mystery of Christ's passion God the Father brings about our salvation in a most generous way, and in a way that honors the humanity He saves. In Christ He allows a man to bring Him gifts in every way worthy and sufficient to redeem mankind. "Man merited death. . . . A man by His dying would conquer death. . . . It was better for us to have been delivered by Christ's passion than by God's will alone" (St. Thomas Aquinas).

4. Why was Christ's passion and death a perfect act of redemption?

First of all, the passion was a perfect act of redemption because it reveals the greatness of God's love. When the Son of God in His humanity freely laid down His life for us, He taught us how much we are loved by God, and He enabled us to love God in return. Secondly, the cross teaches us vividly the gross malice of sin. Thirdly, in the heroism of the passion Christ gave us a pattern for the obedience, humility, and steadfastness that we need to serve God faithfully, and He showed us the need to do works of justice and mercy even if we are being treated unjustly. Finally, the passion of Christ is also an immense comfort to those burdened with pain, fear, contempt, loneliness, or fear of death. They can know that God Himself has freely endured such evils and that He fully understands us when we invoke Him in our trials.

5. Why is Jesus Christ called our Mediator?

Jesus Christ is called our Mediator because when all mankind was alienated from God by sin He restored us to peace with the Father, bringing together in Himself God and humanity. He mediates, brings together, and unites humanity and God in His very person, and by His saving passion He enables all human persons to be reunited with their God.

> Others by their grace-filled acts may play a role in the saving work of Christ, but only in a secondary way. Jesus is the indispensable Mediator of peace. "For there is one God, and there is one mediator between God and men, the man Christ Jesus" (1 Tim. 2.5).

6. Does Catholic faith and devotion center on the passion of Jesus?

From the beginning the Church focused her attention on the infinite love that shines from the cross of Christ. "We preach Christ crucified" (1 Cor. 1.23). "Far be it from me to glory except in the cross of our Lord Jesus Christ" (Gal. 6.14). When the Gospels were written, the longest single section of each was the history of the passion. The Eucharist, which was and is the central liturgical act of the Christian community, is a memorial of His death.

His passion and death are recalled in such devotions as the Stations of the Cross and the sorrowful mysteries of the rosary. Popular Christian devotion has always stressed meditation on the saving sufferings of Jesus. "In the cross is salvation; in the cross is life; in the cross is protection from enemies" (Thomas à Kempis).

7. How is the Last Supper related to the passion of Jesus?

In each of the Gospels the passion narrative begins with an account of the Last Supper. At this sacred banquet on the night before Jesus died for us He clarified the meaning of His passion. He there revealed the greatness of His saving love. "Having loved His own who were in the world, He loved them to the end" (John 13.1). At this supper He instituted the sacraments of the Eucharist and the priesthood, through which He would be with us forever, constantly recalling and making present to us the saving love of His death.

At the Last Supper, Christ promulgated the most sublime precept of fraternal love: "A new command I give to you, that you love one another; even as I have loved you, that you also love one another" (John 13.34). He prayed that splintered humanity might be brought together in unity, a unity that the immense love of His passion would make possible. There too He revealed the utterly unselfish nature of His love, the only love that brings peace to a broken world. "Peace I leave with you, My peace I give to you" (John 14.27).

8. What sufferings did Jesus endure before His crucifixion?

After the Last Supper, in a garden on the Mount of Olives, in which He was accustomed to pray, He underwent a terrible spiritual agony. As He prayed to the Father, He was almost overcome with dread at the sufferings to come; yet He remained steadfast: "Nevertheless, not as I will, but as You will" (Matt. 26.39). After this He suffered the pain of being betrayed by one of His own apostles, Judas Iscariot, into the hands of those who wished to kill him. "Then all His disciples forsook Him and fled" (Matt. 26.56). Before the priests, Herod, and Pilate, He was humiliated by unjust accusations and unfair judges. He was mocked, scourged, spat upon, and crowned with thorns. At length Pilate sentenced Him to death.

9. How did Jesus die for us?

Jesus freely endured the agony and humiliation of crucifixion for us. He suffered not only extreme physical pain, but also loneliness and desolation, and the sorrow of seeing unfathomable pain in His mother, Mary. But even in the torment of these hours, Jesus retained patience and greatness of soul.

Some insight into His mind and heart may be gained from His "seven last words" as recorded in the Gospels. "Father, forgive them, for they know not what they do" (Luke 23.34). To a thief who had been crucified with Him, and asked for mercy: "Truly, I say to you, today you will be with Me in Paradise" (Luke 23.43). To His mother and the apostle John: "Woman, behold, your son! . . . Behold, your mother!" (John 19.26-27). From a prophetic psalm: "My God, My God, why have You forsaken Me?" (Matt. 27.46). "I thirst" (John 19.28). "It is finished" (John 19.30). Again in words drawn from a prophetic psalm: "Father, into Your hands I commend My spirit" (Luke 23.46).

10. Why is Jesus called a priest and His death called a sacrifice?

The New Testament clearly calls Jesus the "great high priest" (Heb. 4.14) of the new and everlasting covenant. As a priest of a new order, superior to every former priesthood, He announced the New Covenant with God at the Last Supper. By offering the one perfect sacrifice of Himself on the cross, He gave perfect worship to the Father and won eternal salvation for us.

His dying for us is called a sacrifice because it fulfills most perfectly the nature of a sacrificial act. A sacrifice is an act of worship of God, in which a gift is offered to God by a suitably chosen priest in a way suited to express absolute recognition of God, for example, by the destruction of the offering. Jesus, the perfect priest, chosen from eternity by the Father, offered to the Father Himself all His love and obedience, His body and His blood.

Clearly Christ did not kill Himself; others slew Him. But He as priest freely gave Himself as the victim in a perfect sacrifice. Christ appeared before the Father in His priestly work as the representative of all humanity, for He was the new Adam, the head of redeemed mankind.

11. What are the effects of Jesus' sacrifice on the cross?

By His sacrificial death Jesus redeemed us; He set us free from sin and from eternal damnation. He reconciled us to the Father, and He won for us anew the life of grace and the hope of everlasting life. He merited for us the sublime gifts that make us children of God and able to participate in God's life. He crushed the power of Satan, and He made possible for us a holy life in this world, and life forever in His kingdom, in which every evil which flows from sin will be entirely overcome.

12. Did Jesus die for every human person?

Yes. God "desires all men to be saved" (1 Tim. 2.4), and so Christ "died for all" (2 Cor. 2.15). It is true that Christ does not force anyone to accept eternal life; but He saves all who, moved by His superabundant grace, freely come to Him and freely live His new life.

"And let him who is thirsty come, let him who desires take the water of life without price" (Rev. 22.17).

13. Why is the cross central to Christian life?

Nothing of Christian life can be understood apart from the cross. By His cross we are saved and brought to life. The Eucharist and the other sacraments by which we cling to Christ are sacred signs by which the Lord communicates to us the fruits of redemption from the tree of the cross. In the cross Christ teaches us the patient, forgiving, and generous love that must illumine and guide all Christian living.

"Christ also suffered for you, leaving you an example, that you should follow in His steps" (1 Peter 2.21). "If any man would come after Me, let him deny himself and take up his cross daily and follow Me" (Luke 9:23).

CHAPTER • 10

By Rising He Restored Our Life

"This is the night when Jesus Christ broke the chains of death and rose triumphant from the grave" (Roman Missal). The Church celebrates the resurrection of Jesus with surpassing joy. Not only Easter, but every Sunday of the year is a celebration of the Lord's resurrection. For the rising of Jesus not only confirms the Church's faith, but is the central mystery through which God calls us to life. The hope to which we are born in coming to faith is "a living hope through the resurrection of Jesus Christ from the dead" (1 Peter 1.3).

In this chapter we speak of the mystery of the resurrection, of what it means to believe in the resurrection, and of the reality of the Lord's rising in the flesh, in the very body which was crucified. We also speak of the ascension of Jesus, in which His enduring presence among men acquired a new form.

1. Did Jesus rise from the dead?

Yes. Jesus Christ truly rose from the dead, and appeared to His apostles, living a new and transformed life in the same flesh in which He had suffered.

> The Catholic faith has always taught, and yet teaches against all denials, that Christ's rising from the dead was an historical event for which there is convincing evidence. Jesus Himself gave evidence "by many proofs" (Acts 1.3) to His apostles; and even up to the present day He gives signs of His resurrection, to lead men to faith.

2. Did Jesus rise by His own power?

Yes. Because He is the Son of God as well as fully human, He was able to, and did, restore Himself to life in the flesh.

> Jesus said: "I lay down My life that I may take it up again. . . . I have power to take it again" (John 10.17-18).
>
> God the Father may also be said to have raised Jesus to life: "God raised Him up" (Acts 2.4). For the power of the one God belongs to the Father and the Son equally. When the power of the resurrection is seen as the seal of the Father's approval, the glorification of Jesus' humanity is viewed as the work of the Father. When it is seen as a manifestation of Jesus' divine power and personality, it is viewed as the act of the Son Himself.

3. Was Jesus' resurrection literally a resurrection of the body?

Yes. The Gospel accounts of the resurrection and the enduring faith of the Church stress that Jesus rose again in the very flesh in which He had suffered for us.

For example, when the apostle St. Thomas refused to believe in the resurrection unless he could see and touch the wounds in the once-crucified hands and side, Christ enabled him to have the signs he longed for. "Put your finger here and see My hands; and put out your hand and place it in My side; do not be faithless, but believing" (John 20.27). Another Gospel account of Jesus' appearance to His disciples, who were startled and inclined to doubt, recalls His words to them: "See My hands and My feet, that it is I Myself; handle Me, and see; for a spirit has not flesh and bones as you see that I have" (Luke 24.39).

Faith in the bodily resurrection is entirely essential to Christianity. Faith teaches that Christ is fully alive now; that He is our living Brother, living in human body and soul as well as in His divinity. His living body in the Eucharist is at the center of Catholic worship. Our belief that we too will rise from the dead in a bodily resurrection is grounded in our faith that Jesus so rose. "If Christ has not been raised, your faith is futile" (1 Cor. 15.17).

4. Did eyewitnesses actually see the risen Lord?

Yes. Not only the apostles, but very many of the disciples of Jesus saw Him risen from the dead.

"He was raised on the third day in accordance with the scriptures. And He appeared to Cephas, then to the twelve. Then He appeared to more than five hundred brethren at one time, most of whom are still alive, though some of them have fallen asleep" (1 Cor. 15.4-6).

Those contemporaries who did not themselves see Jesus had many signs to help them know Jesus had in fact risen from the dead. The testimony of many eyewitnesses was especially persuasive, for these were people who had been transformed by the graces of the Holy Spirit that surrounded the Easter mystery. Their utterly new lives confirmed the truth of what they said. The tomb of Jesus, which had been guarded, was found empty, so that no one could effectively contradict their testimony. Jesus, moreover, had given the disciples power to perform miracles in compassion and as helps toward faith. And the message they taught was the Good News Jesus had proclaimed. Above all, the power of the Holy Spirit was present, enabling those who had seen important signs of the truth to come to a personal faith in the whole mystery that the apostles testified to.

"And we are witnesses to these things, and so is the Holy Spirit, whom God has given to those who obey Him" (Acts 5.32).

5. Were His disciples slow to believe that Jesus had risen to life again?

Yes. They had not understood His teaching that He must die and rise again. In the course of His passion their faith and courage failed, and they all abandoned Him. Faith does not easily rise to life again; even when they saw Him risen they were inclined to doubt for a while what they could actually see.

> "Jesus Himself stood among them. But they were startled and frightened, and supposed that they saw a spirit. And He said to them, 'Why are you troubled, and why do questionings rise in your hearts? See My hands and My feet, that it is I Myself. . .' " (Luke 24.36-39).

6. How did the apostles come to faith in the resurrection?

The mercy and grace of Christ gently led them to faith. There were stages in their return to belief in Him. First He overcame their irrational fears and refusals to believe what He enabled them to see, that is, that He was indeed alive again and with them. But belief in the resurrection implies more than recognizing that the man Jesus was astonishingly alive again. To believe fully in Christ's resurrection is to believe that by His own power He had been raised to a new and unending life, and also that He is the saving Lord and God who calls all to eternal life in Himself.

> Such faith requires more than seeing one who has been restored to life. The presence and grace of Jesus gradually led the apostles back to faith, and made their faith far stronger than it had been before the passion.

7. What visible signs today lead toward faith in the resurrection?

Believers today do not see the same evidence for the resurrection that the disciples and others in apostolic times saw. Nevertheless, many signs of His resurrection and His living presence still shine in the Church that is built upon Christ. Of these signs or marks we shall speak in treating the Catholic Church.

> The Pharisee Gamaliel spoke of such signs when, in apostolic days, he sought to discourage those who wished to kill Christ's followers. He gave them this advice: "If this plan or undertaking is of men, it will fail; but if it is of God, you will not be able to overthrow them. You might even be found opposing God!" (Acts 5.38-39). Christianity is shown to be from God and to be true by its growth and endurance, by the unparalleled unity of belief and hope that it has created in the hearts of many, and by the great goodness it has made possible in those who walk in the light and strength that faith makes accessible.

> To see the striking signs that bear witness to the truth of Christianity does not require faith, just as recognition of the risen Jesus did not itself require faith. It does, however, require a certain openness of heart and

mind. And to progress from seeing the signs of the truth to personal faith requires free acceptance of the grace of Christ.

8. Had the resurrection of Jesus been foretold by the prophets?

Yes. Catholic faith proclaims that He rose "on the third day in accordance with the scriptures" (1 Cor. 15.4). His death was not an accidental tragedy, and His rising was not an improvised solution to an unexpected problem. His paschal mystery was predestined from the beginning of creation. All the promises of God that God Himself would save His people are fulfilled in the death and resurrection of Jesus.

Jesus said to two disciples on Easter day: "O foolish men, and slow of heart to believe all that the prophets have spoken! Was it not necessary that the Christ should suffer these things and enter into His glory?" (Luke 24.25).

9. What is meant by "the power of Christ's resurrection"?

When Scripture speaks of "the power of His resurrection" (Phil. 3.10) it reminds us that the resurrection is far more than a sign bearing witness to the Person of Jesus and confirming the truth of the Good News He had proclaimed. Through His passion and resurrection Christ won the eternal glory that shines forever in His humanity. Since His incarnation He had been the true Son of God; but in the resurrection His divine glory became manifest in the splendor of His risen humanity, and His power to sanctify and save the world became more evident. It is the risen Lord who brings to the whole world faith, hope, love, and His own mighty peace.

At the Last Supper Christ had told His apostles that those who believed in Him would do "greater works" (John 14.12) than He Himself had done on earth. His disciples did indeed proclaim His message in ways that led the multitude of nations to faith; they brought the "power to become children of God" (John 1.12) to every age. But it is the risen Lord who teaches through their words, who sanctifies when they administer the sacraments, and who works within by the power of His grace.

Our personal hope for eternal salvation rests upon the power of His resurrection. "If Christ has not been raised, your faith is futile. . . . But in fact Christ has been raised from the dead, the first fruits of those who have fallen asleep" (1 Cor. 15.17, 20).

10. What is meant by the ascension of Jesus?

There are two aspects to the ascension of Jesus. First of all, it is a glorification of Jesus in His humanity. With our human nature He "ascended far above all the heavens" (Eph. 1.20) and "sat down at the right hand of God" (Mark 16.19). Secondly, the ascension marked the completion of His visible ministry on earth, and the beginning of a new and even more intimate way of being present to and caring for all who belonged to Him.

St. Luke notes that forty days elapsed between the resurrection and the ascension. But the time is not the important point. So also the saying that He "ascended above all the heavens" does not imply that He is now far from us. Jesus in His ascension is not abandoning us. But His relationship to earth is no longer limited to specific times and places. By His ascension Jesus comes to the Father as the eternal High Priest, "able for all time to save those who draw near to God through Him, since He always lives to make intercession for them" (Heb. 7.25).

But the risen Lord also retains a most intimate presence among us. Scriptural accounts of the ascension relate the event to the sending of the Holy Spirit and the mission of the Church. Though He deprives us of his visible presence for a time that He might send the gift of the Spirit, Christ will be with the Church always, in her life of faith and prayer, in her works of charity, and in her sacramental contacts with His glorified humanity.

CHAPTER 11

The Holy Spirit

"We believe in the Holy Spirit, the Lord, the Giver of life, who proceeds from the Father and the Son" (Roman Missal). The Holy Spirit is a Person of the Blessed Trinity, truly and eternally God. He is the Paraclete, the Comforter that Christ promised the apostles would be given "to be with you for ever" (John 14.16). "God's love has been poured into our hearts through the Holy Spirit who has been given to us" (Rom. 5.5).

In this chapter we speak of the Holy Spirit, of His work in the Church, of His presence in each member of the faithful, and of the gifts He gives, distributing them "to each one individually as He wills" (1 Cor. 12.11).

1. Who is the Holy Spirit?

The Holy Spirit is the third Person in the Blessed Trinity. He is coeternal and coequal with the Father and the Son.

Catholic faith believes that God dwells with us most intimately by the gift of the Holy Spirit. The Spirit is sent by the Father and by Jesus to give light, comfort, and strength, and to stir up within us newness of life. The Holy Spirit seals our friendship with God, and He unites us with one another by the divine love He pours forth within our hearts.

2. Was God the Holy Spirit revealed in the Old Testament?

In the centuries of salvation history there was a gradual revelation of the Holy Spirit. The Old Testament taught that God was present in the world and in the hearts of people by His Spirit, and that in Messianic days the life and joy given by the gift of God's Spirit would be abundant. But the mystery of the Trinity, the truth that there are three persons in the one God, was not distinctly revealed in the Old Testament, and the Holy Spirit was not revealed as a distinct divine Person.

Spirit (in Hebrew, "Ruah") signified the dynamic force under which a person acts. We read, for example, that "the Spirit of the LORD came mightily upon David" (1 Sam. 16.13) when he was anointed by Samuel. The Spirit of the Lord descended on the prophets; under His impetus they could proclaim the word of the Lord with courage and absolute faithfulness. The Old Testament looked forward to Messianic days when God would pour out His Spirit richly: "I will pour My Spirit upon your descendants, and My blessing on your offspring" (Isa. 44.3). But upon the Messiah Himself the fullness of the Spirit would come: "Behold My servant, whom I uphold, My chosen one in whom My soul delights; I have put My Spirit upon Him" (Isa. 42.1).

3. How is the Holy Spirit spoken of in the New Testament?

It is Jesus who revealed to us the inner life of God in the Blessed Trinity, and it is through Jesus that the Spirit of God was revealed as a Person distinct from the Father and the Son, as the personal Love within the Trinity who is the source and pattern of all created love.

The Gospels, written after the coming of the Holy Spirit and under His inspiration, speak often of the Holy Spirit even in describing events occurring before the paschal and pentecostal mysteries. At the Annunciation Mary was told: "The Holy Spirit will come upon you, and the power of the Most High will overshadow you" (Luke 1.35); then Mary "was found to be with child of the Holy Spirit" (Matt. 1.18). When Mary visited them, Elizabeth and Zechariah were "filled with the Holy Spirit" (Luke 1.41, 67). John the Baptist said of Jesus: "This is He who baptizes with the Holy Spirit" (John 1.33).

The New Testament speaks most clearly of the Holy Spirit as a Person distinct from the Father and the Son in the discourses of Jesus at the Last Supper, in His words after the Resurrection, in the events surrounding the coming of the Holy Spirit at Pentecost, and in accounts of the activity of the Holy Spirit in the life of the early Church.

4. Did Jesus foretell the coming of the Holy Spirit at Pentecost?

Yes. Jesus told the apostles at the Last Supper: "It is to your advantage that I go away, for if I do not go away the Counselor will not come to you; but if I go, I will send Him to you. . . . When the Spirit of Truth comes He will guide you into all the truth" (John 16.7, 13). At His ascension "He charged them not to depart from Jerusalem, but to wait for the promise of the Father. . . . Before many days you shall be baptized with the Holy Spirit" (Acts 1.4).

5. What was the first major manifestation of the Holy Spirit to the young Church?

On the day of Pentecost, ten days after the Lord's ascension, the Holy Spirit came in a decisive way upon the apostles. "And they were all filled with the Holy Spirit" (Acts 2.3). They had new energy and courage, and spoke with unaccustomed boldness of the mystery of Jesus. Peter spoke to crowds who had come to Jerusalem for the Jewish feast of Pentecost. The Holy Spirit gave such warmth and persuasiveness to his words that about three thousand were converted and asked for baptism.

From that time on the grace and power of the Holy Spirit accompanied the preaching of the Gospel.

6. How did the activity of the Holy Spirit affect the life of the Church?

The scriptural accounts of the early Church, especially in the Acts of the Apostles and in the epistles of St. Paul, show that the guidance and grace of the Holy Spirit were central to the life of the early Church. The early Fathers of the Church insisted that the Church and the Holy Spirit are inseparable. "Where the Church is, there also is the Spirit of God; and where the Spirit of God is, there is the Church" (St. Irenaeus). The Holy Spirit is the "soul," the inner life-giving principle, of the Church, which is the Mystical Body of Christ.

So forceful is the presence of the Spirit in the life of the early Church that the New Testament narrative of the Church's early growth, the Acts of the Apostles, is often called the "Gospel of the Holy Spirit."

It is the Holy Spirit "who, with His heavenly breath of life, is to be considered the Principle of every vital and saving action in all parts of the Body. It is He who, though He is personally present in all the members and is divinely active in them, yet also works in the lower members through the ministry of the higher ones" (Pope Leo XIII).

All the gifts of Christ are poured out upon the Church by the Holy Spirit "for building up the body of Christ" (Eph. 4.12). Of primary importance, therefore, are those gifts that minister to the faith, love, and unity of the whole Church, that is the hierarchical and sacramental gifts of Christ and His Spirit to the People of God. "The whole flock of Christ is preserved and grows in the unity of faith through the action of the same Holy Spirit" who gives the "charism of the Church's infallibility" (LG 25) to the successor of Peter and the "sure charism of truth" (DV 8) to the successors of the apostles. But the ministry of the word is aimed ultimately at love, that divine love which "has been poured into our hearts through the Holy Spirit which has been given to us" (Rom. 5.5).

7. Does the Holy Spirit guide individual Christians as well as the whole Church?

Though the Holy Spirit works in the People of God corporately as the Church, His warmth and love are directed also to each individual Christian. With personal concern He wishes to sanctify each and lead each to the perfection of charity. The process of becoming holy begins at baptism, when the Holy Spirit begins to dwell in the soul, to endow it with sanctifying grace, to implant in it faith, hope, love, and the special gifts of the Holy Spirit.

"Any one who does not have the Spirit of Christ does not belong to Him" (Rom. 8.9).

8. What are charismatic gifts?

In addition to the hierarchical and sacramental gifts given to the whole

Church to serve unity and holiness, and in addition to the inner gifts that make individuals holy, there are also many charismatic gifts, or "charisms." These charisms are not given simply for the sake of the individuals who receive them, but for the benefit of others, "for building up the body of Christ" (Eph. 4.12). They are signs of the presence of God, and sources of encouragement to holiness of life. They include such gifts as those of healing, speaking in tongues, and especially prophecy and the discernment of spirits.

Charismatic gifts "are to be received with thanksgiving and consolation, for they are exceedingly suitable and useful for the needs of the Church. Still extraordinary gifts are not to be rashly sought after. . . . In any case, judgment as to their genuineness and proper use belongs to those who preside over the Church, and to whose special competence it belongs, not indeed to extinguish the Spirit, but to test all things and hold fast to that which is good (cf. 1 Thess. 5.12; 19.21)" (LG 12). All the charisms are by their nature ordered toward "a still more excellent way" (1 Cor. 12.3), that is, the way of Christian love.

9. What is the charism of prophecy?

Prophecy is the charism by which persons moved by the Holy Spirit are led to speak God's words and God's will rather than their own. Often "prophecy" is used for "foretelling the future"; and under divine inspiration there have been prophets who foretold future events. But the charism of prophecy is more frequently concerned with proclaiming God's will for the present. Prophecy calls the Christian community to faithfulness to God and to performance of deeds of justice and mercy.

10. What is meant by discernment of spirits?

The discernment of spirits, or the "ability to distinguish between spirits" (1 Cor. 12.10), is a charism enabling one to determine whether voices or inclinations apparently speaking in the name of God are authentic or not. Such a gift is important for the Church, since it is possible for us to be deceived, and to think that the Holy Spirit is urging us when really we are being moved by some deep desire of our own, or even by hidden and unworthy motives, or by a spirit of the world, or by an evil spirit. Spirits, then, that is, active voices or forces inclining us toward action in the name of the Lord, are to be tested.

"Beloved, do not believe every spirit, but test the spirits to see whether they are of God; for many false prophets have gone out into the world" (1 John 4.1).

Jesus gave us the basic criterion for the discernment of spirits: "You will know them by their fruits" (Matt. 7.16). Utterances and deeds that lead to unity and peace in faith and love are the works of the Holy Spirit; those that turn from faith and disturb the unity of Christian love are not from the Holy Spirit.

11. Was the Bible written under the inspiration of the Holy Spirit?

Yes. All the books of the Bible are sacred because, "having been written under the inspiration of the Holy Spirit (cf. John 20.31; 2 Tim. 3.16; 2 Peter 1.19-21; 3.15-16), they have God as their Author" (DV 11). God chose men and used them in such a way that they "made use of their own powers and abilities," so that "with Him acting in them and through them, they, as true authors, consigned to writing everything and only those things which He wanted" (DV 11).

Since "everything asserted by the inspired authors or sacred writers must be held to be asserted by the Holy Spirit," it must firmly be acknowledged that the books of Scripture "teach firmly, faithfully, and without error that truth which God wanted to put into the sacred writings for our salvation" (DV 11).

12. What is the enduring mission of the Holy Spirit in the Church?

"The Spirit dwells in the Church and in the hearts of the faithful as in a temple (cf. 1 Cor. 3.16; 6.19). In them He prays and bears witness to the fact that they are adopted sons (cf. Gal. 4.6; Rom. 8.15-16, 26). The Spirit guides the Church into the fullness of truth (cf. John 16.13) and gives her a unity of fellowship and service. He furnishes and directs her with hierarchical and charismatic gifts, and adorns her with His fruits (cf. Eph. 4.11-12; 1 Cor. 12.4; Gal. 5.22). By the power of the Gospel He makes the Church keep the freshness of youth, perpetually renews her, and leads her to perfect union with her Spouse. The Spirit and the Bride say to the Lord Jesus, 'Come!' (cf. Rev. 22.17)" (LG 4).

CHAPTER • 12

The Holy Trinity

The central mystery of Christian faith is the mystery of the Holy Trinity. "The history of salvation is identical with the history of the way and the plan by which God, true and one, the Father, the Son, the Holy Spirit, reveals Himself to men, and reconciles and unites with Himself those turned away by sin" (General Catechetical Directory).

In this chapter we speak of the mystery of the Trinity, and of what it means to believe in the Trinity, "three persons equal in majesty, undivided in splendor, yet one Lord, one God, ever to be adored" (Roman Missal). We discuss how the mystery of the Trinity transcends human reason but is not contrary to it; how the works of the Trinity in salvation history reveal to us something of the inner life of the Triune God; and how the Persons of the Trinity work in Unity in Their saving deeds for us.

1. What is the doctrine of the Blessed Trinity?
The doctrine of the Blessed Trinity is the central Christian teaching about God. There is only one God, and there are three distinct divine Persons, the Father, the Son, and the Holy Spirit, who possess equally and eternally the same divine nature.

To say that there is only one God or one divine nature is to say that there is only one Wisdom, one Love, one Life that is God, the source and goal of all. This singular divine nature is possessed by three Persons who are coeternal and coequal, the Father and the Son and the Holy Spirit. Thus the inner life of God is a life of interpersonal love; the one God is a Trinity of Persons with whom we can enter into personal relationships through grace. When Christ sent the apostles out to "make disciples of all the nations" (Matt. 28.19), He instructed them to baptize in the name of the Trinity: ". . . baptizing them in the name of the Father and of the Son and of the Holy Spirit" (Matt. 29.19).

2. Why is the doctrine of the Trinity the most basic in the hierarchy of Christian truths?
The doctrine of the Trinity is the most basic in the hierarchy of Christian truths because it is the most essential teaching about God. Moreover, this mystery illumines many other teachings of the faith, and it is presupposed by many other revealed truths.

From the earliest centuries the Church's professions of faith have proclaimed belief in the Trinity of the Father, the Son, and the Holy Spirit. "Now the Catholic faith is this: that we worship one God in the Trinity, and the Trinity in unity. . . . The Father is a distinct person, the Son is a distinct Person, and the Holy Spirit is a distinct Person; but the Father and the Son and the Holy Spirit have one divinity, equal glory, and coeternal majesty" (Creed "Quicumque").

3. How is faith in the Trinity presupposed by other truths of Catholic faith?

One could not believe that Jesus is the Son of God, and true God, sent by the Father, if one did not believe in the plurality of Persons in one God. And one could not grasp the meaning of eternal life, or of the grace that leads to it, without believing in the Trinity, for grace and eternal life are a sharing in the interpersonal life of the Trinity.

"It is impossible to believe explicitly in the mystery of Christ without faith in the Trinity, for the mystery of Christ includes that the Son of God took flesh, that He renewed the world through the grace of the Holy Spirit, and, again, that He was conceived by the Holy Spirit" (St. Thomas Aquinas).

4. What is meant by calling this teaching a mystery?

The Trinity is in the strictest sense a mystery of faith. It is one of those "mysteries hidden in God which, unless divinely revealed, could not come to be known" (First Vatican Council). Some truths of revelation are open to rational investigation and discovery, but mysteries like that of the Trinity can be grasped only by believing God, and only by those who have recognized His testimony as giving full assurance about the message of faith.

The fact that strict mysteries can be grasped only by faith is no affront to human reason. The divine mysteries are not contrary to human reason, nor are they incompatible with the principles of human thought. Although experience and rational reflection cannot fully grasp how these things can be, neither can they find any contradiction in the divine mysteries.

The things God tells us of His inner personal life can be learned only from Him; but reason, enlightened by faith, can come to some understanding of His revelation. "And indeed reason, illumined by faith, when it seeks earnestly, devoutly, and prudently, does attain by a gift from God some understanding of mysteries, and that a most fruitful one" (First Vatican Council).

5. Did God reveal the Trinity from the beginning of salvation history?

No. Only gradually did God make known to us this basic truth about

Himself. In the Old Testament there were foreshadowings, but the mystery of the Trinity was not formally revealed. In the New Testament the mystery is revealed; the Son and the Holy Spirit are made known, and are recognized as God and as distinct from the Father. But for the Church to attain a clearer synthesis of these truths with the enduring truth that there is only one God, took prayer and reflection, and the guidance of the Holy Spirit, through the first centuries of Christian faith.

The word "Trinity" does not appear in the New Testament; and the meaning of the words "person" and "nature," in the precise senses in which these words are used to bear the message of God, had to be carefully refined to bear that message rightly. But what the New Testament teaches is in truth captured with care and reverence in the exact statements of the early councils of the Church.

6. To what extent was the Trinity revealed in the Old Testament?

The Old Testament proclaims part of the mystery of the Trinity, for it proclaims clearly that there is but one God. But it does not speak of a plurality of Persons in God or reveal the inner life of God. Still there are some passages in the Old Testament which seem to be veiled references to, or in a way preparations for the revelation of, distinct persons in God. Many of the Fathers saw such suggestions in the frequent use of the plural noun (Elohim) and the plural personal pronoun for the one God, and in the triple repetitions of the divine name or attributes. More significant are the special names and titles, such as "Wisdom of God" or "Spirit of God" used in ways that suggest some distinction in the divinity.

7. How was the Trinity revealed in the New Testament?

Jesus Christ, by His presence, by His promise of the Holy Spirit, and by His teaching, made known the mystery of the Trinity. In many ways the Gospels proclaim what is essential to the Trinitarian mystery: that there is but one God; that Jesus is the true Son of God, truly God, a divine person distinct from and sent by the Father; and that the Holy Spirit is God, a divine Person sent by the Father and the Son to console and enlighten the faithful.

At times the New Testament speaks in compact sentences the mystery of the Trinity. Christ instructs the apostles to baptize "in the name of the Father and of the Son and of the Holy Spirit" (Matt. 28.19). At the Last Supper Jesus declared that He, the Son, had been sent by the Father and that He would ask the Father, and the Father "will give you another Counselor, to be with you for ever, even the Spirit of truth" (John 14.16-17).

St. Paul often refers to the three Persons of the Trinity in a single passage: "The grace of our Lord Jesus Christ and the love of God and the fellowship of the Holy Spirit be with you all" (2 Cor. 13.14). "Now there are varieties of gifts, but the same Spirit; and there are varieties of service, but the same Lord; and there are varieties of working, but it is the same God who inspires them all in every one" (1 Cor. 12.4-6). Here, as often in the New Testament, "God" is used to name the Father, the first Person of the Trinity.

8. What is meant by the historical missions of the Trinity?

Jesus revealed the Trinity by revealing His own mission and that of the Holy Spirit. He had been sent forth by the Father into history at a certain time and in a certain place to save His people. After His glorification, the Father and He would send another divine Counselor, the Spirit. But the temporal missions of the Son and the Holy Spirit reflect also the eternal "processions" within God. Through His saving deeds among us, God reveals His inner life to us.

9. What is meant by the eternal Trinity?

The historical missions of the Trinity reflect the eternal mystery of the Trinity. Within the Trinity the Son proceeds eternally from the Father, and the Holy Spirit proceeds eternally from the Father and the Son. Faith in the Trinity is faith in three divine Persons living always the eternal personal relationships of the Trinity. The Father is always the Father to the eternal Son, who is always His only-begotten and uncreated Son. From the Father and the Son proceeds forever the Holy Spirit as the Person who expresses always the eternal love that binds the Father and the Son.

The second Person is Son to the first Person, the Father, and is also the "Word" of the Father, who dwells with the Father eternally, with Him "in the beginning" (cf. John 1.1-3). The Son is the perfect image of the Father, perfectly mirroring and expressing all that the Father is.

The Father is absolutely without origin. The Son is uncreated, eternal, equally God; but without beginning and eternally He proceeds from the Father. He is truly the Father's Son, but the eternal, unchanging, infinite Son who is God equally with the Father.

The Father and the Son love each other with a boundless love, a love that fully expresses all their reality, a love which is as personal and living as are the Father and the Son; and this personal love proceeding from the Father and the Son is the Holy Spirit.

10. How does the mystery of the Trinity illumine our lives?

The Blessed Trinity is the model and the goal of all personal life and of its fulfillment in perfect community. In the Trinity, distinct and perfectly fulfilled Persons dwell in the unity of most perfect life and peace. "The Lord Jesus, when He prayed to the Father, 'that all may be one . . . as we are one' (John 17.21-22), opened up vistas closed to human reason. For He implied a certain likeness between the union of the divine Persons and the union of God's sons in truth and charity" (GS 24).

The mystery of the Trinity is of central importance in faith both because of what it tells us of God and because of the way it illumines human personal life. While there is but one God, and He is the Source of all else that is, God is not an utterly solitary Person. The Trinity, the one true God, is a community of Persons eternally bound together in perfect understanding and love. In seeking to grasp the mystery of the Trinity, we realize that divine life can be shared, and shared even by us created persons, who as adopted sons and daughters can be brought into the joy of the perfect community.

11. Why were early councils of the Church so insistent in proclaiming the mystery of the Trinity with great precision?

The early councils took care to define the mystery of the Trinity with great preciseness because the mystery of God is the most important of the mysteries of faith. Led astray by human philosophies and by worldly attitudes, the heretics who denied elements of what faith believed concerning the Trinity were denying that Jesus is really God; they were rejecting the divinity of the Holy Spirit; and they presented a very faulty understanding of God the Father. The truths of the Trinity are ever defended with fervor by the Church, for only orthodox Trinitarian belief sustains faith in Jesus and keeps alive the heavenly hope of the community of faith.

12. Are all the works of God done by all the Persons of the Trinity?

No. The acts which make up the inner life of the Trinity are not equally shared by all the persons. For example, it is only the Father who eternally generates the Son; and only the Son is begotten by the Father. But the external acts of God are by the three divine Persons together. It is the Blessed Trinity, the Father, Son, and Holy Spirit, who create the world and keep it in being, by the one power of God which each Person possesses.

Certain works done by all the Persons of the Trinity are fittingly attributed by Scripture to One of the Persons when those works or actions reflect that which is most proper to one Person. The technical word for such attribution is "appropriation." To the Father are attributed especially the works of power, like creation; to the Son, the works of wisdom; to the Holy Spirit, the works of love.

Yet some truths are spoken literally only of the Son, and not of the other Persons. The Son, "One of the Holy Trinity" (Second Council of Constantinople), alone became man and suffered for us. When the Trinity created the human nature of Jesus, that nature was united immediately only to the second Person of the Trinity. Hence it would be false to say that the Father or the Holy Spirit suffered for us on the cross. But the eternal divine love of the Son for us is shared equally by the Father and the Spirit.

13. Why is the Trinity the goal of all human life?

We were made to come to the fullness of life, wisdom, and love, but all these exist in their fullness only in the Trinity. We are made to grasp all that is true and good in the personal love of the Father and the Son and the Holy Spirit, to share in God's inner life of wisdom and love.

This the just will do in eternal life to come, and they will be eternally happy, "with a joy very similar to that with which the most holy and undivided Trinity is happy" (Pope Pius XII).

CHAPTER 13

The Catholic Church

The Catholic Church belongs entirely to Christ. He is the Head of the Church, its Founder, its Spouse, and its Savior. He continues to do His saving work in and through the Church. In the New Testament we see His preparation for the Church, His promises concerning it, and the beginning of their rich fulfillment.

In this chapter we speak of the Church as the continuation of Christ in the world and as the sacrament of His presence; as a reality illumined in Scripture by many titles and images; as a visible family of faith sealed with many marks to show that it is Christ's, and as a community having a design and a structure fashioned by Christ Himself.

1. What is the Catholic Church?

The Catholic Church is a society made up of those who have been incorporated into Christ through baptism. It is the People of God, an organized and visible society, sharing the same faith and governed by the successor of Peter and the bishops in communion with him. Through these leaders Christ Himself teaches, rules, and sanctifies in the Church, and enables all the members to share in His prophetic, royal, and priestly tasks in accord with the conditions proper to each, so that the mission of the Church may be accomplished.

The mission of the Church is to proclaim the saving truth of Christ, to lead toward holiness by teaching His sanctifying precepts and administering His sacraments, and to shepherd the Church, so that in unity and peace all may draw near to the Father in Christ through the power of the Holy Spirit.

2. Did Jesus Christ establish the Catholic Church?

Yes. Christ inaugurated the Church, which is "the kingdom of Christ now present in mystery" (GS 3), when He preached the good news and gathered disciples about Him, taught them His saving precepts, and gave them His sacramental gifts. He gave the Church being and life by His death upon the cross. He manifested His Church by sending the Holy Spirit upon her with great power on Pentecost.

3. Does Christ remain with His Church?

Yes. Christ remains intimately present to the Church in all its sacred of-

83

fices of teaching, sanctifying, and ruling. He is the Teacher of the Church in every age, who yet teaches in those who teach in His name, and who is recognized as Teacher by those who come to personal faith. He is the principal minister of every sacrament. He is the shepherd who never abandons the flock, who governs it in those who exercise pastoral authority in His name.

To come to Catholic faith is to see that the Church acts for Christ. It is to understand that when a priest gives us a sacrament it is Christ who gives us the sacrament through Him. It is to know that when the Church speaks His word to us, it is He who speaks and calls to faith. It is to recognize in the teaching and ruling authority of the Church the shepherding of Christ.

"All authority in heaven and on earth has been given to Me. Go therefore and make disciples of all nations, baptizing them in the name of the Father and of the Son and of the Holy Spirit, teaching them to observe all that I have commanded you; and lo, I am with you always, to the close of the age" (Matt. 28.18-20).

4. Does the Holy Spirit dwell in the Church?

Yes. "The Holy Spirit dwells in the Church and in the hearts of the faithful as in a temple" (LG 4). He dwells in the bishops, enabling them to carry out the tasks of teaching, sanctifying, and shepherding that Christ has committed to them. The same Holy Spirit dwells in the hearts of the faithful, conferring on them gifts of faith and grace that enable them to assent freely to the faith and to share fruitfully in the gifts that Christ has given the Church.

The Holy Spirit is called the "soul" of the Church. He gives to the whole Church life from within, and gives a living unity to the whole Body of Christ, that is, the Church.

5. Why is the Church called a sacrament of Christ?

A sacrament is a sacred sign. Now the Church is itself a visible reality. It is a society of persons; they are gathered together by visible sacraments; in their midst the word of God is publicly proclaimed. These visible realities are signs of the presence of Christ who, in and through them, carries out His saving work.

6. Is the Church a visible society?

Yes. The Church exists for us human persons, and is made up of those who profess faith in Christ and are sealed by His sacraments. It is a family of faith endowed with visible signs or marks that reveal it as belonging to Christ. While it has spiritual dimensions that are not themselves sensibly perceptible, they are dimensions of that one visible reality which is the visible Church of Christ.

> "The earthly Church and the Church endowed with heavenly things
> . . . form one interlocked reality which is comprised of a divine and a human element. . . . This is the unique Church of Christ which in the Creed
> we avow as one, holy, catholic, and apostolic" (DV 8).

7. Why are many images used to describe the Church?

The Church is a mystery rich with many dimensions. To grasp more fully the reality of the Church it is necessary to draw upon the many ways of speaking of her that we find in Scripture and Catholic tradition. Thus the Church is to be grasped as both the People of God and as the Kingdom of God. It is the Bride of Christ and our Mother, but it is itself also the Body of Christ.

> All that is said of the Church under the various images is true and precious. It is not appropriate to believe of the Church only that which would seem to fit some particular image of the Church. We are to learn of her mystery by the aid of all the ways in which faith grasps her reality.

8. Why is the Church called the People of God?

To call the Church the People of God is to recall the concrete reality of the Church. The Church is not an abstract idea; neither is it merely its bishops and other leaders. The Church is made up of all the members of the family of faith. The people are the Church; all members of the Church share in its dignity, and are called to contribute, each in his or her proper way, to the saving mission of its Founder, Christ, "Priest, Prophet, and King" (LG 11-13). The People of God is not merely a collection of diverse individuals, but a society of persons with the same faith, and sanctified by the same sacraments, and acknowledging the same pastoral leaders to whose care Christ has committed the Church.

> The expression "People of God" was often used in the Old Testament for the chosen people, the Jews. For this reason it serves to show the continuity between the Old and New Covenant.

> The title People of God suggests the fundamental equality of all members in the Church. But it does not at all suggest that there is no difference in the roles of diverse members of this ordered community.

> "But you are a chosen race, a royal priesthood, a holy nation, God's own people. . . . Once you were no people, but now you are God's people" (1 Peter 2.9-10).

9. Is the Church the kingdom of God?

The kingdom of God is present to the extent that God is present to rule

His people with His saving mercy and they are with Him as His faithful people. The kingdom will be present in its fullness only in eternity, when God will bring all things to completion. But the Church is a realization of God's kingdom on earth. Christ taught that His kingdom is "not of this world" (John 18.36); the spirit of His kingdom is not of this world nor is its fulfillment here. Yet Christ proclaimed the coming of the kingdom here on this earth. In many parables about the kingdom He made it clear that the kingdom on earth, the Church, would be a visible reality, containing both the good and the bad. But God would make the kingdom grow in numbers and in holiness until the time of the final judgment.

To call the Church the kingdom of God is to recall that God rules in the midst of His people, and that those who belong to His kingdom gladly serve Him.

10. Why is the Church called the Bride of Christ?

To call the Church the Bride of Christ is to recall Christ's great love for the Church, and His merciful promise that the Church will always be a faithful spouse to Him.

Christ's love makes the Church a resplendent bride, "without spot or wrinkle or any such thing . . . holy and without blemish" (Eph. 5.27). The Fathers liked to call the Church the new Eve; as Eve was formed from Adam's side, the Church was formed when Christ on the cross was pierced by the lance. She is the faithful spouse of the new Adam, formed from His side as He slept in death on the cross.

"By the power of the Holy Spirit the Church has remained the faithful spouse of her Lord and has never ceased to be the sign of salvation on earth. Still she is well aware that among her members, both clerical and lay, some have been unfaithful to the Spirit of God. . ." (GS 43).

11. Why is the Church called our Mother?

"Holy Mother Church" is a phrase which has its roots in the earliest years of Christian history. The Church is called a mother because, in virtue of Christ's love, she gives birth to many children. "By her preaching and by baptism she brings forth to a new and immortal life children who are conceived of the Holy Spirit and born of God" (LG 64).

Those who recognize the Church as Christ's faithful bride, through whom they have been reborn as children of God, owe unfailing loyalty to her. "You cannot have God for your Father if you have not the Church for your mother" (St. Ambrose).

12. Why is the Church called the Body of Christ?

The Church is called the Body of Christ because of the profound and living unity of the members of the Church with Christ their Head. In a real way the Church is Christ, and those who belong to the Church make up His mystical body. Christ often identified Himself with those who belong to Him. We make one complete living reality with Christ our Head. "I am the vine, you are the branches" (John 15.5). "Now you are the body of Christ and individually members of it" (1 Cor. 12.27).

Of its very nature the Church is a living personal reality, filled with Christ's Holy Spirit. In this living body the various members have diverse functions. The diversity of roles does not harm, but serves the unity of the body. "If all were a single organ, where would the body be? As it is, there are many parts, yet one body" (1 Cor. 12.18-20).

> Christ "is the head of the body, the Church" (Col. 1.18). "We are to grow up in every way into Him who is the head, into Christ, from whom the whole body, joined and knit together by every joint with which it is supplied, when each part is working properly, makes bodily growth and upbuilds itself in love" (Eph. 4.15-16).

13. What are the marks of the Church?

In ancient creeds the Catholic Church identifies itself as "one, holy, catholic, and apostolic." These words refer to what are traditionally known as the four "marks" of the Church, that is, traits that make it possible for one to recognize the Church as an entirely exceptional reality belonging to God.

14. Why do we call the Church "one"?

In a splintered world the Church has an astonishing unity. In every century and in every land the faithful believe the same faith and have unity in their communion of life. They are united in worship, all live in communion accepting the pastoral rule of the bishops, and all the Churches are united in a common obedience to the Pope, who is a sign and servant of unity.

15. Why is the Church called holy?

The Church is called holy principally because Christ and His Holy Spirit remain with the Church and act in it. For this reason the teaching of the Church remains holy, its worship is holy, and the sacraments it administers make it possible for the members of the Church to grow in faith, hope, and love. The Church invites all to a holy life. Many members heed this call, and there are many holy members of the Church.

16. Why is the Church called catholic?

The Church is called catholic, or universal, because it was made to flourish among all nations and in all centuries. It teaches all the whole teaching of Christ, in obedience to His command to "make disciples of all nations" (Matt. 28.19).

17. Why is the Church called apostolic?

Christ founded the Church on the apostles: they were its first teachers and pastors. They, moved by the Spirit of Christ, chose others to assist them in their ministry; and they had successors to carry on the mission of the Church, which Christ willed to continue until the end of time. When we call the Church apostolic we mean not only that the teaching of the apostles yet flourishes in the Church, but also that the Church today is the same living community that grew from the preaching of the apostles.

18. Are there flaws that obscure the marks of the Church?

Yes. Side by side with the divine signs given the Church there are visible in her the many imperfections and sins of her members. Many are far from holy; many in disobedience wound the unity of the Church.

19. Are the marks convincing evidences of the authenticity of the Church?

Yes. The unity, holiness, catholicity, and apostolicity of the Church remain astonishing facets yet visible to the world, in spite of the manifest faults of many who are Catholic. The presence of sinners in the Church suffices to explain the flaws one finds in her total concrete reality. But it is only because God is with her, enabling her to flourish as no other society of human persons has ever flourished, that she can appear in every age as one, holy, catholic, and apostolic.

20. In what sense is the Church historical?

The Church is immersed in history; in every age it lives as a reality of that age. Yet it is not a purely historical reality. It transcends each historical age because Christ dwells with it, guarding in her unchanging truths and good that are always precious. Though the Church may speak in the language and concepts of a particular culture, it is not subjected to it. When a culture perishes and its great cultural institutions die, the Church endures. It survives every cultural transition, for the Lord of history has promised that she will endure until the end of time.

21. Who has authority in the Catholic Church?

All authority in the Catholic Church belongs to Jesus Christ, and, under Him, to those who by His will and in His name teach or rule in the Church.

"All authority in heaven and on earth has been given to me. Go, therefore, and make disciples of all nations, baptizing them . . . , teaching them to observe all I have commanded you; and lo, I am with you always" (Matt. 28.18-20).

22. Did Christ give a hierarchical pattern to the Church?

Yes. From the beginning of His public life Jesus chose disciples to be close to Himself. From these He selected twelve, whom He called apostles. These He prepared for leadership roles. To them He gave a special participation in His authority that they should teach in His name and shepherd His flock. He chose them to be ministers of His sacraments, especially of the Eucharist. They did not replace Him as shepherd of the Church, but through and in them He Himself continues to rule, teach, and sanctify His Church.

> The New Testament bears witness in very many ways to the hierarchical nature of the Church. Anticipations of the hierarchy or sacred rule are seen throughout the Gospels; the early exercise of leadership is traced in the Acts of the Apostles and in the New Testament epistles. The history of the early Church finds Christian faith inseparably united with the conviction that God Himself authorizes and empowers those who have leadership tasks in the Church.

23. Was any special leadership role given to St. Peter?

Yes. In many ways the Gospels suggest the entirely exceptional role of St. Peter in the Church. Always He is mentioned first among the apostles, and always he is treated as a leader among them. After he had solemnly professed faith in Jesus in the name of all, Christ told him: "You are Peter ['Peter' means 'rock'], and on this rock I will build My Church, and the powers of death shall not prevail against it. I will give you the keys of the kingdom of heaven, and whatever you bind on earth shall be bound in heaven, and whatever you loose on earth shall be loosed in heaven" (Matt. 16.17-20). At the last supper Christ said to him: "I have prayed for you that your faith may not fail; and when you have turned again, strengthen your brethren" (Luke 22.32). After the resurrection Jesus told him three times to shepherd His flock. The Acts of the Apostles reveals how in the early Church Peter acted as a leader and chief spokesman for the Church.

24. Did Christ intend the apostles to have successors in whom He would continue to govern His Church?

Yes. St. Peter and the other apostles were mortal, but the mission given them was to be carried out until the end of time. "For this reason the apostles took care to appoint successors in this hierarchically structured society" (LG 20). The third successor of St. Peter, Pope St. Clement of

Rome, wrote that the apostles themselves "laid down a rule once for all to this effect: when these men die, other approved men shall succeed to their ministry."

It is, of course, true that the roles of St. Peter and the other apostles were in many ways unique. They were privileged personal associates of Jesus, witnesses of His resurrection, and first leaders in the Church. Still their responsibilities in teaching, shepherding, and sanctifying were essential to the Church for all time; they are indispensable for guarding the Church in unity of faith and in love. The pope and bishops are their successors in these enduring aspects of their mission.

25. How did Christ wish authority in His Church to be exercised?

Christ taught that all who exercised authority in His name should do so in humility and as exercising an important service. He also insisted that all should recognize and accept the authority of those who shepherd the Church by His will. Pastoral service is to be a work of unselfish love, but it is to be exercised with vigilant care.

Hence a bishop or priest who failed to serve his people by proclaiming the faith clearly and firmly, or who failed to remind them of their duty to live lives worthy of their calling would be derelict in his duty.

Christ can rule even through those whose lives are not worthy of their sacred offices. Speaking of such He said: "Practice and observe what they tell you, but not what they do" (Matt. 23.3).

26. Who are the successors today of St. Peter and of the apostles?

The pope, the bishop of Rome, is the successor to St. Peter, the leader among the apostles and the first bishop of Rome, the rock and visible center of unity upon whom Christ built His Church. The whole body or "college" of bishops, living in communion with one another and with the pope, are the successors to the apostolic college.

The Church has solemnly defined the doctrine that by the will of Christ there has been a continuous line of successors to the office of St. Peter as chief shepherd of Christ's flock, and that the pope does succeed to Peter's primacy over the whole Church. The pope then has the right and duty to teach and to shepherd the whole flock of Christ. He is bishop not only of Rome but of the whole Church. His authority over each member of the Church is immediate; that is, each Catholic is required to accept the pastoral direction of this first shepherd.

The bishop of each local church or diocese has responsibility to teach and to give pastoral care to that Church. In his diocese the bishop is the authentic teacher of faith; he is the sign and center of unity. In communion with the pope and one another the bishops have a collegial responsibility for the care of the Church throughout the world.

90

27. Is the Catholic Church alone the Church of Jesus Christ?

Yes. The Catholic Church has always steadfastly believed and taught that she is the one and only Church of Jesus Christ. To say this is not to say that other Christian communities are without value, or insincere, or that their members are not dear to Christ. But it is to say that Christ willed that those who believe in Him should be bound together in unity in one family of faith, a Church that has existed from the time of Christ, a visible community governed by the successors to St. Peter and the other apostles. It is to say that the saving mercy of Christ requires that all who come by grace to recognize this Church as what it is, the sacrament of His presence, should adhere to this Christ in His Church, in which He guards all the gifts of truth and sources of holiness intended for His faithful.

> "This is the unique Church of Christ which in the creed we avow as
> one, holy, catholic, and apostolic. . . . This Church, constituted and or-
> ganized in this world as a society, subsists in the Catholic Church, gov-
> erned by the successor of Peter and the bishops in communion with him"
> (LG 8). To say that Christ's Church "subsists" in the Catholic Church is
> to say that it is a concrete historical reality, and that this concrete reality
> is found in the living, visible Catholic Church, the community cared for
> by the pope and the bishops in communion with him.

28. Can salvation be found in the Catholic Church alone?

God wills all men to be saved, and all who seek perseveringly to find God and to do His will can be saved. At the same time the Church has constantly taught that "outside the Church there is no salvation" (St. Cyprian). Now those who have never known or recognized the Church as Christ's yet intend in their hearts to do all that God requires of them are excluded neither from the hope of eternal life nor from a certain membership by desire in the Church. Still there is a note of urgency in the teaching that the Church is needed for salvation. If one were to recognize the reality of the Catholic Church and the personal will of Christ that we live in it, and yet deliberately disobey so important a call, one would be turning away from the Savior and from salvation.

CHAPTER • 14

Christ Shepherds His People

The Church traditionally has spoken of three offices of Christ the Savior. He is Prophet or Teacher of truth; He is King or Ruler who shows the way; and He is above all the Sanctifier who gives His people abundant life. Christ performs His work not only personally, but also through the Church. He is with His Church, acts in it, and enables the whole Church, each member in his own role and task, to share actively in His saving work.

Jesus is present in a special way to His bishops. Through them His teaching, ruling, and sanctifying care still touches the whole flock. "In the bishops . . . our Lord Jesus Christ, the supreme High Priest, is present in the midst of those who believe" (LG 21). Pope St. Leo the Great spoke of this in a homily in the fifth century: "The Lord Jesus Christ is in the midst of those who believe in Him; though He sits at the right hand of the Father. . . , He who is the supreme Bishop is not separated from the full assembly of His bishops."

In this chapter we speak of how Christ teaches, rules, and sanctifies in His Church. The chapter treats especially the teaching mission of the Church: why sacred teaching is needed, to whom the teaching is committed, and the various ways in which the teaching office of the Church guides the life of the faith.

1. Is Christ Himself our Teacher?

Yes. During His public life He personally proclaimed the good news, making known the mystery of God and of His saving will. The common title He received was "Teacher." At the end of His earthly life He declared: "For this was I born, and for this have I come into the world, to bear witness to the truth" (John 18.37). Jesus Himself teaches also through those whom He sends to speak in His name. When He sent His apostles to preach, He told them: "I am with you always, to the close of the age" (Matt. 28.20). Anyone who did not accept the word of those He sent would be rejecting not mere men, but Him, whereas acceptance of their word would be acceptance of Christ.

2. Do we need to be taught by the Lord?

Yes. We human beings need to be taught by God. In our fallen state we would fail to grasp with certainty and without many errors admixed even the naturally knowable truths about God, about the meaning of our lives, about good and evil, a knowledge of which is necessary for leading good and authentically human lives. Without revelation we could not know at all the saving truths that God has revealed about Himself and His saving plan that we need to know to pursue the supernatural goal God has mercifully assigned to our lives: that of coming to share God's life in friendship with Him forever.

It is true that human intelligence can learn many things, even about God, and the meaning of our lives, and about good and evil. Yet without revelation human answers to such questions remain incomplete, flawed, and uncertain. Moreover, God has called us to friendship with Himself, to know Himself personally and to share His life. Now human wisdom does not extend to a knowledge of God in His personal life, of God as Father, Son, and Holy Spirit. Neither could we know the ways God wished us to walk to enter into friendship with Him unless He Himself teaches us these ways. We come to an adequate knowledge of God only through Jesus. "No one knows the Father except the Son and anyone to whom the Son chooses to reveal Him" (Matt. 11.27).

3. Can human words express the truth about God?

Yes. When Jesus and the prophets before Him spoke about God and His saving plan they spoke the truth. It is true that human language cannot speak adequately the whole truth about God. "No eye has seen, nor ear heard, nor the heart of man conceive. . ." (1 Cor. 2.9) the fullness of the divine mystery. Still human language is able to bear the message that God wills it to bear.

The very creation of the world was concerned with the communication of truth. God made human beings that they might come to a knowledge of the truth; despite the imperfections of the world the heavens and the earth were made to "declare the glory of God" (Ps. 19.2). The mystery of the incarnation too is concerned with manifesting the saving truth to us. God Himself became man to teach us in human language and ways the saving truths of God. God is able to make human language speak the truth about Himself.

4. What is faith?

Divine faith is believing God. Because of the entire confidence we place in Him, we assent with certainty to the saving truths He makes known.

Even human faith differs from other human ways of knowing. Much of our grasp of truth comes from experience and reflection. But much that we know to be so we grasp by believing those who tell us it is so. Such faith can be very intelligent. We believed our parents, and we now believe our friends, because we know of their goodness and truthfulness, and often realize that they are aware of things we cannot now verify by ourselves. Human faith is fallible, because the goodness and wisdom of human witnesses is limited. But faith in God can be entirely confident. We may believe God's word absolutely, because He who is entirely reliable has borne witness to the truth.

5. How could we know that words spoken in God's name are really His words?

Faith is certain because it is based on the power and truthfulness of God.

God is able to provide outer signs, such as the miracles of Christ, or the astonishing unity of the Church, that cause one to take first steps toward faith. He is able to give us inner graces that enable us to realize that it is indeed He who provided such signs, and that He is near to us, calling us to realize in the light of His grace that it is He Himself who speaks in those whom He has sent. Faith does not arise from long arguments, but from the presence and power of God, who is able to lead us gently toward personal faith in Himself and in the words that He Himself causes to be proclaimed and to be marked with signs of their truth.

6. Did the apostles teach faithfully the truths Jesus had entrusted to them?

Yes. Jesus entrusted to them His saving message, and commanded them to teach His words to all the nations. He promised that the Holy Spirit would guard them in the truth so that they would not fail in this critically important task. He assured them that He would Himself be with them always so that they could preach with confidence in His name.

7. Do those who teach in Christ's name have a duty to hand on His message faithfully?

Yes. The New Testament stressed the duty of those called to teach in Christ's name to preach the whole message of faith with loving care, to guard "the truth that has been entrusted to you" (2 Tim. 1.14).

This is the work of apostolic love that the apostles showed and that their successors in the bishopric must always show: to care that the people of Christ hear the saving words of God. The message of Christ is to be handed on in its entirety to the faithful, in the very sense in which Christ and His Holy Spirit have led the Church to grasp it.

"Preach the word, be urgent in season and out of season, convince, rebuke, and exhort, be unfailing in patience and in teaching" (2 Tim. 4.2). Such vigilant care is necessary in teachers of the faith, because even in those who would want to believe and serve Christ faithfully there are re-

94

current temptations to compromise the faith. Many are tempted to seek out versions of the Gospel that seem less demanding, more in tune with worldly philosophies or less excellent forms of life. The faithful teacher may have to suffer much for the faith, but he will have great consolations also. For God does make it possible and easy for His people to recognize His voice when it is proclaimed faithfully by those He has sent. Bishops today share the joy St. Paul experienced: "We also thank God constantly for this, that when you received the word of God which you heard from us, you accepted it not as the word of men but as what it really is, the word of God, which is at work in you believers" (1 Thess. 2.13).

8. Where can this saving message of Christ be found?

This saving message of Christ is found in Sacred Scripture, in the living tradition of the Church, and in the teaching of the magisterium, or teaching office of the Church.

Sacred Scripture is always to be read in the light of the faith that continues always to be handed down in the tradition of the Church; tradition is always to be animated by reverent reflection on the writings of Sacred Scripture; and the whole faith is always rightly guarded by the Holy Spirit in a special way through the care with which He protects from error the bishops to whom Christ's will has committed the teaching of the faith.

"It is clear, therefore, that sacred tradition, Sacred Scripture, and the magisterium of the Church, in accord with God's most wise design, are so linked and joined together that one cannot stand without the others, and that all together and each in its own way under the action of the one Holy Spirit contribute effectively to the salvation of souls" (DV 10).

9. What is meant by tradition?

Tradition means "handing on." All that the Church receives from Christ and His Holy Spirit that God wishes her to hand on to the faithful of every age belongs to sacred tradition. The Church is responsible for handing on from one generation to the next the whole saving message of Christ: His doctrine, His saving precepts, the sacraments and other sanctifying gifts He has given His Church. Tradition means also "that which is handed on," the content of Catholic faith. "Now that which was handed on by the apostles includes everything which contributes to the holiness of life, and the increase in faith in the people of God; and so the Church, in her teaching, life, and worship, perpetuates and hands on to all generations all that she herself is, all that she believes" (DV 8).

There can also be in the Church human traditions. These traditions may be of only temporary value. The Holy Spirit enables the authentic teachers of the Church to distinguish that which is the enduring word of

95

God, and must be faithfully handed on, from that which is of only limited and passing worth.

10. What is Sacred Scripture?

Sacred Scripture consists of all those books gathered together in the Bible which are recognized by the Church as written under the inspiration of the same Holy Spirit who guides the Church in faithfully handing on sacred tradition.

Among the Scriptures the Gospels "have a special preeminence, and rightly so, for they are the principal witness of the life and teaching of the incarnate Word, our Savior" (DV 18). These four Gospels, together with an account of the events of the young Church, that is, the Acts of the Apostles, and with twenty-one letters, or epistles, and the book of Revelation, make up the New Testament. These writings, joined with the sacred books of the former, or Jewish, dispensation, which are known collectively as the Old Testament, make up the entire Bible.

The Church has profound reverence for all of Sacred Scripture, for all of it was written under the inspiration of the Holy Spirit to confirm and enrich faith. With special care she reflects on the Gospels and other writings of the New Testament. These had their origin within the living Church to preserve for all time a faithful account of Christ's message, which had been preached and was being preached by the apostles and lived in the whole Church. From the beginning these writings have been proclaimed by the Church's own teachers, and have been believed and understood in the light of the whole living tradition and faith of the Church.

It is "not from Sacred Scripture alone that the Church draws its certainty about everything which has been revealed" (DV 9). Sacred tradition and Sacred Scripture form "one sacred deposit of the word of God, which is committed to the Church" (DV 10) and both "are to be accepted and venerated with the same sense of devotion and reverence" (DV 10).

11. What is the magisterium of the Church?

The magisterium is the teaching office of the Church. Certain members of the Church have the divinely given responsibility to bear witness authoritatively to the message of Christ. These are the Holy Father and the bishops who are in communion with him. Christ promised to be with these teachers and to be with them in the truth, so that those who come to faith in Him may learn securely from their teaching what Christ wills us to believe and to do.

12. Does God continue to give the Church new revelation in every age?

No. God revealed Himself and His saving plan fully in Jesus, "and now no new public revelation is to be expected before the glorious manifestation of our Lord Jesus Christ (cf. 1 Tim. 6.14 and Titus 2.13)" (DV 4). That is, the faith that the Church teaches to all in the name of Jesus was completely revealed in the times of Jesus and His apostles, and the task of the Church was to hand on the good news that had already been fully announced.

Revelation can be said to continue in certain senses, however. The living God remains with His people, and by His continuing care and His gifts of grace He Himself enables His people to recognize and love Him and the good news of the Gospel. Moreover, there can be private revelations, such as those God has made to some of His saints. These do not add to the content of the Gospel, but they stir God's people to more earnest concern to hear and be faithful to the words already proclaimed in the family of faith.

13. Is there a development of doctrine in the teaching of the Church?

Yes. The Church teaches and believes a living faith; she does not hand on her doctrine in static ways. As centuries pass, the prayer and study of the Church, and the guidance of the Holy Spirit, lead the Church into an ever-greater understanding of the divine word.

Genuine development of doctrine always proceeds along consistent lines. It is growth from partial to fuller vision, so that what has been believed continues to be believed, though its depths and consequences are more and more fully realized. Hence development of doctrine never means abandonment of doctrine, or the substitution of new doctrine for old; it never means that what the Church once firmly assents to, it will ever deny. "Hence also that meaning of the sacred dogmas which has once been declared by holy Mother Church must always be retained" (First Vatican Council).

14. Why are the pope and the bishops recognized as the authoritative teachers of Catholic faith?

Divine revelation is a gift of God and He Himself chose ways to guard its faithful transmission through the ages. The Catholic Church teaches that the Holy Father and the bishops are by Christ's will the successors of the apostles as authentic teachers and witnesses of the faith. Hence Christ has given to them uniquely the charism of truth that does not fail. In them Christ guards the word with divine care, not to glorify them, but to make them centers of unity and truth for those He calls to faith.

Other teachers assist the bishops in their work. Priests preach the Gospel, as officially sent by their bishops to this task. Parents are "the first and foremost educators of their children" (GE 3). Very important teachers also are those who teach the faith in schools and catechetical centers. All these draw their certainty from the divinely given gift of faith in the message publicly proclaimed in the Church, a message which Christ guards in the bishops He has called to be His witnesses.

15. Are theologians and scholars authentic teachers of Catholic faith?

No. Theologians and other scholars concerned with questions touching faith also teach the word, and help the Church to penetrate its depths. But they are not authentic teachers of faith, as bishops are. Christ has promised to be with the bishops always in their proclamations of faith; and those who have faith in Christ are enabled by Him to recognize as true that which is proclaimed by those He has sent. Theologians do not have this crucial role in grounding faith. In fact, their own faith needs to see the witness of the Holy Father and the bishops so that they may recognize the message of faith as assuredly coming from Christ.

The bishops of the Church, however, need and rejoice in the help of faithful theologians, who ground their studies on principles of faith that they have learned from Christ in the teaching Church.

16. Must bishops themselves believe the faith of the Church?

Yes. The Holy Father and the other bishops are servants of the word of God. They have a duty to believe the Scriptures and the entire message of faith that has been handed down in the Church by the bishops and apostles who preceded them.

It is God who enables the bishops of the Church to be faithful in handing on the word, not simply for their sake, but in order that all who wish to believe Christ may have the true message of faith taught to them in its purity. It is the Spirit of God who gives the charism of truth to authentic teachers, and the charism of faith both to these teachers and to those who hear them.

17. Is the faith of the Christian community infallible?

Yes. Christ promised to send His Holy Spirit to those who believed in Him to guide them in all truth, and He promised to remain with those who teach in His name until the end of time. That those of all ages would be able to believe securely the priceless good news that He taught, He gave to the whole believing Church, and to the teaching Church, the gift of infallibility, so that they could faithfully teach precisely His message.

By infallibility we mean a certain inability to err in believing or teaching the saving words that Christ has entrusted to the Church.

Only God is completely infallible. Humans are by nature capable of falling into error. Obviously faith does not give believers entirely certain knowledge in everything. But it does give them light and certainty in some matters that are of immense importance for salvation. The God who gives the Church a share in the light of His own knowledge by faith grants to the Church also a certain participation in His own infallibility. What the whole Church believes, instructed by Christ and those whom He has sent, and strengthened by the Holy Spirit, is certainly true.

"The body of the faithful as a whole, anointed as they are by the Holy Spirit (cf. 1 John 2.20, 27), cannot err in matters of belief" (LG 12).

18. Are those commissioned by Christ to teach the faith infallible in their teaching?

Christ has given to the Church the infallibility that it needs to proclaim the Gospel message faithfully. The authentic teachers of the Church are certainly not infallible in all things. But when they teach decisively in Christ's name matters of divine faith or morals, they teach infallibly.

19. When is the Church infallible in its ordinary teaching?

The ordinary teaching of the Church is found in its preaching and its catechetical instruction. It is manifested in the Church's forms of prayer and worship, in the instructions and pastoral letters in which bishops instruct their faithful, and in the day-to-day care that the bishops of the Church show in guarding intact the faith. Now what all the bishops, in communion with each other, teach insistently as the saving message of Christ is infallibly taught. They teach the message of Christ infallibly "even when they are dispersed around the world, provided that while maintaining the bond of unity among themselves and with Peter's successor, and while teaching authentically on a matter of faith and morals, they concur in a single viewpoint as the one which must be held conclusively" (LG 25).

Thus the basic teachings of Catholic faith and morality that have always and everywhere been taught by the Church as the word of Christ are taught infallibly.

20. What is the extraordinary magisterium of the Church?

The extraordinary magisterium is the teaching of the Church that is exercised in unusual and especially solemn circumstances. It has two forms. The first of these is in the solemn decisions of ecumenical councils. The second is in solemn (sometimes called *ex cathedra*, that is, "from the chair") definitions of doctrine by the Holy Father.

21. What is an ecumenical council?

Ecumenical, or general, councils are meetings of all or a large number of the bishops, together with the pope as the head of the college of bishops.

The authority of ecumenical councils was foreshown in the Acts of the Apostles by what is said there of a council of apostles and apostolic co-workers (cf. Acts 15.1-28). It met at a time of crisis in the early Church, confident that Christ and His Spirit would lead them to right decisions. They introduced their report on their shared judgment in these words: "It has seemed good to the Holy Spirit and to us. . ." (Acts 15.28). They rejoiced in this gift of God that freed His people from anxieties in crucially important matters of faith.

In the year 325 the first ecumenical council was held in Nicea, during a time of crisis when Arian heretics were assailing the fundamental Catholic teaching on the divinity of Christ. The Church then too was fully confident that the considered judgment of the bishops gathered together would be guarded from all error. Since that time, when major heresies and discords arose in the Church, or when important pastoral decisions needed to be made, the bishops have met with the Holy Father in ecumenical councils.

22. Are ecumenical councils infallible?

Yes. The Catholic Church has always taught that what the Holy Father and the bishops teach solemnly and decisively in ecumenical councils as the word of God, is indeed His word and infallibly true. "Their definitions then must be adhered to with the submission of faith" (LG 25).

Not everything said by ecumenical councils is meant to be infallible teaching. Some conciliar statements are directed rather at offering pastoral considerations or changeable disciplinary regulations.

But ecumenical councils have often made precise statements of Catholic doctrine, and taught these solemnly to the whole Church as infallibly true. These statements of faith are often called "irreformable" and "unalterable." To say this does not mean that the statements could not also be expressed in other words, perhaps even in more adequate ways. But it does mean that such faith statements do express the teaching of God aptly, and in such a way that "as they are they remain forever suitable for communicating the faith to those who interpret them correctly" (Sacred Congregaton for the Doctrine of the Faith), that is, in the sense in which they were solemnly declared.

23. Has the pope an exceptional teaching role in the Church?

Yes. Because he succeeds to St. Peter's role as shepherd of the whole flock, the Holy Father has a special teaching office among the bishops. He has a duty to care for the faith of the whole Church and to minister to the unity of the faith.

The pope does not derive his authority from the other bishops, or by delegation from the Church, but from Christ. Hence his teaching does not require approval or acceptance from others to deserve reverent acceptance from each member of the Church. Still, it is his practice to consult with other bishops and with theologians before giving authoritative teachings to the Church.

The Church teaches that Christ Himself teaches through the ministry of the Holy Father, to guard His Church in the truth. Even when a pope is unworthy of his office, the Lord guards the Church from false teaching at his hands.

24. Is the teaching of the pope infallible?

The Holy Father is infallible in certain of his pronouncements. The ancient Catholic teaching on this matter, rooted in the scriptural texts concerning St. Peter noted in the preceding chapter, and affirmed with growing clarity through the centuries, was solemnly defined by the First Vatican Council and reaffirmed in the Second Vatican Council. These councils teach that when the pope, using his full authority as shepherd and teacher of all Christians, defines or states precisely doctrines of faith or morals, and presents them as teachings that must be held true by the whole Church, then, by the divine assistance promised to St. Peter, he teaches with that infallibility with which Christ willed His Church to be endowed.

Papal infallibility does not extend to matters of natural science or merely human wisdom. It applies to the same matters as the infallibility of the whole Church, to "doctrine concerning faith or morals to be held by the whole Church" (First Vatican Council).

25. What is meant by authentic Catholic teaching?

Authentic Catholic teaching is the teaching of the Church proposed as true and authoritative by the pope or by bishops in the name of Christ, but not in infallible modes of teaching. Catholic teaching is far more than a limited number of infallibly presented dogmas or articles of faith. The Catholic is expected to give religious assent to all the authoritative teaching of the Church, even when the Church is not using its full infallible authority.

Thus when the pope teaches the whole Church insistently on matters of faith or morals in encyclicals and other such statements, a firm religious assent is to be given by all. Not only the laity, but bishops, priests, and theologians owe such assent; the Holy Father himself owes assent to these teachings.

"When their bishop speaks in the name of the Church in matters of faith and morals, the faithful are to accept his teaching and adhere to it with a religious assent of soul. This religious submission of will and of

101

mind must be shown in a special way to the authentic magisterium of the Roman Pontiff even when he is not speaking ex cathedra" (LG 25). "Such teachings belong to the ordinary magisterium, of which it is true to say: 'He who hears you, hears me' (Luke 10.16)" (Pope Pius XII).

26. Does Christ rule in the Church through His bishops?

Yes. It is in Christ that all authority of the Church natively dwells. "All authority in heaven and on earth has been given to Me" (Matt. 28.18). But He chooses to exercise authority through those whom He has made shepherds of His flock. To St. Peter and the other apostles Christ gave authority to govern His flock, and authority which was to endure in their successors until the end of time.

This ruling office in the Church was discussed in the preceding chapter. Often called the power of jurisdiction, the office of ruling in the Church exists to serve the growth of faith and holiness. The laws of the Church are issued with the authority Christ gave the Church for the good of the People of God. The Code of Canon Law is a collection of laws issued by the Holy See to guide the Universal Church in questions of faith, morals, worship, and discipline. A new Code, taking into account the teachings of the Second Vatican Council, was published in 1983.

The bishops of each country generally list the most notable of the special duties of Catholics which are known as precepts of the Church. These include such obligations as those to attend Mass on Sundays and on certain holy days, and to avoid unnecessary and inappropriate work on such days; to lead a regular sacramental life; to observe the marriage laws; to strengthen and support the Church; to do penance at the appointed times.

27. Does Christ sanctify us through His Church?

Yes. Christ's sanctifying work is the most important of the tasks He performs through His Church. He came to give us the life that is love and holiness. He came to bind us to the Father in friendship, to join us together in Himself as a priestly people, and to associate us personally with the acts by which He redeems and makes holy the universe. Church teaching and ruling is aimed entirely at the more essential goal of promoting holiness in the faithful.

Christ is the principal minister of the sacraments He entrusted to the Church. It is He who baptizes when the priest baptizes; it is He who celebrates the Eucharist through the ministry of priests; it is He who forgives our sins when the sacrament of penance is administered.

Some of the sanctifying powers Christ gave to the Church He gave to all members of the Church. But some of the sanctifying works of Christ are to be done through the shepherds of His flock, the bishops and priests, who alone must preside at the Eucharistic sacrifice and administer the sacrament of reconciliation and certain other sacraments. The sanctifying gifts entrusted to the Church are discussed in the third part of this book.

CHAPTER 15

Mary, Mother and Model of the Church

Mary, the mother of Jesus, was with Him in the hour of His passion. In many ways she was associated with His redemptive work. Jesus has shared with her also, in her Assumption, the glory of His risen life. Because of all that this intimate nearness to Jesus' work implies, Mary has close ties with all those who have been redeemed and called to be members of her Son's Mystical Body.

The first part of this chapter treats Mary's role as Mother of the Church and of each of the faithful. Though she was herself redeemed by Jesus, she shared with great love in His saving work; she is spiritually our mother, and a mediatrix of grace. The chapter then treats Mary's position as model of the Church, the pattern of what the Church should be as the mother of the faithful and as a holy servant of the Lord. The final part of the chapter speaks of the role of St. Joseph, Mary's husband, in Christian life.

1. Why is Mary called "Mother of the Church"?

Mary is called "Mother of the Church" because, as Mother of Jesus, who is forever head of the Church, and as spiritual mother of all who are members of the Church, she has with maternal care given both life and love to the Church.

To call Mary Mother of the Church is to recall especially her special association with the saving work of Jesus, through which, by His mercy, she was enabled in maternal love to assist in bringing to life all those whom Jesus has saved. In this maternal role Mary served as model of the Church, which similarly ministers to bring life to the people of God.

2. Was not Mary redeemed by Jesus?

Yes. Because she belonged to the sinful human race, Mary stood in need of redemption. Mary was, then, redeemed by Christ, who alone is the Redeemer of all. Her redemption, however, like the rest of her role in God's plan, was unique. Christ did not take away Mary's sins, for she had none. Rather, by His redemptive mercy He kept her from incurring sin.

The special way in which Christ applied His redemptive act to Mary is known as her Immaculate Conception, as we have noted above. Mary was thus kept free from sin not only because she was to be the Mother of Jesus, but also because that made her more suited to share with great love in all the redemptive work of her Son.

3. How was Mary associated with Christ's redeeming work?

Mary was enabled to share in Christ's redeeming work most becomingly because she had herself been so perfectly redeemed by Jesus: she was able to be His sinless and holy associate in His saving work. Mary cooperated in our redemption by her free consent to become the mother of the Savior, with all the suffering that implied. She cooperated by enduring the trials of Jesus with Him. Despite the great pain it caused her, she accepted with compassionate and sacrificial love, and in freedom, her Son's passion and death for the life of the world. By receiving the Redeemer into her own life with deep faith, especially at the moments of the Annunciation, Calvary, and Pentecost, she cooperated maternally in Christ's objective redemption of the human race.

St. Thomas Aquinas says that the Blessed Virgin gave her consent to the redemptive incarnation "in place of the whole human race." Mary's "let it be" is a model for us and a meritorious act that helps enable us to accept the fruits of the redemption into our lives.

4. Is Mary our spiritual mother?

Yes. Mary is our spiritual mother because of her special role in communicating to us our life in Christ. Having given her free consent, she became the mother of the Redeemer. She freely associated herself with His saving work. She stood beneath the cross, "in keeping with the divine plan, suffering grievously with her only begotten Son. There she united herself with a maternal heart to His sacrifice, and lovingly consented to the immolation of this Victim which she herself had brought forth" (LG 58). Out of love for each of us for whom Christ died, she freely bore this suffering, and merited to be the new Eve, the "mother of all the living" (Gen. 3.20 NAB), because of her close association with Jesus, the new Adam, in His redemptive work.

The Fathers of the Church and the devotion of the faithful understood the words of Jesus to the faithful disciple John and to His mother from the cross to be applicable to every disciple. "When Jesus saw His mother, and the disciple whom He loved standing near, He said to His mother, 'Woman, behold, your son!' Then He said to the disciple, 'Behold, your mother!' " (John 19.26). A title for Mary that each Catholic finds especially dear is "Mother." She is spiritual mother to all men because her maternal care extends to all for whom her Son died and rose again; and He is the Redeemer of all. In a special way, however, she is mother of all the faithful who are actually members of His Body the Church. For that reason she is called "Mother of the Church."

"In an utterly singular way she cooperated by her obedience, faith, hope, and burning charity in the Savior's work of restoring supernatural life to souls. For this reason she is a mother to us in the order of grace" (LG 61).

5. Why is Mary called "mediatrix"?

Mary is called mediatrix because she intercedes continually for each of us to "procure for us gifts of eternal salvation" (LG 62). She fosters a close union between each of us and her divine Son. "Since Mary is rightly to be regarded as the way by which we are led to Christ, the person who encounters Mary cannot help but encounter Christ likewise" (Pope Paul VI). As she cooperated with Jesus in the whole task of redemption, she mediates and intercedes for us in all things that lead us to her Son and to the Father.

Mary's mediation does not compete with the centrality of Christ as the one Mediator between God and men. For Christ's mediation is essential. It was only Christ's will that His mother should also be called by His mercy to assist gently in drawing us nearer to Christ Himself.

"The maternal duty of Mary toward men in no wise obscures or diminishes this unique mediation of Christ but rather shows His power. For every saving influence of the Blessed Virgin on men originates, not from some inner necessity, but from the divine pleasure. It flows forth from the superabundance of the merits of Christ, rests on His mediation, depends entirely upon it, and draws all its powers from it. It in no way impedes, but rather fosters the immediate union of the faithful with Christ" (LG 60).

6. Does Catholic faith encourage devotion to Mary?

Yes. The Church has always honored Mary, and the faithful have persistently had a devoted love for her. In our own day the Second Vatican Council has warmly encouraged devotion to Mary, a devotion that "proceeds from true faith, by which we are led to know the excellence of the Mother of God, and are moved by a filial love toward our mother and to the imitation of her virtues" (LG 67).

Devotion to Mary, of course, "differs essentially from the cult of adoration" (LG 66), which is given to God alone. Though Mary has sublime dignity as the Mother of God, she is a fellow creature. Personal devotion to Mary ought to imitate the patterns found in the Church's liturgy, in its joyful worship of God and praise of her. We should acknowledge that the goodness and greatness of Mary are gifts of God to her, as she confessed: "All generations will call me blessed; for He who is mighty has done great things for me, and holy is His name" (Luke 1.48-49).

7. How does Mary's intercession differ from that of the other saints?

All the saints intercede for us as fellow creatures, happy to fulfill God's will that in the communion of saints we care for one another and intercede for one another. The difference between Mary's intercession and that of the other saints lies in its universality and in its intensity. When God chose Mary as mother of Jesus and His associate in His redeeming work, and called her to be the spiritual mother of all the faithful, He called her to have a universal loving concern for all who have been redeemed by Jesus. Inspired by her close union with her Son, she embraces all of us in all our needs. She cares with intense personal love for the entire fulfillment of His work of salvation. That is why, under Jesus, she is said to be the mediatrix of graces.

Devotion to Mary is of great importance in our spiritual life. One who has no devotion to her, and refuses to seek her maternal guidance, will not mature as fully in Christian worship and mission as Christ wishes. Devotion to Mary in liturgical worship is always rooted securely in the doctrines of faith, as are the traditional private Marian prayers most honored and most warmly encouraged in the Church, such as the Angelus and the rosary.

Devotion to Mary has often been related to accounts of apparitions of Mary, as at Lourdes, Fatima, and Guadalupe. The Church does not give any definitive teaching on the authenticity of such apparitions. But the Church does study them carefully, and if the fruits of an event breathe the presence of God's providential designs, it approves the consequent devotions. "These providential happenings serve as reminders to us of basic Christian themes: prayer, penance, and the necessity of the sacraments" (Pope Paul VI).

8. Why is Mary called the model of the Church?

Mary is called the model of the Church because of the unique example she gives of Christian virtue.

As St. Ambrose taught, the Mother of God is a model of the Church in the order of faith, charity, and perfect union with Christ. Among the members of the Church she stands out as eminent in holiness. Catholics of every rank and condition find in Mary a model of faith, obedience, purity, poverty of spirit, and generous love. Married couples and parents can be enlightened by her selfless love of Joseph and Jesus; celibate priests and religious, by her virginal consecration to serving God's saving plan; single persons in the world, by her spirit of prayer and dedicated service. In our own times she shows all who seek or enjoy a new liberation how to use freedom in such a way that it does not drift toward the slavery of sinfulness, but becomes instead a source of energy for self-fulfillment and for the transformation of the world.

9. Is Mary's spiritual motherhood like that of the Church?

Yes. We address both Mary and the Church as our mother, because through Mary's intercession and through the prayers and the gifts entrusted to the Church we receive the new life of Christ. Just as Mary is saved by Christ, and mediates to us saving graces, so also the Church is saved by the Lord, yet it is also a saving community within which we receive the graces of Christ.

> As many Fathers of the Church observed, what is said of Mary is also to be said of the Church. The Church is also both mother and virgin; the Church also is both saved and sanctifying.

10. What is meant by Mary's assumption into heaven?

The Church solemnly teaches that after her life on earth was ended, Mary was assumed into heaven, that is, she was taken body and soul into heaven.

> This dogma of Catholic faith is not explicitly stated in Scripture, but it has been handed down as part of the faith from early centuries, and is rooted in scriptural teaching on the holiness of Mary and on the meaning of sin, death, and of the resurrection of the body. Since by special divine mercy she was kept always free from sin, she, like her divine Son, was not to remain in the grave. It was fitting that she who gave birth to Jesus and was intimately associated with Him in His saving work should be with Him bodily in heaven, to adore Him with all her being, and to be a sign of hope for all of us who look forward to the resurrection of our bodies.

> Many centuries of faith and devotion were crowned when the doctrine of the assumption was formally defined by Pope Pius XII. In her Assumption Mary has not been separated from us, but instead remains as a sign of sure hope that each one of us is called to share as she has in the fullness of Christ's glory. She is the model of all that the Church and mankind hope to become in heaven.

11. What is the role of St. Joseph in Christian life?

As the guardian of the Holy Family, most chaste spouse of our Lady, and foster father of our Savior, St. Joseph received from God one of the highest vocations in the plan of redemption. He continues to have a place in the lives and devotion of those who love Christ. He has been seen as a model for fathers of families and working men; but for every person devotion to St. Joseph can lead to a deeper faith, and to a greater closeness to Christ and to Mary.

> Joseph was truly married to Mary, in a virginal marriage, but a marriage of devoted personal love. Jesus was not merely Joseph's adopted Son; He was born of Joseph's wife. While he was not physically the father

of Jesus, "yet to the piety and love of Joseph a Son was born of the Virgin Mary — He who was also the Son of God" (St. Augustine). Like Mary, Joseph must have had a profound influence upon the Child who was "obedient to them" (Luke 2.51).

CHAPTER 16

Faith Lived in a Divided World

The Catholic Church, "God's only flock" (UR 2), carries on Christ's work in a world in which people profess many different religions and indeed many profess no religion at all. The Church does not despise other religions, but rather respects all that is good and true in all religions. It knows that faith is a gift of God, and that the Holy Spirit distributes His gifts as He will; and it knows that God in His mercy and love gives all men and women grace sufficient for salvation if they but respond. For Christ "died for all" (2 Cor. 5.15) and God wills that all be saved.

Yet the Church, "missionary by her very nature" (AG 2), can never forget its mission to proclaim the Gospel to all creation. "All men are called to belong to the new People of God. Wherefore this People, while remaining one and unique, is to be spread throughout the whole world and must exist in all ages, so that the purpose of God's will may be fulfilled" (LG 13).

In this chapter we discuss the Catholic response to the multiplicity of religions in the world today. The chapter also discusses the responsibility of the Church to the world, and the meaning and importance of true religious freedom.

1. Has Judaism a unique place in the history of salvation?

Of all the non-Christian religions, Judaism holds a unique place in the history of salvation. The Old Testament records the history of the Jews, and it shows how God chose them in a special way and revealed Himself to them.

> God entered into a covenant with Abraham and, through Moses, with the people of Israel. He taught this nation to acknowledge Him as the one living and true God. When the Son of Man came among us, He came as a Jew. Those He chose as apostles were Jews. Most of the early disciples were Jews. Christians should always remember that the beginnings of their faith are found already among the patriarchs, Moses, and the prophets. There is a spiritual bond linking the people of the New Covenant with the people of the Old Covenant.

2. Did the Second Vatican Council call for dialogue with the Jews?

In addressing the question of relations between Christians and Jews, the Second Vatican Council recalled the great heritage common to both and encouraged "that mutual understanding and respect, which is the fruit above all of biblical and theological studies, and of brotherly dialogues" (NA 4).

This clearly requires truth and simplicity. "Dialogue presupposes that each side wishes to know the other, and wishes to increase and deepen its knowledge of the other. . . . Dialogue demands respect for the other as he is; above all, respect for his faith and his religious convictions" (Commission for Religious Relations with the Jews).

3. Is anti-Semitism unchristian?

Yes. It is clear that anti-Semitism, that is, hostility toward the Jews or discrimination against them, is unchristian. The Church "mindful of her common patrimony with the Jews, and motivated by the Gospel's spiritual love and by no political considerations, deplores the hatred, persecutions, and displays of anti-Semitism directed against the Jews at any time and from any source" (NA 4).

It is true that the Jews have suffered much abuse or even savage persecution from Christian individuals and from nations called Christian. Certainly there have been many times in history when Jews could hardly have been expected to recognize the Christ witnessed by some Christians as indeed the Prince of peace.

4. What is the ecumenical movement?

The ecumenical movement is the movement supported by many groups of Christians to heal the divisions among Christians and to promote unity among all who believe in Christ.

The Second Vatican Council called on all Catholics to promote the restoration of unity among all Christians. It declared that this unity was one of the chief concerns of the council.

5. What are the sins of schism and of heresy?

The sin of schism is willful and culpable separation from the unity of the Church. The sin of heresy is deliberate and culpable denial or doubt of one or more elements of the Catholic faith.

It is not appropriate to use the words "schismatic" or "heretical" to describe Christians who through no fault of their own do not have the fullness of Catholic faith, because the sins of schism and heresy are both willful acts.

Schism does in fact always involve some heresy, at least in regard to Catholic teaching on the unity and authority of the Church. In practice a sharp distinction between schism and heresy is not always easy to maintain.

6. What are the principal divisions within Christendom?

The principal divisions within Christendom today are the result of separations that took place hundreds of years ago. Primarily they are: the break between the Holy See and the Eastern Patriarch in the eleventh century, and, in the West, the separation of various communions, both national and denominational, from Catholic unity in what is commonly called the Reformation, largely in the sixteenth century. Neither in the East nor in the West was the separation a single historical event; the separations evolved over long periods of time, from different causes, resulting in divisions different in nature.

The Eastern Orthodox Churches, although they are not in ecclesiastical communion with the Holy See, and thus are separated from the Catholic Church, nonetheless "possess true sacraments, above all — by apostolic succession — the priesthood and the Eucharist, whereby they are still joined to us in a very close relationship" (UR 15). Variety in liturgy, customs, and traditions is by no means a bar to Church unity; nor indeed is variety in theological expressions or doctrinal truth.

The Eastern Catholic Churches preserve the rich heritage of the East while living in full communion with the Holy See. These churches "have a special role to play in promoting the unity of all Christians, particularly Easterners, . . . first of all by prayer, then by the example of their lives, by religious fidelity to ancient Eastern traditions, by greater mutual knowledge, by collaboration, and by a brotherly regard for objects and attitudes" (OE 24).

The divisions which developed in the West are of a different type, and here the non-Catholic Christian communions "differ not only from us but also among themselves to a considerable degree" (UR 19), and it is difficult to speak of them in a collective way. But the separations were, and are, more than a rupture of Church unity. Although baptism provides a sacramental bond of unity linking all who are reborn by means of it, these separated Christians "lack that fulness of unity with us which should flow from baptism, and we believe that especially because of the lack of the sacrament of orders they have not preserved the genuine and total reality of the Eucharistic mystery" (UR 22). Nonetheless, they "are bound to the Catholic Church by a special affinity and close relationship in view of the long span of earlier centuries when the Christian people lived in ecclesiastical communion" (UR 19).

7. Is each Catholic called to take part in ecumenical activity?

Yes. All Catholics are called to share in the task of ecumenism. All can contribute in some way to the pursuit of greater unity among Christians.

"Concern for restoring unity pertains to the whole Church, faithful

112

and clergy alike. It extends to everyone, according to the potential of each, whether it be exercised in daily Christian living or in theological and historical studies" (UR 5).

The divisions rooted in centuries past did not come about without fault on both sides. Catholics have an obligation to bear witness to their Catholic faith, and they assist the cause of unity to the extent that they do this well. At the same time, Catholics "must joyfully acknowledge and esteem the truly Christian endowments derived from our common heritage which are to be found among our separated brethren" (UR 4). We should be willing to be edified by God's grace in them, for "whatever is wrought by the grace of the Holy Spirit in the hearts of our separated brethren can contribute to our own sanctification" (UR 4).

8. Does pursuit of unity justify forsaking some truths of Catholic faith?

No. "True ecumenical activity means openness, drawing closer, availablity for dialogue, and a shared investigation of the truth in the full evangelical and Christian sense; but in no way does it or can it mean giving up or in any way diminishing the treasures of divine truth that the Church has constantly confessed and taught" (Pope John Paul II).

"Nothing is so foreign to the spirit of ecumenism as a false conciliatory approach which harms the purity of Catholic doctrine and obscures its assured genuine meaning" (UR 11). Catholics believe that "it is through Christ's Catholic Church alone, which is the all-embracing means of salvation, that all fullness of the means of salvation can be obtained" (UR 3), and they "are bound to profess that through the gift of God's mercy they belong to that Church which Christ founded and which is governed by the successors of Peter and the other apostles" (Sacred Congregation for the Doctrine of the Faith).

9. Is religious dialogue with Moslems important?

Yes. The Moslems, "professing to hold the faith of Abraham, along with us adore the one and merciful God, who at the last day will judge mankind" (LG 16). Though the Islamic faith does not acknowledge Jesus as God, it does revere Him as a prophet, and also honors His virgin mother. Moslems "prize the moral life, and give worship to God especially through prayer, almsgiving, and fasting" (NA 3). Noting that there had been many quarrels and hostilities between Christians and Moslems, the Second Vatican Council urged that all "forget the past and strive sincerely for mutual understanding, and, on the behalf of all mankind, make common cause of safeguarding and fostering social justice, moral values, peace, and freedom" (NA 3).

10. Should Catholics build ties with other non-Christian religions?

Yes. The non-Christian religions, including Hinduism, Buddhism, and many others besides Islam, differ in many ways from the Catholic Church. This, however, does not put their followers who are in good conscience outside the plan of salvation.

"The divine design of salvation embraces all men; and those who without fault on their part do not know the Gospel of Christ and His Church, but seek God sincerely, and under the influence of grace endeavor to do His will as recognized through the promptings of their conscience, they, in a number known only to God, can obtain salvation" (Pope Paul VI).

11. Does the Church encourage dialogue with atheists?
Yes. The Church rejects atheism completely, but some dialogue with atheists is useful and important.

The Church strives to detect in the atheist's mind the reasons for the denial of God, and it invites the atheist to examine the Gospel with an open mind. Moreover, the Church believes that all, believers and unbelievers alike, ought to work for the rightful betterment of this world, and this cannot be brought about without "sincere and prudent dialogue" (GS 21).

12. Does the Church still have a major missionary task?
Yes. The Church "strives to proclaim the Gospel to all men" (AG 1) and is "missionary by her very nature" (AG 2). The Gospel message has not yet been heard, or scarcely so, by many in this world, and there is still a "gigantic missionary task" (AG 10).

Every follower of Christ has an obligation to do his or her part in spreading the faith; indeed, "by its very nature the Christian vocation is also a vocation to the apostolate" (AA 2).

13. Does the Church teach that all have a right to religious freedom?
Yes. Catholic faith insists that religious freedom is a basic human right flowing from the dignity of the human person. This right to immunity from external coercion in religious matters is a right which both governments and individuals have a duty to respect.

This civil right does not in any way negate or alter the moral obligation each person has to seek the truth, especially religious truth, and to adhere to that truth when it is known, and to order one's life in accord with the demands of truth.

God calls men insistently to serve Him, but He does not force them. "It is one of the major tenets of Catholic doctrine that man's response to God in faith must be free. Therefore no one is to be forced to embrace the Christian faith against his will. This doctrine is contained in the word of God and it was constantly proclaimed by the Fathers of the Church. . ."

(DH 10). Indeed, the principle of religious freedom "makes no small contribution to the creation of an environment in which men can without hindrance be invited to Christian faith and embrace it of their own free will, and profess it effectively in their whole manner of life" (DH 10).

Part Three

With Christ:
Sharing the Life of God

CHAPTER • 17

Christ Comes to Give Life

Jesus came to give us life. "I came that they might have life, and have it abundantly" (John 10.10). He offers a life richer than we could ever otherwise have, a life so radically new that we must be born again to have it.

This new life fulfills our deepest longings. It makes what is good in human life far better and richer. It makes our broken lives authenticallly human; it causes us to share in God's life as well. From the beginning God made human persons not merely to be His creatures, but to be His friends. This is indeed the reason why God created the world, why He did all the merciful deeds of salvation history, why He permitted all the sorrows of human history: the ultimate purpose of all things is that, in Christ, all persons made by God's creative love might freely come to Him and share the abundant life of the Blessed Trinity.

The rest of this catechism speaks of the life that Christ offers us, and of how that life is to be received, increased, and expressed.

This chapter first discusses how this new life is an entirely free gift of God in Christ. It then notes some of the basic elements of the new life, and outlines the major ways in which one obtains new life and grows in it.

1. What kind of new life does Christ offer us?

The new life that God offers us in Christ has two aspects. First, Christ has come to a fallen and sinful race to heal us, to make us more fully human and free, more truly what we were made to be. Secondly, He has called us to a new life, so that we might share divine life with our Savior. Each of these enrichments of life begins now in time; each is completely fulfilled only in eternal life.

2. Can we live already the new life that Christ brings?

Yes. Though the fullness of this life is reserved for eternity, already the new life of grace, of faith, hope, and love, and of friendship with Christ can be richly experienced. This new life is as real and present to us as the sorrows of this life are.

Those who teach faith to others should first live that faith themselves. It was not an utterly unknown and unexperienced mystery that the disciples of Christ invited others to share. They had the experience of a living faith "which casts a new light on everything" (GS 11), and they announced the Gospel "so that you may have fellowship with us" (1 John 1.3).

119

3. How does the "mystery of Christ" explain the world?

The "mystery of Christ" (Col. 4.3) is God's plan for the saving of the world. God made the world so that the love which is the inner life of the Trinity might be shared by the persons He made and whom He would call to truth and peace and life in Christ.

In a sinful and broken world the abundance of pain tempts many to reject life as meaningless. Christ enables us to see the meaning of suffering: how it came with sin, which is a rejection of love, and how it can be healed by love such as He showed on the cross. But the richness of the mystery of Christ was much more than a healing of the wounds of sin, for it was above all an invitation to share in the infinitely rich life of God Himself.

4. What are the central elements of the mystery of Christ?

By Christ we are called to freedom from sin and from all the evils in human life that are the effects of sin. We are invited to live freer and more authentic human lives. All humanity is invited to unity and peace in Christ the Lord. God gives us now a share in his own life, so that through faith, hope, and love we may live a new life on earth and confidently expect to enter at length the fullness of life, in the blessed vision of God, shared with all those whom we have loved in Christ.

5. Is the new life we receive from Christ a free gift of God?

Yes. Those who come to a living faith in God, and to the joy of new life in Him, should not imagine that the blessings they have received are due to their own merits. "For by grace you have been saved through faith; and this is not your doing, it is the gift of God" (Eph. 2.8).

6. Do we remain free when God's grace touches our lives?

Yes. God calls us to a new life, but not in such a way that we are forced to respond. God loves freedom, and He wishes from us only a free service and a free faith. Those who in fact accept His grace are enabled to do this freely by the power of His grace. Those who refuse His grace have not been abandoned by God, but they themselves have chosen to reject His gifts. For God "desires all men to be saved and to come to the knowledge of the truth" (1 Tim. 2.4).

7. In what ways is Jesus the life of the world?

God has graced the humanity of Jesus with the fullness of divine gifts. His is the fullness of life; He is always attractive, an invitation to life. In Him the "goodness and loving kindness of God" (Titus 3.4) were made visible to us.

Jesus is also the Teacher and the Exemplar of life. In His words and action we find the best models for living in the ways we most want and need to live.

Even more, Jesus is the source of life. Only by the energy of grace received from Him can we live in freedom and in greatness of soul.

8. How does Christ heal our human lives?

Human integrity has been deeply wounded by sin. The new life Christ brings heals men and women in their very humanity. He enables us to pursue authentic human values with energy and hope. Grace makes each one of us more human, more concerned with the personal and social goods of all and with the attainment of true temporal values.

> Before grace touches our lives we experience bitterly the effects of sin. "I can will what is right, but I cannot do it. For I do not do the good I want, but the evil I do not want is what I do" (Rom. 7.18). God's grace is liberating; it restores to us the power to do good consistently. But our own continuing cooperation with grace is essential. God freely and generously calls us to respond freely and generously.

9. How does one acquire the new life in Christ?

One receives this new life as a gift. God's grace precedes every prayer or work of ours that could merit it. Still, God's grace is offered to us as free persons. When we are moved by His grace and do not resist, He gives us the power to recognize, believe, trust, and love Him. He enables us then to make the free acts of faith and love that initiate divine life within us. By believing in Jesus, and by being baptized in His name, we become children of God and sharers in divine life.

10. What are the chief ways of growing in the new life?

We grow in divine life first by doing works of love, doing the "will of My Father who is in heaven" (Matt. 7.21), that is to say, by keeping God's commandments and by learning to lead generous lives pleasing to Him. Secondly, we grow in divine life through prayer, which is itself made possible by grace. Finally, we grow in divine life by receiving the sacraments.

> These three ways of growing in divine life will be developed at length in the following chapters.

11. Can we merit eternal life by living in faith and love?

To merit something is to acquire a right to it. Of our own power we can do nothing to merit eternal life or any of the gifts that lead to this; all that leads to a sharing in God's life flows from the free mercy of God. But our good deeds, moved by the grace of Christ, do merit eternal life for us. It is, to be sure, His grace that gives such efficacy to free human actions. He gives us the power to do freely sublime acts out of faith, hope, and love; then He freely rewards us for the good we have done in response to His call. "When God crowns our merits, is He not crowning precisely His own gifts?" (St. Augustine).

Scripture commends the justice of God in bestowing eternal life on those who have freely served Him. "Henceforth there is laid up for me the crown of righteousness, which the Lord, the righteous judge, will award to me on that day, and not only to me but also to all who have loved His appearing" (2 Tim. 4.8).

CHAPTER 18

God's Plan for Human Living

Called to a new life in Christ, we must yet live on this earth and in the midst of our human family. As creatures made children of God, and as co-workers of God in bettering the world, we are called to live freely and responsibly. With our natural talents and the gifts of grace, we are to chart out for ourselves a life pleasing to God.

Here we discuss first the problems involved in shaping a good human life. Then we speak of Christ's place in solving these problems. This chapter treats of what conscience is and of how it is to be guided; how God makes known the natural law and the commandments; and how the grace-rooted virtues we have as His gifts enable us to grow in freedom in doing His will.

1. Why is morality important in Catholic life?

Morality is important because our lives are important. Christ came that we may have life, and have it more abundantly. Aided by the grace of Christ, we should live as intelligent love requires. For the moral choices we freely make determine what our lives shall be like and the sort of persons we shall be.

2. Why do some people despair of leading a good moral life?

The experience of human weakness makes many feel that they have no power to lead consistently good lives. Pressures of many kinds make them feel that they have but little freedom and are not likely to acquire much freedom. The problems of life and the skepticism of the world tempt them to judge that no one can come to know how to live life well at all. That is, they are tempted to doubt their own dignity and worth.

3. Are we capable of understanding what is morally good?

Yes. A morally good life is a life in which one does what is genuinely good, what enriches and fulfills the deepest desires of his or her own heart. Our fallen state and the trials of life can make it more difficult for us to recognize what is authentically good. But faith teaches that ordinary human intelligence is in principle capable of learning how to live well.

"When the Gentiles who do not have the law do by nature what the law requires, they are a law to themselves, even though they do not have the law. They show that what the law requires is written on their hearts, while their conscience also bears witness. . ." (Rom. 2.14-15).

123

4. How do we know that anything is really good?

The goodness of many things can be difficult to determine; but all people know the goodness of the most basic of all human values. No one is incapable of knowing that friendship and beauty and peace and life and truth and integrity of heart are really good. Values like these are celebrated everywhere in Scripture, and also in human literature, and the experience of life reveals that they are good. Hence whether guided by natural intelligence or by faith, we can know securely the goodness of these values.

5. Does intelligent reflection help us make sound moral decisions?

Yes. Many of the parables of the Lord guide us to be reasonable and impartial in our moral decisions. The Golden Rule taught by our Lord, "As you wish that men would do to you, do so to them" (Luke 6.31), is a moral directive easily grasped by human intelligence.

6. Does the experience of friendship help us to make good moral decisions?

Yes. Anyone who has experienced real friendship is certain that friendship is part of any person's well-being. But friendship leads one away from selfishness and narrowness. It makes us realize that we are ourselves fulfilled when we see and rejoice in the flourishing of those we love.

Thus friendship reveals a richer kind of love than mere self-love; it makes clear hidden depths of our being. In this way it stimulates a morally sound impartiality in the pursuit of good.

7. Can remembrance that we shall die help us to acquire moral wisdom?

Yes. To see life from the vantage point one would have at its earthly conclusion, at the moment of death, is an effort to see life whole. From this perspective anyone is more readily inclined to approve what is truly worthwhile, what makes life precious and good. Concern about present pleasures and pains then appears less demanding.

"In all that you do, remember the end of your life" (Sir. 7.36). There is added force in this saying for the believer, who knows that after death comes the judgment of the Lord, and that our present ways of living shape our eternal destiny.

8. What is our conscience?

Our conscience is first of all the power God gives us to recognize personally what is good and what is evil. "In the depths of his conscience man detects a law which he did not impose upon himself, but which holds him to obedience. . . . For man has in his heart a law written by God" (GS 16). Conscience is also the judgment that one makes about the goodness or

124

badness of particular acts that we have done or are considering doing. "Always summoning one to love good and do it and to avoid evil, the voice of conscience can when necessary speak to his heart more specifically: do this, shun that" (GS 16).

9. Can conscience err?
Yes. Even when one honestly and earnestly seeks to know what is morally right, the judgments of conscience can be mistaken.

We personally make our own judgments of conscience, and we are not infallible. "Conscience frequently errs from invincible ignorance without losing its dignity" (GS 16).

10. Have we a duty to follow our conscience?
Yes. "Every one of us is bound to obey his conscience" (DH 11). We are obliged to follow our conscience even when, unknown to us, it is quite mistaken. For our conscience expresses our considered judgment about what is really right or required, and what we judge that God desires of us. To act against our conscience would be to do what we ourselves judge to be wrong.

11. Would we sin in doing a morally wrong kind of act if our conscience judged it right?
No. We would not sin if we had seriously sought to know and to do what is really good. But we would not be excused for doing something evil if we care little about truth and goodness, and if we do not try seriously to know what intelligent love requires of us.

When we make judgments of conscience, we should seek to determine what is truly right and good. If we err out of complacency, prejudice, rashness, or self-centeredness, then we will be in the wrong whether we follow or reject the dictates of "conscience."

12. How should one make a judgment of conscience?
In making a judgment of conscience we should seek earnestly to discover what is truly good, what God wills. Hence we have a duty to heed the secure teachings of Christ, and to form our consciences in the light of faith. We must avoid the obvious obstacles to the formation of a right conscience. We must not let ourselves be led astray by thoughtless public opinion, or by the prejudices of special groups, or by our own biased self-interest.

"In the formation of their consciences, the Christian faithful ought carefully to attend to the sacred and certain doctrine of the Church. The Catholic Church is, by the will of Christ, the teacher of the truth. It is her

125

duty to give utterance to, and authoritatively to teach, that truth which is Christ Himself and also to confirm by her authority those principles of the moral order which have their origin in human nature itself" (DH 14).

13. What is the natural law?

The natural law is the fundamental moral law that governs human life. It is not an arbitrary set of rules, but an intelligent guide to life. The natural law shows us how we must live to fulfill our own being and to satisfy the requirements of our own personal and social life.

The expression "natural law" reminds us that we are able by our own natural powers to come to a personal understanding of the basic moral truths that all people need to live by to live well. The expression "natural law" reminds us also that some laws bind all those who share human nature. They are enduringly true and good, because they express the enduring requirements for the fulfillment of our human nature. In this they differ from the positive laws made by the state or by the Church, many of which are appropriately changed as times and circumstances require. The basic precepts of the natural law are the foundation of the inalienable rights of all persons.

14. Has God revealed the natural law?

Yes. Each person is able by native intelligence to grasp the principles of natural law, and each is able to grow in personal understanding of what is good and evil. Still, we live in the midst of our passions and the many pressures of the world, and many have little leisure to study moral questions with great care. That we might not remain in ignorance of what we need to live good lives, God has revealed the fundamental requirements of moral life, and He has given the Church the task of teaching the moral law authoritatively.

"By the will of Christ the Catholic Church is the teacher of truth and it is her responsibility to proclaim and authoritatively to teach the truth that is Christ Himself, and at the same time, by her authority to declare and confirm the principles of the moral order that flow from human nature itself" (DH 14).

15. What are the Ten Commandments?

The Ten Commandments are precepts given by God through Moses to the chosen people as a central part of their covenant with Him. They contain a striking summary of the most important elements of natural law; they guard the dignity and rights of all and ennoble the lives of those who live by them. In summary the Ten Commandments are:

1. I, the Lord, am your God. You shall not have any other gods besides Me.

2. You shall not take the name of the Lord, your God, in vain.
3. Remember to keep holy the Sabbath day.
4. Honor your father and your mother.
5. You shall not kill.
6. You shall not commit adultery.
7. You shall not steal.
8. You shall not bear false witness against your neighbor.
9. You shall not covet your neighbor's wife.
10. You shall not covet anything that belongs to your neighbor.

16. What is the basic meaning of the Ten Commandments?

The Ten Commandments first point out the absolute priority of a free and loving service of God. The author of Deuteronomy summarizes the theme of the first three commandments: "The LORD our God is one God, and you shall love the LORD your God with all your heart, and with all your soul, and with all your might" (Deut. 6.4-5). Christ calls this the first and greatest commandment. The first three precepts spell out some of the fundamental ways in which God is to be loved.

Secondly, the Ten Commandments show that serving God absolutely requires respect for one's neighbor in deeds and in words. Several essential requirements of this respect are spelled out.

Thirdly, the decalogue makes it clear that the deliberate doing of certain types of acts, and, as the last two commandments show, even the inner will to do such types of acts are incompatible with love of God and respect for neighbor. Acts of such kinds are always and everywhere wrong; they may not be done in any situation.

> The decalogue does not identify with complete precision all these types of acts that are incompatible with love. The identification is made in other parts of Scripture, in the reflection of the saints and doctors who, reflecting on Scripture, sought to see as God sees and to love as He loves, and in a special way by "the Church's teaching office, which authentically interprets the divine law in the light of the Gospel" (GS 50).

17. Is Jesus Christ a moral teacher?

Jesus Christ is the most sublime Teacher of morality. He indeed ratified the decalogue, and He also pointed out that every commandment in the law and prophets is rooted in the two fundamental precepts of love of God and love of neighbor.

Though the Old Testament also taught love of God and neighbor, the Lord's precepts were new, because He taught us the right measure of love. We are to love one another "as I have loved you," that is, with a measure of love never seen before on earth. He taught by words and by His life that love essentially involves self-giving and self-sacrifice. We are never deliberately to do evil to anyone to achieve any objective whatever.

The new standard is that of children of God. We are summoned to "be imitators of God, as beloved children. And walk in love, as Christ loved us" (Eph. 5.1-2).

Thus Jesus did not hesitate to give most excellent precepts to His disciples, reminding them that for those made children by divine grace it was not enough to heed the precepts they had heard in the Old Law. They must walk by far better ways. Still the way was not to be bitter or burdensome. His grace would make it possible for all to turn aside from deeds incompatible with love. To make growth in love easier, Jesus commended, but did not impose on all, the evangelical counsels. All were called to live in the spirit of the beatitudes.

The excellence of Christ as a moral Teacher flows from the sublime goodness of His life, the wisdom of His moral teaching, His ability to make goodness attractive, and His power to move His disciples to live the excellent ways He taught them.

18. Can we keep the commandments of Christ by our own power?

No. While the natural power of free will extends to the ability of doing some good deeds, the performance of good actions out of that love which makes them meritorious and pleasing to God is possible only by the grace of Christ.

"Without Me you can do nothing" (John 15.5). It is the grace of Christ and the gifts of His spirit that make the moral life easy and pleasant.

19. What is a virtue?

A virtue is a settled disposition or characteristic of the good person, which inclines the person toward good, loving, and morally right action. There are chiefly two kinds of virtues. Infused virtues are gifts of God that give one the power to act in excellent ways, as the gifts of faith, hope, and love give us power to direct our lives freely toward the Lord. Acquired virtues are learned traits, obtained also by divine assistance, that make it not only possible but easy and pleasant to do that which is good and right.

20. How do we acquire virtue?

Infused virtues are free gifts of God, though they may be efficaciously sought in prayer. Acquired virtues are obtained by freely doing excellent actions in the way that virtuous people do them.

Thus if we seek to acquire chastity we must act in ways that the chaste person does; we must seek to do so out of the same motives, the same love, and the same wholehearted generosity with which the chaste person acts. At first these acts require effort; but persistent effort gives one's mind, memory, imagination, and will a far greater ease and joy in acting in excellent ways.

21. Can people be taught to be good?

Since all persons have free will, and grace is a gift of God, there are no infallible ways of educating people to goodness of life. Yet there are many ways to help people live good lives. The excellence and beauty of right living can be taught, especially by example. By prayer we can obtain graces for those we love. It is possible, especially for parents, to begin early in life to teach children virtue by guiding them to experience the joy of doing very good actions. From the happiness that flows from doing excellent deeds they gradually acquire joy and then ease in performing acts of virtue.

22. Why must a moral life be free?

A person's response to God's call would not be a personal response if it were not free. We cannot please God with acts that are not done with free and willing hearts. God's gift of free will is a basic gift that makes moral striving intelligible. Even more precious is that freedom of the children of God, the help that God gives to make it possible to do what really enriches our lives.

23. Are freedom and moral obligation compatible?

Yes. Everywhere we experience such compatibility. For example, parents are obliged to care for their children; yet they can, and should, carry out these duties in freedom and with great love.

Many kinds of freedom adorn Christian life. Obedience to saving precepts is a work of freedom, since "no one can fulfill a precept of love except of his own free will" (St. Thomas Aquinas). Moreover, specific commandments do not shape most of our lives. God offers us many ways in which we may live excellent and holy lives, and He calls us freely to a wide variety of vocations. Response to the call of grace is commonly a call to a free and creative response to God's free gifts.

129

CHAPTER 19

Living Faith, Hope, and Love

"So there abide faith, hope, and love, these three" (1 Cor. 13.13). The response to Christ's call has a variety of aspects. First, there is recognition that it is God who calls us, and acknowledgment that He is trustworthy and His word is true and good. This is faith. Second, there is a lively confidence that in responding to Him we approach One whose will it is to fulfill our needs and longings more fully than we could otherwise have imagined. This is hope. Finally, there is the fullest response, the gift to Him of one's whole self, of mind and heart and strength, accepting His call to membership in God's family, to friendship with the Trinity and with one another. This is charity, or love.

In this chapter we speak of the place of these theological virtues in the moral life, and of the special obligations they imply.

1. What is faith?

Faith is a gift of God which enables us to recognize that it is God Himself who speaks and teaches in the Scriptures and in the living voice of the Church. It is a gift which "is the beginning of human salvation" (St. Fulgentius), for it initiates our personal relationship with the revealing and saving God. By faith we are enabled to entrust our whole being to God, "offering 'the full submission of intellect and will to God who reveals' (First Vatican Council), and freely assenting to the truth revealed by Him" (DV 5).

> Often "faith" is used in a comprehensive sense, that is, for full response to the word of God, a response lived in hope and in love. But faith is also used in a more specific sense, for an aspect of Christian life distinct from though closely related to hope and love. Faith in this sense is the virtue that enables us to discover the teaching presence of God in the family of faith, and to believe His words because we have found personal faith in Him. "You have the words of everlasting life; and we have believed, and have come to know, that you are the Holy One of God" (John 6.68-69).

2. What duties follow from the gift of faith?

The primary duties of faith are: to believe what we are enabled to recognize as God's word; to seek to have an informed faith; to hold fast to the word of God in its purity, never compromising it or receding from it for any reason whatever. Similarly, pastors and parents who have responsibility for the care of little ones in Christ must be tireless witnesses to the truth that God has revealed, guarding the faith in its entirety, and being "unfailing in patience and in teaching" (2 Tim. 4.2).

3. When are we obliged to profess our faith or defend it?

The Catholic is gravely obliged "faithfully to proclaim his faith, and vigorously to defend it" (DH 14). Especially we are obliged to confess our faith when it is called into question seriously, or when silence on our part would suggest lack of inner faith, or when silence would be a cause of scandal to others.

> "Whoever acknowledges Me before men, I also will acknowledge him before My Father who is in heaven; but whoever denies Me before men, I will also deny him before My Father who is in heaven" (Matt. 10.32-33).

4. Does a Catholic have a duty to believe all that the Church teaches?

Yes. Catholic faith is a gift that enables one to recognize the words of God proclaimed in the family of faith as indeed His words. The instructed Catholic knows that whenever any teaching is proposed infallibly by the Church that the truth of this teaching is confirmed by God. Hence he or she has the power and the duty to assent to it in the freedom of divine faith. Those teachings of the Church that are proposed authoritatively and insistently, though not in decisive or infallible ways, are to be accepted with internal religious assent, in reverent respect for the Lord who rules and teaches in His Church.

5. Could one ever have a just reason for abandoning the Catholic faith?

The Church teaches that faith is an enduring gift of God. He continues to give His grace to those whom He has called to faith, never deserting those who do not desert Him. "Those who have received the faith under the teaching authority of the Church can never have a just reason to change this same faith or call it into doubt" (First Vatican Council).

> One could, of course, encounter many trials and temptations that disturb one's faith. But steadfastness in prayer and intelligent concern to guard faith will, by God's mercy, overcome every difficulty.

6. How does faith enrich human life?

Faith first gives the joy of a personal relationship with the Lord. For it gives one power to recognize the teaching presence of the Lord in the midst of the family of faith. The person blessed with faith knows that, in the midst of all the doubts and anxieties of the world, the teachings of faith are the teaching of God, and are therefore certain and good.

> "Faith throws a new light on everything, manifests God's design for

man's total vocation, and thus directs the mind to solutions which are fully human" (GS 11).

7. What is hope?

Hope is a supernatural virtue, a free gift of God, that enables us to trust God utterly. By hope we look forward with confidence to the fulfillment of all God's promises.

8. Have we a duty to hope in God?

One of the strongest demands God makes of His people is that they trust Him entirely.

> In Scripture the Lord constantly assures us: "It is the LORD your God who goes with you; He will not fail you or forsake you" (Deut. 31.6).

9. For what should we primarily hope from God?

First of all we confidently hope that God will give us all the graces that we need to serve Him faithfully and bring us at length into His eternal life. Hope does not absolutely assure us that we shall persevere in faithfulness to God; but it makes us certain that He shall always be faithful to us, and patiently urge us toward the crown of everlasting life.

> The Christian hopes also for God's mercy in earthly matters as well. We know that He loves us and is concerned about all the details of our lives. Yet the virtue of hope does not give absolute assurance that any particular earthly goods will be obtained.

10. Is it selfish to hope for one's own salvation?

No. The Lord Himself calls us to hope for everlasting life in Him. Each person is to seek eternal life as one of many brothers and sisters who will inherit the kingdom together. There is no conflict between love of God and neighbor and hope for personal salvation, for God is glorified in the salvation of His people.

11. Should hope for eternal life make us care less for justice on earth?

No. Eternal life begins for us here on earth. The good works that we are called to do by Christ are such as serve justice and tend toward the truest fulfillment of this world. But at the same time they make us worthy of the final kingdom, in which all the goods done in love in this world will be found again, "but freed of stain, burnished, and transfigured" (GS 39).

12. Do those who live in hope avoid doing evil that good may come of it?

Yes. One who lives in Christian hope will not do even a "small evil" for the purpose of achieving a great good or avoiding a great hardship. For even a small sin is, in the eyes of faith, more grievous than any amount of physical evil. One who believes in God and hopes in Him knows that He is indeed the Lord of Providence and will care for us if we faithfully pursue good ends only by good means.

13. What is despair?
Despair is a deliberate refusal to trust that God will enable one to be saved.

14. What is presumption?
Presumption is a sin against hope, a pretense that one could find salvation without God's help and without prayerfully seeking this help, or a pretense that salvation can be had without personal cooperation with God's grace.

15. What is love of God?
Love of God is a supernatural virtue that God pours into our hearts; it is also our free response to God, made possible by that gift and His actual graces. The first and greatest commandment is that we should love God with our whole heart, mind, soul, and all our strength.

> Love of God is the heart of Christian life. We are able to love God rightly only by the aid of God. It is He who pours charity into our hearts, and so enables us to love Him freely and generously.

16. What should motivate love of God in us?
We should love God because He is most excellent in Himself, full of mercy, love, forgiveness, awesome in power and grandeur, and also because He has freely chosen to love us before we could love Him. When we sinned, the Father sent His true Son, equally God with the Father, to dwell among us as a brother. Gladly God the Son chose even to suffer and die for us. Only in loving God above all can we be true to what we are and find the fulfillment for which we long.

17. How important is love to Christian morality?
Love is absolutely basic. All the precepts of Christian morality simply unfold the requirements of a true love of God and of neighbor. Jesus Himself taught that all the moral teachings of the law and the prophets flow from the two great commandments of love.

18. Why does a personal love of God require keeping all of God's commandments?
If one believes God, one knows that all that God commands us is really

good. It is His wisdom and mercy that teach us ways to live. If one loves God, one wishes to do His gracious will. Christ died for each one of our human brothers and sisters, and He wills that we share His love for them.

"Love does no wrong to a neighbor; therefore love is the fulfilling of the law" (Rom. 13.10).

19. What is sin?

The basic kind of sin is actual sin, that is, any thought, word, deed, or omission contrary to the saving law of God. Sin is the great enemy to and the obstacle to the love of God and love of neighbor; it leads to a "state of sin." One who sins gravely, or mortally, and does not properly repent, begins to live a life enduringly alienated from God. There is also the "original sin" in which we were born, a state implying absence of God's grace and causing disorder in our inner lives, inclining us toward actual sin.

20. What is the difference between formal sin and material sin?

Some of the bad actions we perform are done freely and with the knowledge that they are contrary to God's will. These are known as formal sins. If the act in question is a gravely wrong kind of act, the formal sin in doing such an act separates us from the love of Christ and the secure hope of salvation. Some actions which are in themselves wrong are done without personal guilt, because the doer acts without freedom or in ignorance. These are called material sins.

Pastors, parents, and educators must help those in their care to avoid even material sin also. For the commandments of God direct us in ways that are truly good, and necessary for the fulfillment of our lives and of his saving plan; and to do evil deeds even without formal guilt is to do something harmful to oneself and to others.

21. What is a mortal sin?

A mortal sin is a sin that separates one from friendship with God, or deepens one's alienation from God. A formal mortal sin involves doing an act that is or is thought to be a gravely evil kind of act, and doing this with sufficient knowledge and freedom.

From Scripture and from the constant teaching of the Church we know that there are certain kinds of actions that objectively are gravely wrong kinds of actions.

22. What are the consequences of mortal sin?

Those who deliberately and knowingly commit mortal sin lose sanctifying grace and that participation in divine life which Christ won for us. Moreover, one who sins gravely forfeits all the merits for good acts formerly done, and ceases to be an heir to the kingdom of heaven. To die separated from the grace of God is to face the terrifying prospect of God's judgment and the eternal separation from God about which He has warned us.

23. Are all sins equally serious?

No. It is clear from Scripture and constant Church teaching that not all sins are equally serious. St. James refers to lesser kinds of sins that do not separate us from friendship with God: "For we all make many mistakes" (James 3.2). Even the closest disciples of Jesus were taught to ask forgiveness of their sins: "Forgive us our trespasses. . . ."

24. What is a venial sin?

A venial sin is a less serious offense than a mortal sin. A venial sin is not a turning away from God, not the doing of a deed that of its nature is incompatible with love of God and neighbor. But it is a shortcoming, a hesitation or misstep, as it were, in following Christ.

> Some sins are venial because the wrong done is not so base or serious a disorder that it involves turning from the love of God, even if it is deliberately done. An example of this would be carelessness about keeping a promise to do a slight favor for a friend, when such carelessness might disappoint but not seriously hurt. Sometimes a sin is venial because it violates a serious responsibility in only a slight degree. An example would be the theft of a very trivial item. Sometimes a sin is venial because, although the action performed is a gravely evil kind of deed, one does not perform it with the knowledge and freedom required to make it a fully deliberate human action.

25. Is venial sin a matter of great importance?

Yes. Although venial sin does not separate us from the love of God, it weakens our love of God and can pave the way for the commission of mortal sins. A venial sin is the greatest of all evils except for mortal sin.

26. What is meant by a "fundamental option"?

In recent years many Christian thinkers have adopted the expression "fundamental option" as a name for the persistent will or attitude that shapes a person's life. One may exhibit a basic intent to live as one who believes God's word and accepts His call to live a new life, or may decline to do so. Such fundamental stances do in fact determine many of the choices we make. Certainly the act of faith and love by which one turns to God is not an isolated act. It has its roots in prior responses to graces, and, when it is entirely sincere, it establishes the fundamental orientation of one's life.

Similarly, a mortal sin ordinarily has roots in prior acts of unfaithfulness, and it endures in a life deliberately lived without genuine love of God.

27. Could a single mortal sin change one's "fundamental option"?

Yes. We tend to become established in a rooted loyalty to God, which makes service of Him more easy and pleasant, or we tend to become more set in the selfishness that turns us away from God. But this does not mean that those who have exhibited some lasting loyalty to God cannot commit mortal sins.

We have many frailties. Our venial sins can, without themselves changing our fundamental stance toward God, make us drift toward an act of disloyalty and disobedience so radical that it brings about and reveals a different orientation toward God. It would be presumptuous to claim that one's life has been so steadfastly turned toward God that it would not be possible for one to change the essential direction of one's life by a single act of lust or abortion or blasphemy. For if one deliberately does an act that is gravely evil, and known to be opposed to the will of God, and does this with sufficient awareness and freedom, one reveals that one is not firmly devoted to God.

So, also, a single act of repentance, made possible by God's merciful grace, can change the whole direction of a sinful life and restore one to friendship with God. One sees many such instances in Scripture, as, for example, that of the Good Thief.

28. Must one believe in God to commit a sin?

No. Failure to believe in God, when one has been given sufficient grace to do so, is itself sinful. However, there are many who, though they do not explicitly believe in God, recognize the existence of some Reality that requires them to do good and avoid evil. While they may not explicitly know that this Reality that calls us to do good and avoid evil is God, their evil actions are in reality rejections of the God they are obscurely aware of.

29. Which commandments speak of the duties that flow from faith, hope, and love of God?

The first three commandments of the decalogue speak of the duties that flow from faith, hope, and love, the three theological virtues.

30. What duties are implied by the first commandment of God?

The first commandment obliges us to recognize the one true God and to worship Him alone. We have a duty to live in the faith, hope, and love that God has infused into our hearts at baptism, and actually to express these commitments at certain times.

Sins against faith include apostasy, or the abandonment of faith entirely, and heresy, the deliberate denial of some revealed truth or truths. One would sin against hope by presumption or by despair. The most bitter sin against love is hatred of God. The first commandment forbids also sins of superstition and sacrilege.

We are required to make acts of faith, hope, and love at times like these: early in life, when we begin to realize our duty to relate ourselves to God freely in these ways; often in life, to keep these dispositions earnest in our lives; in times of temptation, when these expressions of commitment are needed to guard loyalty to Him. The act of love is the most important of these. At the moment of death we should, if possible, explicitly express our love for our heavenly Father.

In superstition, one seriously attributes to created things power to shape events or to foresee the future in ways that are possible only to God. Sacrilege is the mistreatment of what is sacred, of persons or things consecrated to divine worship. Especially serious is sacrilegious reception of the sacraments, that is, receiving while in the state of grave sin sacraments that symbolize and demand of recipients love of God in their hearts (Eucharist, Confirmation, Holy Orders, and Matrimony).

31. What duties flow from the second commandment?

The second commandment requires reverence for God's name. God's name is dishonored by perjury, that is, when one lies after calling upon the name of God as a pledge that one will speak the truth. Similarly, God's name is dishonored by violations of one's vows (promises that are seriously made to God and sealed by His name). One also dishonors God by cursing, that is, by calling upon God to do harm to others; and especially by blasphemy, that is, by any words or actions intended to express contempt for God.

32. What duties flow from the third commandment?

The third commandment requires that we keep the Lord's day holy. Church law specifies for the Catholic certain fundamental ways he or she is to do this. Thus the Catholic has the grave duty to attend Mass on Sundays and on certain holy days. Likewise Catholics are required to avoid needless labor and unnecessary commercial dealings on such days; that is, they must avoid activities that hinder the spirit of celebration, joy, and prayer.

At times one is dispensed from these special duties of worship and rest, especially if some real necessity or an urgent requirement of charity is pressing. Worship is a great duty, but charity is a greater one.

137

33. Should we have love for ourselves?

Yes. There is a proper order of love. After love of God comes love of self. Christ commanded: "You shall love your neighbor as you love yourself" (Mark 12.31). But the love that is set as the standard of love for one's neighbor is a right love of self, a love that is governed and guided by love of God. One who does not have a right love of self, a love that flows from a grateful love of God, is not able to love his neighbor rightly.

Every individual should think of his or her salvation as a primary responsibility. We can and must do much to help one another in building up the kingdom of God. But each of us can and must do for ourselves in this pursuit much that our neighbor cannot do for us.

34. Is self-love ever sinful?

Yes. Disordered love of self is the root of all sin. There can be only one center of a person's life. That center can be God, or it can be oneself. The second choice is pride, from which all sin flows.

35. Why must we love our neighbor?

"This commandment we have from Him, that he who loves God should love his neighbor also" (1 John 4.21). In a sense nature itself demands that we love one another. For we are members of one human family, and we cannot live well if we do not bear one another's burdens. But it is in Christ that our duty to love one another becomes most clear. Christ loved, and died for, each one of our brothers and sisters, and He has so identified Himself with each of them in love that we cannot love Him without loving them also.

CHAPTER 20

A Life Worthy of Our Calling

Faith calls us not only to share in a new and divine life with Christ, but also to guard all human values as well. Catholic moral teaching requires us to care for earthly goods too.

Only by cultivating "natural goods and values" can a person come to "an authentic and full humanity" (GS 53). If human values are to be protected as they should be in a world that threatens them so seriously, we must have the "perspective of humanity redeemed by Christ" (GE 2). For "faith throws a new light on everything, manifests God's design for man's total vocation, and thus directs the mind to solutions which are fully human" (GS 11). Only in that light can we make judgments on all that concerns our daily life.

In this chapter we consider how, in the light of faith, Christian hope and love should heal and perfect our attitudes toward three basic human values: life, procreation (the transmission of life), and truth.

1. Does Catholic faith require reverence for every human person?

Yes. The Church has always proclaimed the dignity of each human person. Because each human being is the image of God, and is called through Christ to share in the personal life of the Trinity, each one is precious before God. The dignity and rights of each person are always to be respected.

2. Must reverence for human life be stressed in our day?

Yes. Few ages have seen violations of the dignity of man as our age has seen. Today in a special way the Church must cry out against "whatever is opposed to life itself, such as any type of murder, genocide, abortion, euthanasia, and willful self-destruction. . . ; all these things and others of their like are infamies indeed. They poison human society, but they do more harm to those who do them than to those who suffer the injury. Moreover, they are a supreme dishonor to the Creator" (GS 27).

On the other hand, providence has mercifully stirred up at this time a sensitivity to the worth of each person. "There is a growing awareness of the exalted dignity proper to the human person, since he stands above all things, and his rights and duties are universal and inviolable" (GS 26).

3. Is respect for human life satisfied by abstaining from certain evil acts opposed to life?

No. The duty to honor human life is fundamentally positive. It is not

139

enough simply to restrict one's activities, to do no murders, to oppress no one. Rather, we are called to show personal and positive love by causing the basic values to flourish concretely in our own lives and in the lives of others.

4. Is life the only value that always demands respect?

No. Our lives are fulfilled and made human by concern for every human value: for truth and friendship, for beauty and peace, for integrity, and for every rich value celebrated in Scripture and hungered for by the human heart.

No one can make each one of these values the focus of his life. As Christians we must have a concern for every human value, but we may be specially dedicated to serving one or more particular ones. For example, some may have a special concern for peace or for advancing truth through scholarship. Many will dedicate themselves especially to the service of life, perhaps as doctors or nurses, or firemen, or, less directly, as farmers, and so on. But all of us are obliged to reverence life through care for the safety of others and through works of mercy. Moreover, each of us is strictly bound never to act directly against life, as we are bound never to act directly against any basic value.

5. What is meant by acts "opposed to life itself"?

Christian tradition is unwavering in its condemnation of actions "opposed to life itself" (GS 27). There are acts in which individual, concrete human lives are treated as though they were not good, not worthy of respect. Acts of murder, genocide, abortion, or suicide, for example, are of their nature direct attacks on the precious good of human life; they are acts "opposed to life itself." Such acts should never be done for any reason whatever.

The Church rejects the idea of weighing, balancing, or attempting to calculate circumstances in which one might do such deeds. No circumstance could justify treating a person as a mere means to some desired end; no circumstance could justify abortion, killing an innocent person, or the like. Such direct attacks on a basic form of human goodness are always evil.

6. Does faith condemn every act that causes harm to human lives?

While faith insists on reverent concern for every human life, it does not teach that every act which causes harm to another, not even every act which might cause death, is necessarily "opposed to life itself." Some acts performed in defense of human lives and other human values may, despite the good intentions of those who do these acts, cause harm to the lives of others. Such acts are not necessarily wrong.

Thus, those who are attacked unjustly may have a right to resist, even though their acts of self-defense may harm those who attack them. Officials responsible for defending justice in a community have a duty to defend the helpless when they are assailed; under certain conditions they might even be called upon to perform defensive actions that result in the death of the assailants. Indeed, in times when there has seemed to be no other way of preventing the unjust violence of a criminal, the Church has not condemned the execution of a criminal according to law by properly constituted authorities. Many, however, reasonably oppose capital punishment in our day, especially since it is often applied unfairly; it is far more likely to be inflicted on criminals from poor or underprivileged classes than on other criminals.

7. What is the difference between directly doing harm and indirectly causing harm?

In complex questions in which one must guard against directly attacking life and yet must also take care to protect life or other values, this distinction is often essential. When one directly does harm, as in an act of deliberate murder, one intentionally brings about the harm that occurs. But one is said to cause a harm indirectly when one in no way intends the bad effect that happens to follow from one's action. It is always wrong to directly do evil, but sometimes even virtuous acts indirectly cause harm.

The case of a martyr can be illuminating here. St. Thomas More, for example, chose not to swear falsely, but to proclaim the truth, and remain faithful to his God. However, he could foresee that many evils would follow if he remained faithful. He would die; his family would suffer greatly; the king and his servants would do many wicked deeds. But Thomas More did nothing that directly caused these evil effects. He did not desire these evils in themselves or for the sake of achieving anything else. He did not want the evil effects, though he knew they would follow if he acted faithfully. Though his decision had a death-dealing effect for himself, and resulted in harm to others, his was clearly not a choice "opposed to life itself."

In a complex world the support of justice and other essential values will at times have bad side effects. To maintain purity of heart one must indeed care about those unwanted side effects, and seek to create a world order in which they do not occur. We must never do evil, and we must never want evil consequences to occur.

8. Why is it wrong to do even a slight evil to attain a great good?

It is wrong to do any evil even in the hope of attaining great goods because of the decisive importance of free human actions. No hope for goods could justify doing an evil or sinful action. God indeed wishes us to care about accomplishing good in this world, but He wishes us to achieve our good ends only by good actions.

One could readily imagine cases in which great harm could occur unless we were willing to do something evil to prevent it. But faith reminds us both of the limits of our vision and of our role in serving providence. The doing of an evil action does not of itself bring about anything good. In a world ruled by providence the performance of evil deeds is never justified. Evil kinds of acts remain evil even if the performance of them now seems likely to bring about good effects in the world.

Many saints were tested by trials in which it seemed that the direct doing of evil would have far better fruits than abstaining from doing evil. To St. Thomas More it might well have seemed that a false oath would really do little harm. By a false oath he could save his life, preserve his family, remain as a wise counsellor to the king. But he knew that deliberate evil deeds always pervert the heart. A good person who can find no good means to achieve a desired end should judge that he has now no means to attain that end. But he may and should struggle to change the world, so that good can be achieved in good ways.

9. Is direct abortion always gravely sinful?
Yes. From the first centuries the Church taught that direct abortion is gravely immoral.

In modern times science has shown clearly that a new human life begins at conception. Hence to procure an abortion directly is to kill a human being. Some deny that all human beings are persons, and argue that it is permissible to kill these most helpless human beings. But faith recognizes every human being as a person, a bearer of rights given by God.

10. Is the life of the child more important than that of the mother?
No. The Church sees every human life as precious. It would clearly be wrong to kill the mother in order to save the child, just as it would be wrong to kill the child for the mother's sake. The good person never deliberately kills any innocent person.

"Any deliberate attack on innocent human life, in whatever condition it is found from the first moment of its existence, is wrong. This principle holds good both for the life of the child and for that of the mother. Never and in no cases has the Church taught that the life of the child must be preferred to that of the mother. . . . There can be but one obligation: to make every effort to save the lives of each" (Pope Pius XII).

11. What is the difference between direct abortion and indirect abortion?
One who performs a direct abortion intends to end the life of the un-

142

born child, and performs acts to achieve that end. One who causes an in-
direct abortion neither intends to end the life of the child nor does anything aimed at ending that life, but he performs an act from which the
death of the child follows as an unwanted consequence.

It is always gravely wrong to choose or perform a direct abortion; but
it is not always immoral to cause an abortion indirectly. For example, if a
physician were to give a pregnant woman a treatment now needed to save
her life, even though he foresees that the child may be aborted as a consequence of the treatment, his action would not be immoral.

12. Are sex and sexual activity essentially good?

Yes. The Church has always recognized sex as a good and important reality. It is God who made mankind male and female. He established marriage, and wished to have His human family enlarged through the sexual
expression of love by spouses.

"Have you not read that He who made them from the beginning made
them male and female, and said, 'For this reason a man shall leave his father and mother and be joined to his wife, and the two shall become
one?' " (Matt. 19.4-5).

13. Is sex essentially related to important human values?

Yes. Basic and indispensable human goods are served by the right use of
sex. Three basic goods toward which the use of sex is ordered are faithful
love, the procreative good, and the sacramental good.

The deep loneliness of the human heart is remedied by the faithful love
of the human spouses who commit themselves to each other uniquely and
irrevocably. The procreative good satisfies the great human longing to be
fruitful, to have new life spring out of the love one has for one's spouse;
and to provide a place in which faithful love can care rightly for the child
and happily bring it to maturity. Married sexual love mirrors also the
kind of love that God has for his people, that Christ has for his Church.

14. Why are some kinds of sexual acts sinful?

The Church has always taught that abuses of sexual love are seriously
wrong. For this reason it declares gravely sinful acts of masturbation, fornication, incest, adultery, homosexual acts, contraception, deliberate cas-
ual provocation of lust, and even lustful desires. These are not wrong because sex or sexual activity is itself suspect, but because sex is good and
important, and sexual sins fail to respect the dignity of sexual activity and
the goods toward which it is ordered.

15. Is family planning of itself immoral?

No. "Children are really the supreme gift of marriage," and "spouses

143

should regard as their proper mission the task of transmitting life and educating those to whom it has been transmitted" (GS 50). Still, it would not always be wise for a couple to bring a new child into being. Spouses should always respect the procreative good and never act against it. But parents will at times wisely decide to limit the size of their families.

Husband and wife "will thoughtfully take into account both their own welfare and that of their children, those already born and those which may be foreseen. For this accounting they will reckon with both the material and the spiritual conditions of the times as well as of their state of life. Finally, they will consult the interests of the family group, of temporal society, and of the Church herself. The married partners themselves should make this judgment, in the sight of God. In their manner of acting, however, spouses should be aware that they cannot proceed arbitrarily, but must always be governed according to a conscience dutifully conformed to the divine law itself, and should be submissive toward the Church's Magisterium, which authentically interprets that law in the light of the Gospel" (GS 50).

16. What is contraception?

Contraceptive acts are acts which seek directly to prevent the conception of a child. The Catholic faith has always taught that contraception is a grave violation of the law of God, a direct attack on the procreative good and on the meaning of sexual love.

"Every act that intends to impede procreation must be repudiated, whether that act is intended as an end to be attained or as a means to be used, and whether it is done in anticipation of marital intercourse, or during it, or while it is having its natural consequence" (Pope Paul VI).

17. Is natural family planning permitted?

Yes. Natural family planning is very different from contraception. Couples who use natural family planning do not act against the procreative good. They do not engage in an act that is of its nature life-giving and then engage in other acts to repress the possible beginnings of life. Rather, they treat each other and marital activity with full respect. Understanding well their own fertility, they know when conception is likely to result from intercourse and when it is not. With self-possession and responsible reverence for all the goods that sexual activity is related to, they make their free choices in the light of this knowledge.

In every area of moral life, faith recognizes that it is wrong to act directly and deliberately against any basic human good, while it is not always obligatory to act in favor of such goods. Thus it is always wrong to directly kill an innocent person, even for a good motive, for example, to

144

spare one great pain. But it is not immoral to abstain from using extraordinary means to preserve a life. It is always wrong to act against the truth, to swear falsely or lie deliberately, in order to escape the harms that might come from revealing an important secret; but it is not wrong to seek suitable ways to escape revealing the secret.

Similarly, contraception directly attacks a basic human good, the procreative good. Natural family planning does not do that; it simply refrains from having intercourse at times when this would probably result in the conception of a child, if it would not be wise to have a child at this time. The difference between the two is like the difference between telling a deliberate lie to protect our secrets, and being silent to protect them. It is like the difference between euthanasia, directly killing a person to prevent suffering, and declining to give extraordinary care that would prolong the dying of a person in great pain. In every area of morality it is always wrong to directly attack basic goods, to attack the truth by lying, to attack life by killing; but it is sometimes wise and good to abstain on the matter of truth or not to prolong the life of one who is dying in pain. It is always wrong to attack the procreative good, but it is sometimes right not to promote it.

The difference between contraception and natural family planning "is a difference which is much wider and deeper than is usually thought, one which involves in the final analysis two irreconcilable differences of the human person and of human sexuality" (Pope John Paul II).

18. Is natural family planning a practical alternative for married couples today?

Yes. Contemporary forms of natural family planning are easy to learn and are very secure. They provide a morally acceptable form of family planning, and they have no harmful physical side effects. Moreover, the cooperation required in natural family planning can give the relationship of man and wife a more humanly loving character, foster their consideration for one another, and help each of them to avoid selfishness. The self-restraint that it requires is very moderate.

The ecclesial community has the duty to help couples escape the many moral and physical evils associated with contraception by making accessible knowledge about natural family planning and by "offering practical help to those who wish to live out their parenthood in a truly responsible way" (Pope John Paul II).

"A very valuable witness can and should be given by those husbands and wives who through the joint exercise of periodic continence have reached a more mature personal responsibility with regard to love and life" (Pope John Paul II).

19. Are impure thoughts and desires sinful?

Yes. The deliberate intention to commit seriously wrong sexual sins, or a deliberate will to delight in them in the imagination, is itself gravely sinful. Other sexual fantasizing, when it is deliberate, may be immoral for another reason: to the extent that it tends to stir up passion unreasonably and becomes an occasion for sinful desires, acts of masturbation, and the like.

Similarly, it is gravely sinful for unmarried persons to engage in kisses or embraces precisely to stir up the passion of lust in oneself or another.

20. What is modesty?

Modesty is an important safeguard to chastity. It is a virtue that governs our choices and conduct in many things that affect purity. Modesty is concerned with many matters that can affect sexual attitudes and behavior, for example, with forms of dress, with entertainment, reading, conversation, and with signs of affection, such as kisses and embraces. Modesty inclines one in all such matters to act with intelligent concern for all the values that guard self-possession and purity of heart.

Specific standards of modesty will vary. In matters of dress, for example, that which is suitable for the beach is not suitable for church or places of work. A style of clothing that would in one culture correctly be counted scandalous and lust-provoking might in another culture be entirely appropriate. But this does not mean that one may rightly conform to any standards of modesty accepted in one's culture. For we live in a world that is often hostile to the spirit of Christ. Some magazines and entertainments popular in our culture are certainly intended to be lust-provoking and are serious occasions of sin for many.

Kisses and embraces are often appropriate ways of expressing a right affection. But they can also be used to arouse passion or to lead to lustful behavior. One schooled in modesty can distinguish that which is offensive to purity of heart from that which is not.

21. Is it excessively difficult in our age to be chaste and modest?

No. Christian modesty and chastity can certainly be lived even in an age of great sexual laxity. But intelligent care is needed to acquire peaceful possession of these virtues. These are not burdensome virtues. Rather they establish conditions that make possible enduring and unselfish love.

Sound growth in these virtues does not lead to narrowness or prudery, but to self-possession, joy, and peace. Growth in chastity and modesty is assisted by tranquil vigilance, by a spirit of prayer, by reception of the sacraments, and by devotion to the Blessed Virgin Mary.

146

22. Why is love for truth important?

Love for truth is central to human dignity. Christ came into this world "to bear witness to the truth" (John 18.37), and we can live excellent lives pleasing to God only if we faithfully pursue that which is true and truly good.

Earnest care for truth, especially religious truth, requires effort and personal involvement. Christians have a special duty to reveal that "undeviating honesty which can attract all men to the love of truth and goodness, and finally to the Church and Christ" (AA 13). Without interior honesty even the most brilliant intellectual life is inwardly corrupted by hypocrisy such as that which the Lord vehemently condemned.

23. What is a lie?

A lie is a deliberate assertion of something which one believes to be false.

At times, because of the context in which they are spoken, the words that one speaks do not really come within the range of the value of truth at all. The novelist, for example, does not lie in narrating events that never really happened. Obvious jokes are not lies simply because they are not literal truths. Conventional greetings and phrases such as "You look well today" are rightly interpreted as words of encouragement rather than a considered medical judgment.

24. Is lying always wrong?

Yes. Even if one hopes to obtain great good, or to avoid serious harms, the choice to make false assertions is always wrong. A lie can never be justified by an appeal to expected good consequences.

The eighth commandment explicitly forbids the most serious kind of lie: "You shall not bear false witness against your neighbor" (Exod. 20.16). But the Church has understood it to forbid every kind of lie: malicious lies (lies that deliberately deceive or hurt another), officious lies (lies told to achieve some apparently good end), and even jocose lies (untrue assertions, sometimes tinged with cruelty, that deliberately mislead others for the pleasure of doing so).

"Therefore, putting away falsehood, let everyone speak the truth with his neighbor" (Eph. 4.25).

25. Are some lies more seriously wrong than others?

Yes. Some lies are mortally sinful. Deliberate perjury is always a grave sin, whatever the reason or occasion. Malicious lies, intended to harm another seriously, are also gravely sinful. But officious lies, or lies of convenience, are often only venially sinful.

26. Can one have a duty to guard secrets?

Yes. While we must never speak against the truth, there are some truths that we must guard with reverent silence. One can have a serious duty not to reveal secrets.

Those who have promised to guard a confidence, or whose lifework gives them access to sensitive secrets of others (as psychologists or confessors) have especially grave duties to guard secrets. The reasonable demands of privacy and the need to maintain interpersonal harmony require of all the proper keeping of secrets.

27. How can one guard secrets without being untruthful?

No simple rule provides a satisfactory answer for all such cases. Prudence demands that we not carelessly put ourselves in circumstances in which it would be difficult to guard important secrets from the prying of others. In each such instance we must carefully consider whether silence, or reproach, or an evasive response would fairly serve all the interests rightly involved, and at the same time avoid any contradiction of what we judge to be the truth.

"Do not lie to one another," for you "have put off the old nature with its practices and have put on the new nature, which is being renewed in knowledge after the image of its Creator" (Col. 3.9-10).

CHAPTER 21

Building a Just and Good Society

We were made to live in society. Community with others not only helps us secure such basic goods as knowledge and life itself, but is itself a basic element in our well-being and fulfillment as persons. Each one's life is deeply affected by the society in which he or she lives; each has a duty to share in the task of shaping and guarding a just and humane social order.

The first part of this chapter discusses the principles that underlie social life. The chapter then treats of the basic forms of this social life: the family, economic society, the political community, and the family of nations.

1. Should the Gospel affect the social life of mankind?

The social teaching of the Gospel is an essential part of its whole message. From Christ Himself the Church learned that we should not selfishly seek earthly treasure, that as children of one Father we should share property generously, show special solicitude for the poor and afflicted, and seek to structure our earthly lives in such a way that the kingdom of God may begin to appear in our midst.

The Church's social teaching is an unfolding of certain elementary requirements of faith, hope, and love.

2. What fundamental principles underlie the whole social teaching of the Church?

First, we human persons are social beings. We are called to love our brothers and sisters in Christ, and we can find fulfillment only by living in community with others, so that in our lives we serve and are served, love and are loved. Secondly, our lives cannot be entirely fulfilled by our social ties with one another. Each must have also a deep personal commitment to God. Though each human being is a social being, he or she has a transcendent dignity, and is called to an immediate personal relationship with God.

3. Are all human persons equal?

All human persons are basically equal. Each has a transcendent dignity because of his or her sublime vocation before God. Because of each person's eternal destiny, no one may ever be simply subordinated to the good of another or to the good of any society.

"True, all men are not alike from the point of view of varying physical power and diversity of intellectual and moral resources. Nevertheless, with respect to the fundamental rights of the person, every type of discrimination, whether social or cultural, whether based on sex, race, color, social condition, language, or religion, is to be overcome and eradicated as contrary to God's intent." Why? "Because all men, having a rational soul and being created in God's image, have the same nature and origins, and because all men, having been redeemed by Christ, enjoy the same divine calling and destiny" (GS 29).

4. Why must we seek to make society just?

Those who suffer from unjust discrimination, whose lives are bruised by the unjust attitudes and structures that sin has implanted in our society, are persons of transcendent worth. They are our brothers and sisters in Christ. To despise the fraternal and social implication of the Gospel is to fail in basic responsibilities. We cannot love God if we do not love our wounded brothers and sisters, and do not seek justice and mercy for them.

5. What gives a community its unity?

A community is bound together by a "common good," that is, by a goal that is shared, loved, and sought after together by its members.

6. What is the "common good"?

This expression can be understood in a number of ways. God's goodness can be called the common good for all, for all need to be fulfilled in Him. The basic human goods, life, truth, beauty, friendship, and the like, may, taken together, be called the common good of mankind; for pursuit of these pervades all human life.

In its social teaching the Church uses the phrase "common good" in this sense: the common good of society "consists chiefly in the protection of the rights and the performance of the duties of the human person" (DH 6). The Church therefore often speaks of the common good as "the sum of those conditions of social life which allow not only groups, but also their individual members to achieve their own fulfillment more fully and readily" (DH 6) than they otherwise could.

7. Are human societies natural or artificial?

Some of the social ties that bind people together spring immediately from the demands of their nature. To live well we clearly need such societies as the family and the political community. Other communities (such as unions, cooperatives, corporations, professional, cultural, and recreational societies) are made and developed freely. Though such societies can have their dangers, they are ordinarily formed to enrich human lives and to safeguard human rights.

8. What is the principle of subsidiarity?

This is a principle aimed at guarding personal freedom and dignity in a world in which massive institutions tend to overwhelm the rights and the freedom of the individual person. It teaches that choices and decisions should be made by individual persons and by small groups, such as families, whenever that is possible. Decisions should be made by larger groups, such as states, only when the matter is too large or too complex for resolution by smaller groups; and then decisions should be made in ways that enlarge as much as possible the rights and freedoms of individual persons.

"Just as it is wrong to withdraw from the individual and commit to the community at large what private initiative and endeavor can accomplish, so it is likewise an injustice, a serious harm, and a disturbance of proper order to turn over to a greater society, of higher rank, functions and services which can be performed by smaller communities on a lower plane. For any social undertaking, of its very nature, ought to give aid to the members of the body social, and ought never to destroy and absorb them" (Pope Pius XI).

9. Why is the family the first vital cell of society?

The family is the first vital cell of society because it is the most basic and intimate of societies, most suited to serve with special love the most essential human values.

Although each marriage is contracted by the free decision of the man and woman involved, it is neither they nor the laws and customs of their community that determine what marriage is. "For God Himself is the author of matrimony, endowed as it is with various benefits and purposes" (GS 48).

10. Has public authority any responsibility toward the family?

Since society cannot flourish unless the family does, public authority has many responsibilities to the family. "Public authority should regard it as a sacred duty to recognize, protect, and promote the authentic nature" of marriage and the family, "to shield public morality, and to favor the prosperity of domestic life" (GS 52).

In particular, "attention is to be paid to the needs of the family in government policies regarding housing, the education of children, working conditions, social security, and taxation" (AA 11).

11. Are there limits to the rights the state has in directing the life of families?

Yes. States may not assume the right to make the decisions that belong properly to husbands and wives. They may not tell parents how many children they may have, and they may not dominate the education of children. The state should assist families, providing the conditions in which they can perform their proper tasks. When families need assistance of the community to attain necessary goals they cannot achieve on their own, they should receive the assistance of the state.

12. What are the basic obligations of parents toward their children?

Parents have the duty to love, care for, and educate their children. "Since the parents have conferred life on their children, they have a most solemn obligation to educate their offspring, and so must be acknowledged as the first and foremost educators of those children" (GE 3).

The education that parents owe their children is far more than an academic one, or a preparation for economic security. The parents must seek to educate their children in virtue, to guide them toward a mature freedom and responsibility, and to assist them to grow in faith, hope, and love.

13. What role does the state have in the education of children?

Civil society does have duties and rights in relation to the education of children. Civil society plays its part "by guarding the duties and rights of parents and of others who have a role in education, and by providing them with assistance; by implementing the principles of subsidiarity and by completing the task of education, with attention to parental wishes, whenever the efforts of parents and of other groups are insufficient; and, moreover, by building its own schools and institutes, as the common good may demand" (GE 6).

The principle of subsidiarity requires that "no kind of school monopoly arise" (GE 6). Governments "must acknowledge the right of parents to make a genuinely free choice of schools and of other means of education" (DH 5).

14. What basic relationships must exist within the family?

Spouses are equals in human dignity and in fundamental rights. Each has a claim on the other's respect, affection, sexual attentions, and assistance of every kind.

Marriage usually requires a specialization of function. Ordinarily one partner works in the wider community for the support of the family while the other devotes time more directly to the at least equally important task of giving time more directly to the upbringing of the children. The Church teaches that the mother ordinarily has a "domestic role which must be safely preserved" (GS 52). Young children in particular need the security and loving attention of a parent at home.

All Christians ought to be "subject to one another out of reverence for Christ" (Eph. 5.21), honoring the various forms of priority and dignity that each has in his or her role. Thus when St. Paul speaks of the way in which a wife should be subject to her husband, he does not compromise her dignity. She is not related to the husband as a child is to its parents, but as the Church is to Christ; and between the Church and Christ there is a mutual service. Sincere personal love should be the basic form of relationship between husbands and wives.

15. What duties do children have to their parents?

Children owe their parents obedience in their formative years, and all their lives they must honor their parents and have concern for them. Parents need to insist on obedience in children, not to dominate them, but to guide them toward authentic maturity and freedom. Rightly educated children will become able, as they mature, to "come to decisions on their own judgment and in the light of truth, govern their activities with a sense of responsibility, and strive to pursue whatever is true and right, by willingly joining with others in cooperative effort" (DH 8).

The obedience of children should be motivated not by fear but by love, gratitude, and humility. When they have grown into young men and young women, they must make decisions which their parents have no right to make for them, such as choosing their own vocation in life.

16. What does faith teach about the goals and the meaning of human work?

Human work and economic life are not aimed only at the production and exchange of goods. The work that human persons do ought to be fully human and enrich their lives. By work mankind can not only dominate the earth, but also become more free, more human, and more open to divine grace. Jesus Christ conferred an immense dignity on labor, showing how it can be an exercise of love and how it enables free persons to bring God's creation to perfection.

17. Why is private property legitimate?

The principal purpose of private property is to provide everyone with a necessary area of independence. The right of private property is abused when some amass great fortunes and refuse to use their property in ways that benefit all. Indeed, the principal original source of private property lies in concern to give independence to persons and families, and for providing opportunities for the creative use of human freedom.

18. Is ownership of property absolute?

No. "God intended the earth and all that it contains for the use of all human beings and all peoples. Therefore, created goods ought equitably to flow to all, with justice as the guide, accompanied by charity. . . . In using his lawful possessions, therefore, a man ought to regard them not merely as his own, but also as common property in the sense that they can be of benefit not only to himself but also to others" (GS 69).

Hence the wealthy are obliged to come to the relief of the poor; and one in extreme necessity has the right to take care of personal needs from the riches of others.

19. How should freedom and order be guarded in economic life?

Intelligence and care are needed to shape a humane economic life. There are no automatic economic laws that guarantee justice and prosperity in society. The spontaneous activities of individuals, corporations, banks, and other powerful economic forces must not only aim at serving the common good, but must also be coordinated with the efforts of public authorities.

In accord with the principle of subsidiarity, economic authority "must not be entrusted solely to the authority of the government" (GS 65). Government should assist rather than totally dominate the economy: "at every level the largest possible number of people should . . . have an active role in the directing" (GS 65) of economic development.

20. Does the Church acknowledge the right to form labor unions?

Yes. Just as the Church recognizes the right of private ownership of productive goods, it also acknowledges the right to form trade unions and set up ways of assisting the participation of workers in the economy as a whole.

The purpose of economic life is not simply to create many things or to provide a few with power over the many, but it is to enable all to live and work with as much freedom and dignity as possible. "Therefore . . . the active participation of everyone in the running of enterprises should be promoted" (GS 68) so that all persons, whether they have skills in management and organization or manual skills, should find mutual respect.

21. Why does the state exist?

The state exists to serve the common good. "Individuals, families, and various groups which compose civil society are aware of their own insufficiency in the matter of establishing a fully human condition of life" (GS 74). The political community was established for the protection of the rights of all, to provide for the common safety, to assist individuals and groups in developing education and aesthetic activities, and for the promotion of every aspect of the common good.

The particular ways in which a given state may carry out these tasks will, of course, vary "according to the particular character of a people and its historical development" (GS 74).

22. Is authority within political life legitimate and necessary?

Yes. It is essential that there be real authority in a political community. The many people who make up a community will inevitably have different opinions about how things ought to be done. "Now if the political community is not to be torn to pieces as each person follows his own viewpoint, authority is needed in order to direct the energies of all citizens toward the common good" (GS 74).

Authority must recognize that its purpose is to serve the freedom and richness of life of the citizens. Efforts must be made to have each person's active participation in public affairs, just as this is important in any true community.

"It is obvious that the political community and public authority are based on human nature and hence belong to an order of things preordained by God, though the choice of government and the designation of leaders is left to the free choice of the citizens" (GS 74).

23. Must citizens obey the laws of the state?

Yes. When public authority is exercised within the limits of the moral order and on behalf of the common good, citizens "are conscience-bound to obey" (GS 74).

This moral obligation can extend even to laws which might reasonably have been different, such as speed limits and tax rates, but which nonetheless are intelligibly related to the needs of the common good and are established in good faith.

24. Should immoral demands of the state be obeyed?

No. If civil authorities issue laws or decrees which are in contravention to the moral order, "and therefore against the will of God," these "cannot be binding on the consciences of the citizens, since 'one ought to obey God rather than men' (Acts 5.29)" (Pope John XXIII).

"If any government does not acknowledge human rights, or violates them, not only does it fail in its duty, but its orders are wholly lacking in binding force" (Pope John XXIII). It is lawful for citizens to defend their own rights and those of their fellow citizens against the abuse of public authority, provided that in so doing they observe the limits set by the natural law and the Gospel.

25. How should the state guard the rights of men?

There are two basic kinds of human rights. First, there are those rights which are inalienable and which must be supported in every situation whatever. An example is the right of an innocent person to life. Many rights are inalienable and inviolable in a somewhat different sense. An example here is the right to a good education. These rights too belong to all persons as such, and may never be discounted or treated as irrelevant by other persons or by public authority.

But the positive fulfillment of this second kind of rights is subject to other moral considerations, for it is not always possible to provide for the full realization of all such rights. The government has a duty to assist citizens in the exercise of these rights in ways compatible with the common good and with what is possible in all the circumstances of time and place.

26. Has civil authority the right to direct the consciences of its citizens?

No. The political community is a "complete society" in the sense that it has in principle all the means necessary for advancing the temporal good of man. But the political society is not the only "complete society," and it has no legitimate supremacy over the spiritual life of its citizens.

Because Christ rules in the Church, the Church can rightly speak directly to the conscience, and can exercise jurisdiction over even the interior life.

27. What is justice?

Justice is a virtue that disposes a person to render to everyone his or her due.

28. What is commutative justice?

Commutative justice is the form of justice that governs relationships between individuals.

The commandments speak of the basic duties we have in justice, each toward his neighbor. Each person is required not to kill, or slander, or steal from another. Should one person violate the rights of another, a duty to make restitution arises.

Thus, one who has taken the property of another must return the property or its equivalent. If the theft was a gravely sinful one the duty of restitution is also grave. Similarly one who has injured the neighbor in other ways, as by slander or physical harm, must find suitable ways to atone for the offense.

29. What is social justice?

Social justice is the form of justice that governs the relations between the citizen and the state. Each should see to it that the civil authority and powerful forces in society act with justice, and that laws are structured to promote the common good.

"Let the laity by their combined efforts remedy any institutions and conditions of the world which are customarily an inducement to sin, so that all such things may be conformed to the norms of justice and may favor the practice of justice rather than hinder it" (LG 36).

Often injustices have complex roots, and corrective measures require intelligent planning as well as good will. Education for justice is an integral part of Christian education. This education for justice "demands a renewal of heart, a renewal based on the recognition of sin in its individual and social manifestations" (Second General Assembly of the Synod of Bishops).

30. Why must we be concerned with the common good of all the peoples of the world?

Today the whole human family on earth constitutes in an important way a single society which must be the concern of all nations. Instantaneous communications, rapid transportation, and a host of economic and cultural ties bind ever more closely all the peoples of the world. All of us share concern for peace in a nuclear age.

"Consequently the moral order itself demands the establishment of some general public authority . . . set up with the consent of all nations" (Pope John XXIII).

31. Are governmental leaders obliged to obey the natural law?

Yes. Nations and their leaders are not above the demands of morality and of the natural law. The same principles that govern the dealings of individuals with one another and call for a just organization within states must also govern the relations of political communities with one another.

32. How does the principle of subsidiarity apply to international questions?

Some world problems are so large and complex that only an international organization established with the consent of the nations and having real authority could deal effectively with them. There are, for example, the issues of war and peace, and justice in international trade. Such a world organization, however, while needed, must not be allowed to destroy the proper independence, diversity, and separate functioning of smaller groups.

33. Why must Christians seek to promote peace and to stop the arms race?

The peace that is hoped for is so great a good, and modern war is so great an evil, that every effort must be made in pursuit of world peace.The arms race itself makes war more probable. Moreover, the poor are injured when the state spends too much public money for instruments of war.

We have a duty "to strain every muscle as we work for the time when all war can be completely outlawed by international consent" (GS 82).

Still the Church does not teach that defensive war is always immoral, for the evils that would come upon the world by the domination of an atheistic and inhuman tyranny are also unbearably grave.

34. Can peace be secured by merely political structures?

No. Peace can be only the fruit of justice and of charity. The radical causes of dissension must be rooted out. The economic injustices that impoverish so many nations must be overcome. Other causes of dissension are the irrational quest for power and contempt for personal rights, "distrust, pride, and other egotistic passions" (GS 83).

To have peace, mankind needs most of all a profound change of heart.

35. Is Christian hope aimed chiefly at establishing peace and justice in this world?

No. Christians have a serious duty to bring the spirit of Christ to social life at every level, and to make this earth an image of the eternal kingdom by laboring to penetrate it with mercy, justice, and peace. Still, we are uncertain about the measure of success we can achieve in this world; we cannot have absolute confidence in earthly success. The future of this world is "as uncertain as it is changing" (Pope Paul VI).

CHAPTER 22

Ways of Living a Christian Life

"I came to cast fire upon the earth; and would that it were already kindled!" (Luke 12.49). There are many vocations in which God can be served, but there is basically only one Christian vocation: to serve God's saving plan by loving Him and one another, and to share God's life in holiness and joy. "All the faithful of Christ of whatever rank or status are called to the fullness of the Christian life and to the perfection of charity" (LG 40). It is within that one call that there is a variety of forms of Christian life.

In other chapters we speak of the special duties and blessings in the lives of those called to holy orders or to matrimony. Here we treat of the universal call to perfection, of minimal service to God, of the vocation of the Christian in the world, and of the religious vocation.

1. What is the basic vocation of every Christian?

The basic vocation of every Christian is to love God with the whole heart, and to love each of our human neighbors as we love ourselves, even as Christ has loved us. We are to grow in the new life of Christ by learning to believe in God, to trust Him, and to love Him personally and in our brothers and sisters in Christ. "You shall love the Lord your God with all your heart, and with all your soul, and with all your strength, and with all your mind; and your neighbor as yourself" (Luke 10.27).

2. How should one live to follow this basic vocation?

There are many ways of carrying out the twofold commandment of love, which in fact sums up all that is asked of us. God can be served in a rich variety of forms of life. Yet each should seek to follow the special vocation that God wishes him or her to follow.

3. Does every Christian have a vocation?

Yes. Every Christian has a vocation. That is to say, every Christian is called by God to some particular way of carrying out the one great ministry of love.

"There are varieties of gifts, but the same Spirit; and there are varieties of service, but the same Lord" (1 Cor. 12.4-5).

4. How does one learn one's special vocation?

There are diverse inner and outward signs of the form of lifework that

159

one should choose in serving God. Young people should be taught to pray that they will wisely discern their special vocation in life. Partly this is learned through self-knowledge and through understanding of the needs of the world in which one lives.

That is, we come to learn, through personal reflection and perhaps with the help of friends and advisors, our special abilities and interests and the inclinations of our hearts. External realities help speak to us of the will of God; for example, one who hoped to serve God as a physician may know that another choice is required if one cannot meet the requirements or cannot be accepted into any medical school.

Sometimes individual vocations are somewhat generic. For example, one may be called to serve God in the lay life, but have no discernible divine call to especially this or that profession or form of service, so that one could with equal wisdom choose any of a number of forms of lay life. Or one might have a vocation to religious life, with no clearly discernible vocation to this or that community. But at times vocations are more specific, as, for example, a vocation to a special contemplative community.

5. What is the least measure of true love of God?

We have no love of God at all if we are not resolved to keep His commandments. "He who has My commandments and keeps them, he it is who loves Me" (John 14.21). To have true or saving love we must love God with the whole heart at least to this extent, that we are determined to prefer nothing to remaining in the love of God. Even the least measure of true love, then, requires that we be determined to do nothing that would separate us from the love of Christ. That is, our will to love and serve God requires a determination never to commit any mortal sin.

Hence, even minimal love of God requires a determination to give God essentially the first place in our lives. It would not be divine love at all if it did not wish to remain in God's favor and grace more than anything else. However a minimal love wishes to do no more than it must to remain in God's grace and to reach eternal life. Minimal love can be perilous, since it may lead one to be complacent about sins that are not mortal but incline one toward mortal sin. Moreover, one who does not seek to grow in grace and to be generous in love can begin to find worldly attractions so alluring that one ceases in fact to keep God in first place at all.

6. What are some characteristics of the lay Christian vocation?

Every person is called to grow in love and in friendship with God. Moreover, "on all Christians is laid the splendid burden of working to make the divine message of salvation accepted by all men throughout the world" (AA 7). The laity have a special obligation to permeate the temporal order with the spirit of the Gospel.

160

To care for the temporal order is to care for the goods of life and of the family, for culture and business, for the arts and professions, for political and social institutions. "This order requires constant improvement. It must be founded on truth, built on justice, and animated by love" (GS 26). It is not possible to serve the temporal order well unless one seeks to grow in personal holiness.

7. What is meant by the lay apostolate?

The lay apostolate is the task given by Christ first to the apostles: to heal and sanctify the world by proclaiming the kingdom, to lead to faith, hope, and love, and to transform this world to the extent possible into an image of the eternal kingdom, and to help all God's people to become worthy of entering everlasting life. But this is not a task for the hierarchy and clergy alone. It is one to be carried on by the Church "through all its members" (AA 2). The laity are called to play their proper role in the work of the whole Church.

The laity "exercise a genuine apostolate by their activity on behalf of bringing the gospel and holiness to men, and on behalf of penetrating and perfecting the temporal sphere of things through the spirit of the gospel" (AA 2).

8. What preparation is needed for those called to the lay apostolate?

Spiritual formation is most important. One can advance the kingdom effectively only if one's own life is firmly rooted in faith. The lay apostle must love the world out of love for the Creator, and care to save it out of love for Christ. In addition to spiritual formation, one needs doctrinal instruction in the faith, and in the sciences and skills relevant to the work one plans to do in the apostolate.

9. What are the "gospel counsels"?

The gospel counsels, known also as evangelical counsels, are attitudes and patterns of conduct commended by Christ to free those who live by them "from those obstacles which might draw one away from the fervor of charity and the perfection of divine worship" (LG 44). They enable one to live more freely in the spirit of Christ's kingdom. Three gospel counsels are especially commended: poverty, chastity, and obedience.

Evangelical poverty guards one from the danger of the love of riches and the power wealth brings; chastity frees one from dangers of subservience to pleasure and from earthly burdens that hinder wholehearted service of Christ and His people; obedience helps to liberate one from selfishness and pride and puts one fully at the service of the family of faith.

10. What is religious life in the Church?

Religious life is a form of Christian living in which groups of persons live in communities consecrated in a special way to divine service. They freely bind themselves to live in Gospel poverty, chastity, and obedience, and to further the special works of the Church for which the community was formed.

Religious communities have existed in the Church since the fourth century; they grew out of the spirit of the Gospel. There is a rich variety of forms of religious life. Some are devoted especially to contemplative prayer; some are devoted to special apostolates such as teaching or health care; some are essentially contemplative, but directed also toward apostolic works that flow from contemplation, such as preaching or teaching faith. In addition to religious communities, strictly speaking the Church has other groups committed to cooperating in consecrated lives, guarding poverty, chastity, and obedience, such as the so-called secular institutes.

Religious life is a consecrated life aimed first at serving God more intensely. It promotes the perfection of charity and the life of grace in its members, and thus enables them to serve more perfectly the good of the whole family of God.

11. How do religious serve the Church?

While religious serve the Church in many ways through their apostolic works, they serve her primarily by their consecrated life. The total commitment of religious life is a blessing to the whole Church and a visible sign that strengthens the whole family of faith.

"Without this concrete sign there would be a danger that the charity which animates the entire Church would grow cold" (Paul VI).

12. What is the special gift of contemplative religious to the Church?

Contemplative religious dedicate their lives to personal closeness to the Lord in faith and love, to prayers of adoration, praise, and of petition for the needs of all the Church. They serve the Church in an especially generous way, and forcefully remind the Church of the importance of earnest prayer for any great works to be accomplished.

Great renewals in the Church have always begun with small groups who cared enough to go out into the desert or to the hermitage or to the cloister to wrestle alone with God and Satan in the solitude of contemplative prayer. Contemplative religious "will always have a distinguished part to play in Christ's Mystical Body" (PC 7).

CHAPTER 23

To Share in the Divinity of Christ

The Son of God became man so that we might share in the life of God. This is the mystery of God's love in the Incarnation. "What has revealed God's love among us is that the only-begotten Son of God has been sent by the Father into the world so that, being made man, the Son might by His redemption of the entire human race give new life to it and unify it" (UR 2). Daily the Church prays that we may "come to share in the divinity of Christ, who humbled Himself to share in our humanity" (Roman Missal).

In this chapter we speak of the various ways in which we share in the life of God. The chapter discusses the various kinds of grace, how God Himself dwelling in us is the uncreated grace, and how God transforms His people with the created gifts of grace. Finally, it shows why it is necessary for those who have been justified to grow in the life of grace.

1. What is grace?

The word grace means gift or favor. Grace signifies the free generosity or favor with which God blesses us. Grace is used also to name the gifts that flow from this favor or mercy of God through the merits of Christ. All the gifts of grace are intended to enable us to share now in God's life, and to come at length to the full possession of God in the beatific vision.

> All that we have received from God, including our very nature and being, is His free gift. But gifts of grace are called "supernatural" gifts, because they go far beyond all the reasonable expectations of our nature. The gifts of grace are aimed at enabling us to share in the very life of God, something that no created reality could expect or consider itself in any way entitled to.

2. What is justification?

Justification is the act of God by which He freely calls us from the sinful state in which we were born or from our sinful ways of life to newness of life in Christ.

> In all the stages of justification, from the first invitation of grace to its full flowering, divine freedom arouses human freedom. If we do not reject his early gifts, God moves us to have a holy and useful fear of His justice, to have hope in His mercy, to begin to love Him, and so to hate and turn away from sin so that we repent and come to the new birth of baptism.

In justification we receive "not only remission of sins, but also a sanctification and renewal of the inner man through the voluntary reception of the grace and gifts whereby an unjust person becomes just and from being an enemy becomes a friend, that he may be 'an heir according to the hope of everlasting life' (Titus 3.7)" (Council of Trent).

3. What is uncreated grace?

Uncreated grace is the greatest of all God's gifts to us, for it is the gift of Himself. God gives Himself to us in many ways. He gives us Himself in Christ, in whom "the fullness of deity dwells bodily" (Col. 2.9). He gives Himself as a friend in the gifts of revelation and charity. By the uncreated grace, known also as the divine indwelling, He gives Himself in a most special way.

"If a man loves Me, he will keep My word, and My Father will love him, and We will come to him and make Our home with him" (John 14.23). The Father and Son cause the Holy Spirit also to dwell in our hearts as Consoler and Advocate (cf. John 14.26). Thus the Blessed Trinity comes to us in a personal way though the divine indwelling.

This presence of God is far more than ordinary presence of God as Creator of all that is. By his creative omnipresence God keeps all things in being. But by this supernatural presence He is present as a Friend, inviting us to an ever deeper knowledge of Him and an ever richer sharing in His life.

This mystery of God's indwelling is truly a beginning of heavenly life. Yet, while God is so in us and with us, He remains God and we remain creatures.

4. What are created gifts and graces?

Created gifts and graces are realities distinct from God, but they lead us toward union with Him and toward activity that leads us toward eternal life. Among the created gifts of God are sanctifying grace, infused virtues and gifts, and actual graces.

5. What is sanctifying grace?

Sanctifying grace is a divine gift that makes us sharers in God's nature and life, and causes us to be children of God and heirs of the kingdom of God. God dwells personally in those who possess sanctifying grace.

One who has sanctifying grace is said to be in the "state of grace." It is a basic duty of the Catholic to guard and nourish this relationship with the Blessed Trinity.

6. Is sanctifying grace a permanent gift?

Yes. Sanctifying grace radically changes us and makes us enduringly sharers in the nature of God. For this reason it is also called habitual grace, or the state of grace. The state of grace can be lost only by deliberate mortal sin.

7. What virtues do we receive with sanctifying grace?

Together with sanctifying grace God gives the just person the virtues of faith, hope, and love, so that those who have become in reality children of God may be able to do the works of God. These virtues are called the "theological virtues," because they orient our new life directly toward God.

> To please God in our lives we need other virtues as well, such as the cardinal virtues of prudence, justice, temperance, and fortitude. There are natural cardinal virtues that can be possessed even by those who do not live in God's grace. But in this state virtues promote only excellent human living, and they do not promote friendship with God or merit life everlasting. Now grace and charity can transform natural virtues, and plant in the heart dispositions to do all humanly good deeds in a way that makes them expressions of divine love.

8. What are the "gifts of the Holy Spirit"?

The gifts of the Holy Spirit are permanent gifts by which "the soul is furnished and strengthened to be able to obey God's voice and impulse more easily and promptly" (Pope Leo XIII). The Church has persistently taught that the gifts of wisdom, understanding, counsel, knowledge, fortitude, piety, and fear of the Lord are conferred on all the faithful with the gift of sanctifying grace. These gifts correspond to gifts that Messianic prophecy declared that the Spirit would confer upon the Christ. These gifts are important in every stage of the spiritual life, but they are especially important in the lives of those who are becoming more mature in grace.

9. How do the gifts of the Holy Spirit affect a mature Christian life?

Those who are weak and unpracticed in serving Christ often find it hard to recognize and to do God's will, for, though grace be present, the whole person is not yet attuned to receiving the gentle guidance of the Spirit. As one grows in friendship with the Lord, his or her life is led less by merely human reflection, even reflection illumined by faith. As the person freely and gladly wishes to do God's will, the Lord through the gifts of the Spirit enables him or her to do excellent deeds of love with ease and with joy. The more one is led by the quiet guidance of the Spirit rather than by one's own determination, the more perfect and free one's acts become.

10. What is a beatitude?

A beatitude is a blessing proclaimed by the Lord, commending a characteristic of life that is most precious and dear to God. By the gifts of the Holy Spirit one is led toward the sublime dispositions that the beatitudes praise and the blessedness that they promise. These were pronounced by Christ at the very beginning of His public preaching:

- Blessed are the poor in spirit, for theirs is the kingdom of heaven.
- Blessed are those who mourn, for they shall be comforted.
- Blessed are the meek, for they shall inherit the land.
- Blessed are they who hunger and thirst for righteousness, for they shall be satisfied.
- Blessed are the merciful, for they shall obtain mercy.
- Blessed are the pure in heart, for they shall see God.
- Blessed are the peacemakers, for they shall be called children of God.
- Blessed are those who are persecuted for righteousness' sake, for theirs is the kingdom of heaven.

11. What are actual graces?
Actual graces are gifts that God gives us in specific circumstances to enable us to act in ways that lead toward salvation. By actual graces God enlightens our minds to see His ways and strengthens our resolve to walk in them, or to return to them if we have gone astray.

12. Is "dying to sin" still necessary even after justification?
Yes. Even after justification there remains in us something that inclines us toward sin. One can be in the state of grace and at the same time experience concupiscence, the inclination to sin. Even when we rejoice in the grace of God, we must yet acknowledge that we are sinners, born in original sin, and experiencing often tendencies toward sin. Hence the struggle against sin is an enduring aspect of Christian life on earth. As athletes must deny themselves much in training if they desire victory, so we must discipline ourselves if we truly care about eternal life. The Lord Himself came to "free and strengthen man" (GS 13); but we ourselves must act in the "dramatic struggle between good and evil" (GS 13).

13. What are the capital sins?
Capital sins are sins or sinful dispositions which tend to lead us into many other sins. The capital sins are pride, covetousness, lust, anger, gluttony, envy, and sloth.

14. What are the sins against the Holy Spirit?
These are sins which offend against the very gifts of the Holy Spirit that are most needed to turn in conversion toward God; hence they make the heart less disposed to seek forgiveness. These sins are impenitence, ob-

duracy in sin, presumption, despair, rejection of the known truth, and envy of the grace others enjoy.

15. Why must we struggle against the flesh?

"Flesh" in this sense does not mean the body, but it means against all those inclinations and temptations we experience within ourselves that are hostile to God. Concupiscence inclines us toward every capital sin and toward their dismal fruits. The Gospel often speaks of the paradox of our need to die (that is, to put to death certain inclinations really found within us) if we are to come to life.

"And those who belong to Christ Jesus have crucified the flesh with its passions and desires" (Gal. 5.24).

16. In what sense must we struggle against the world?

The created world in itself is "very good" (Gen. 1.31), and "God so loved the world" (John 3.16) that He sent His Son to save it. But Scripture also speaks of the world in another sense, of the "world" as an alignment of forces that do not believe and love God. Against this world we must struggle, for it conspires with our own baser inclinations against all that is good.

"If anyone loves the world, love for the Father is not in him" (1 John 2.15).

17. Must we also struggle against the devil?

Yes. Although we do not understand fully what role God permits the devil to have on this earth, the reality of malign spirits is only too evident in the despondent pain of the unbelieving world and in the tragic sorrows in the record of history.

18. Is it possible to grow in grace?

Yes. Grace is a gift of life, and we must grow in it. At the beginning of our new life we are really only infants in grace, but we are to grow up in faith, in doing deeds of love, growing up in every way to mirror the splendid maturity of Christ our head.

Christ has called us to a perfection that is not quickly reached. Every Christian is called to great holiness of life; to accept our vocation requires great efforts. "One thing I do, forgetting what lies behind and straining forward to what lies ahead, I press on toward the goal for the prize of the upward call of God in Christ Jesus" (Phil. 3.13-14).

CHAPTER • 24

Christ and the Life of Prayer

"Lord, teach us to pray" (Luke 11.1). The disciples, seeing the Lord so long at prayer, asked that they might learn to pray. And Jesus taught them.

In this chapter we treat of prayer in the life of one who has accepted Jesus as Lord and Teacher. Here we discuss Christ as Model and Teacher of prayer, the necessity of prayer for the Christian life, the effects of prayer, the definition and types of prayer, and the necessity of grace for prayer.

1. Did Christ pray much during His earthly life?

Yes. All the Gospels, especially that of St. Luke, often describe Christ at prayer. He prayed publicly and privately. Before the great acts and decisions of His ministry He prayed earnestly. Often He spent long periods in prayer; prayer was the constant background of His life.

The evangelist John explains Jesus' continual prayer to the Father in the light of His special relationship to the Father. Jesus prayed the divinely inspired prayers that were the heart of the Jewish tradition, especially the Psalms and the Shema: "Hear, O Israel! The Lord our God is one Lord. . ." (Deut. 6.4).

Jesus prayed also in simple and direct words flowing from His heart. He addressed God the Father as "Abba," the simple, familiar address used by a child to his father.

2. Did Jesus teach that prayer is important for us?

Yes. Jesus frequently taught us the importance of prayer. "Watch and pray" (Mark 14.38). "And He told them a parable, to the effect that they should pray always, and not lose heart" (Luke 18.1). He taught us the Our Father, a perfect form of prayer; and He taught us the spirit in which we should pray both by His example and by His words.

3. What is prayer?

Prayer is raising the heart and mind to God, and at times our voices also.

The chief forms of prayer are prayers of adoration, thanksgiving, petition, and contrition.

4. What are the fruits of prayer?

Through prayer we merit needed graces; prayer obtains every kind of benefit from God; and prayer brings spiritual refreshment to the mind and heart.

Prayer is essential for growth in faith, in love, and in every form of holiness.

While our activity can be penetrated with a prayerful spirit, and become a kind of prayer, this is not possible unless we give time to explicit prayer. Those who wish to obey the Gospel precepts of prayer must take time to pray with personal fervor to the Father in solitude and with others.

5. What is prayer of petition?

The prayer of petition is "the request for fitting things from God" (St. John Damascene).

Christ taught us to ask God for the things that we need. "If you ask anything of the Father, He will give it to you in My name. . . . Ask, and you will receive, that your joy may be filled" (John 16.23-24). It is fitting to pray to God for all things that we need or may reasonably desire. Nothing which is important to us is insignificant to God, who loves us.

6. Does God answer our prayers?

Yes. Whenever we pray in Christ's name, that is, with the proper dispositions and for something that will truly benefit us, God hears and answers our prayers.

This clearly does not mean that all our prayers will be answered at once, or that we shall always receive from God the specific thing we asked for. God wishes us to pray perseveringly and in trust; He often leads people to holiness by aiding their constant prayers over long periods of time. Moreover, we often ask for things that could in fact harm us more than help us. God often hears prayers by granting the good things we need rather than the apparent goods we mistakenly ask for. Clearly it is not necessary to inform God of our needs; He knows our needs before we ask Him. But prayer is needed to express our acknowledgment that we depend entirely upon God and to express our confidence in His mercy.

7. What qualities should our prayer have?

We should pray with attention, devotion, confidence, and perseverance.

To pray with attention is to pray with the mind and heart, and not with the lips alone. To pray with devotion is to pray with a will seeking to give God the first place we should give Him in all things. We pray with confidence when we pray in faith, and with trust that God will show His mercy to us. We pray with perseverance when we patiently await His favor, refusing to be discouraged or to lose heart.

8. To whom do we pray?

The Christian prays to God, the Blessed Trinity. Most commonly we address our prayer to the Father through Christ in the Holy Spirit.

One may direct prayer to all three Persons of the Trinity or to one Person. Thus in the New Testament, in the liturgy, and in popular devotions some prayers are directed to Christ. Other prayers, as the "Come, Holy Spirit," are addressed to the Holy Spirit.

When we invoke the Blessed Virgin or the other saints our prayers are still ultimately addressed to God. For our petition to the saints is that they intercede for us with God.

9. Is grace necessary for prayer?

Authentic prayer is made possible in us only by the gift of God. Prayer is not mastered merely by human efforts, but it is God who enables us to lift up our hearts freely to Him.

"The Spirit helps us in our weakness; for we do not know how to pray as we ought, but the Spirit Himself intercedes for us with sighs too deep for words" (Rom. 8.26).

10. Why is Christian prayer called filial prayer?

The foundation of all Christian prayer is the new relationship we have with the Father through Christ in the Spirit. In Christ we have come to share the life of God; we have been made sons and daughters of the Father in Jesus. Hence we do not pray simply as creatures to their God, but as children to their Father.

"When you pray, say: 'Father...'" (Luke 11.12). "When we cry, 'Abba! Father!' it is the Spirit Himself bearing witness with our spirit that we are children of God" (Rom. 8.15-16).

11. Is prayer a conversation with God?

Yes. We speak with God in prayer because God has first spoken to us. "For in the sacred books, the Father who is in heaven meets His children with great love and speaks with them" (DV 21). Our prayer is a response, supported by divine grace, to the words God has spoken to us.

God often speaks to us in prayer, enabling us to understand more fully His saving words, and helping us to realize how we are to serve Him.

12. Does persevering prayer require self-discipline?

Yes. Earnest and persevering prayer requires much self-discipline,

170

though it is also the source of much joy and peace. Efforts to learn prayer cannot be separated from efforts to love God and one another in every aspect of our lives.

Prayer becomes an insupportable burden if we are not seeking to be faithful to God in our lives. And we are not able to be faithful to God in our lives if we do not pray. The invitation to prayer is an invitation to friendship with God in all things; to accept that invitation is to accept a gift that is both supportive and demanding.

CHAPTER 25

Private and Liturgical Prayer

All prayer is personal. In it we are to be personally involved, mind and heart, in speaking with God. There are, however, various kinds of prayer. Sometimes prayer is individual or private; sometimes it is shared with others; sometimes it is public or liturgical.

In this chapter we discuss each of these various forms of prayer and offer some suggestions on learning to pray.

1. Should each person pray to God in solitude?

Yes. Each person should speak individually to God from the heart.

"When you pray, go into your room and shut the door and pray to your Father who is in secret; and your Father who sees in secret will reward you" (Matt. 6.6). Such personal prayer is of basic importance in living a Christian life.

2. What is vocal prayer?

Vocal prayer is prayer expressed in words. All prayer should flow from the mind and heart; but some prayer is expressed also in words, spoken aloud or silently uttered in the heart. In vocal prayer we may use those prayers that are part of the Christian heritage, like the Our Father, or we may pray in words that rise spontaneously from the heart.

3. Should we pray the prayers commonly used in the Catholic community?

Yes. To pray earnestly the prayers of the Catholic community has many advantages. These prayers guide our thoughts and our hearts in right ways, and support our efforts to speak to God in ways that are pleasing to Him.

Christ Himself clearly made use of the customary prayers of the community of faith in which He lived. Regularly He prayed the psalms and other prayers of His people. When the apostles sought guidance in prayer, He taught them the Our Father, which remains a perfect form of prayer for us.

Each Catholic should have firmly in memory the most important prayers: the Our Father, the Sign of the Cross, the Hail Mary, the Apostles' Creed, and acts of faith, hope, love, and contrition.

4. What is spontaneous prayer?

Spontaneous prayer is a form of vocal prayer in which the words we speak are not found beforehand in a fixed formula, but spring to our lips out of the special circumstances of our lives.

There are many forms of spontaneous prayer. At times awareness of God's great goodness to us evokes a personal response of thanks and praise. At other times crosses and anxieties move us to cry out to God for help in our need.

There are moments in which circumstances almost compel us to pray. Our prayer, however, should not be limited to such occasions. We ought to pray faithfully and regularly, even at times when special sentiments do not thrust us toward prayer.

5. What is meant by mental prayer?

Mental prayer is a form of prayer that is unspoken, or in which our words are less important. Such prayer has diverse forms: meditation, affective prayer, and contemplation. In such forms of prayer the mind is glad to immerse itself in the beauty and truth of the saving mysteries revealed in Christ. The heart is given time to respond in grateful love to God.

The Virgin Mary is often seen as the model of mental prayer. "But Mary kept all these things, pondering them in her heart" (Luke 2.19).

6. Is mental prayer important for Catholic life?

Yes. Mental prayer is a major means of growing in the life of grace. Through it our minds and hearts are schooled to know and love God in intimate acts of friendship. Through it we escape from worldly ways of thinking and feeling, and allow the light and warmth of the Gospel to penetrate to the core of our being.

Many followers of Christ may acquire holiness through thoughtful vocal prayers and through works of love. Hence it cannot be said that formal mental prayer is absolutely necessary for all. Still for most people it is a means of grace that cannot be neglected without serious loss. Devoting time each day to mental prayer is for most people an indispensable way of reaching close personal friendship with the Lord.

7. What is meditation?

Meditation is the form of mental prayer most suited to those beginning to live seriously the life of grace. It is characterized primarily by devout reflection on a sacred theme: for example, on the passion of Jesus, on some words of His in the Gospel, on the last things, or on His invitation to serve Him by acts of mercy to the poor.

Through such reflection we seek to make the saving truth of the Gospel deeply our own, to "put on the Lord Jesus Christ" (Rom. 13.14). Meditation aims at helping us to love God with all our heart and with all our mind.

8. How does one meditate?

The saints have taught the Church a variety of ways to approach meditation. Each person should choose a way of meditating that he or she finds helpful. But each form has basic elements. First, one must prepare the mind and heart. Then the body of the meditation is some form of prayerful reflection on the saving truth meant to heal our lives. Finally, this reflection should lead to earnest praise and thanks to God, and to firm resolutions to shape our lives in the light of the Lord.

Remote preparation for meditation is the effort to turn all of our lives to God. Immediate preparation involves such things as withdrawing to a quiet environment, reading some passages of Scripture or a point from some other religious book providing a theme for our reflection, earnestly recalling that we are in fact in the presence of God, and asking Him to assist us in our prayers.

The body of the meditation is devout reflection on a chosen theme. One seeks in this prayer to give God one's whole attention: one's memory, imagination, understanding, and all one's affections. The immediate purpose of meditation is to deepen one's faith, spiritual insight, and convictions, so that we can appreciate more fully the richness of the mysteries of faith, and that our commitment to God and our love of Him may acquire deep and lasting roots.

The conclusion of the meditation may include earnest and deeply personal acts of praise of God or of thanksgiving to Him, or deeply felt petitions, illumined by the saving truths on which we have reflected. Some firm, practical resolution should be made, so that the activity of prayer will affect our lives concretely. Many urge selecting a key idea from the meditation to keep gently in one's thoughts throughout the day.

9. What is affective mental prayer?

Affective mental prayer is a more advanced form of mental prayer. Here probing reflections play a smaller part. One's mind and heart are already firmly rooted in God, and direct themselves more readily toward Him. Yet one longs for a deeper kind of knowing and a greater presence of love, and, moved by grace, gives the heart opportunity to draw near to its Lord.

10. What is contemplation?

Contemplation is the most excellent form of mental prayer. In it those who have come to love God more intensely express their faith and love with the simplicity of hearts that have been brought to great peace through grace. It is a prayer that enjoys a certain rich experience of the divine presence. One comes to such great love through the cross, through dark nights and faithfulness in trials. Yet in contemplation one comes to the overwhelming peace of Christ.

"For as we share abundantly in Christ's sufferings, so through Christ we share abundantly in comfort too" (2 Cor. 1.5).

11. What is shared prayer?

Shared prayer is a form of vocal prayer in which one joins voice and heart with others in praising God, in thanking Him, in asking for His gifts, or in seeking forgiveness.

There is a great power in shared prayer. "If two of you agree on earth about anything they ask, it will be done for them by My Father in heaven. For where two or three are gathered in My name, there am I in the midst of them" (Matt. 18.19-20).

Family prayer is an important form of shared prayer. Charismatic groups also provide opportunities to take part in shared prayer.

12. What is liturgy?

Liturgy is the public prayer and worship of the whole Church, that is, of the family of God united together in Christ.

"The sacred liturgy is the public worship which our Redeemer as Head of the Church renders to the heavenly Father, and which the community of the faithful renders to its Founder and through Him to the eternal Father. It is, in short, the entire public worship rendered by the Mystical Body of Christ, that is, by the Head of His members" (Pope Pius XII).

Liturgical prayer differs in important ways from private prayer. In private prayer, individuals or groups approach God as their own fervor and their own personalities urge them. We participate in liturgical prayer not as individuals, but as members of the Lord's Church. The liturgy is the prayer of the whole Church community headed by Christ.

13. What are the chief liturgical prayers?

The chief liturgical prayers and acts of worship are: the sacrifice of the Mass; the other sacraments of the Church and the prayers associated with them; and the liturgy of the hours.

14. How is private prayer related to liturgical prayer?

Liturgical prayer, the prayer of the community, is the most important form of prayer. However, private prayer is indispensable in preparing our hearts for liturgical prayer. Private prayer, vocal and mental, nourishes the faith and love that must penetrate our participation in the liturgy.

15. What is the most excellent act of liturgical worship?

The first, highest, and central form of all Christian liturgy is the Eucharistic sacrifice, the Mass. The worship of the Church and its whole inner life has always centered on this. Through the ministry of His priests, Christ makes present in the midst of the Church the one saving sacrifice of the cross that is the world's salvation. He unites with Himself His priestly people, enabling them to offer with Him the highest sacrifice of praise to the Father.

16. What is the liturgy of the hours?

The liturgy of the hours, or "Divine Office," is a prayer of praise and thanksgiving constantly offered by the Church. Certain members of the Church have the duty to offer these prayers in the name of the whole Church: bishops, priests, deacons, and certain religious. Others are invited to take part in this public prayer of the Church. This office or liturgy is predominantly scriptural, the Psalms holding a prominent place in it.

The Divine Office "is arranged so that the whole course of the day and night is made holy by the praises of God" (SC 84). It consists of (1) an Hour of Readings, (2) Morning Praises, (3) Midday prayers, (4) Vespers, or Evening Prayers, and (5) a short Night Prayer, or Compline. The Divine Office is a treasury of scriptural, ancient, and modern prayers.

17. What are the basic characteristics of liturgical prayer?

All liturgical prayer is based on the priestly, redemptive work of Jesus Christ. He is the supreme Celebrant of all liturgical worship. Those bound to Christ through holy orders preside over the liturgy. Liturgy is always communal in nature; it is the public worship of the Church, aimed at uniting all in Christ, and calling for the proper participation of all. Liturgy is preeminently sanctifying: it is the sign and source of the true Christian spirit.

"Every liturgical celebration, because it is an action of Christ the priest and of His Body the Church, is a sacred action surpassing all others" (SC 7).

Since liturgy is the worship of Christ and all His Church, responsibility for directing this public prayer rests with those to whom Christ has entrusted the care of the Church, to the Holy Father and the bishops. All who participate are required to use the approved forms established for Church prayer. These forms rightly leave open certain parts of the liturgy to optional forms, and permit suitable elements of spontaneity. But many elements of the liturgy are designed to express the unity in faith and worship of the whole community, and it would be a disservice to the Church to alter these elements without authority to do so.

18. What is the most important form of prayer for Catholics?

The most important form of prayer for Catholics is liturgical prayer, and chiefly the prayer of the Mass. Catholics should learn to participate in this worship with intelligent devotion. Private prayer is important in itself and as a preparation for sharing in the liturgy. These private prayers should include morning and evening prayers. Morning prayers should include acts of faith, hope, and love, and a consecration of the day to the Lord. Evening prayers should include prayers of thanksgiving and of sorrow for the sins of the day. When it is possible, family groups should offer morning prayers in common.

Daily meditation is also of great importance. Those who devote fifteen to thirty minutes a day to such prayer will do much to strengthen their Christian life.

19. Should very young children be taught to pray?

Yes. Parents should be mindful that it is their responsibility and privilege to teach their children to pray. Even the very young should "learn to call upon the God who loves us and protects us, and upon Jesus, the Son of God and our brother, who leads us to the Father, and upon the Holy Spirit, who dwells within our hearts; and . . . Mary, the Mother of Jesus and our mother" (General Catechetical Directory).

The teaching of prayer should take place through experiences of prayer, through the example of prayer, and through the learning of common prayers. "The concrete example and living witness of parents is fundamental and irreplaceable in educating their children to pray. Only by praying together with their children can a father and mother — exercising their royal priesthood — penetrate the innermost depths of their children's hearts and leave an impression that the future events of their lives will not be able to efface" (Pope John Paul II).

CHAPTER 26

Liturgy: The Paschal Mystery and the Sacramental Life

Religion at its core is the quest for God. "One thing have I asked of the LORD that will I seek after; that I may dwell in the house of the LORD all the days of my life" (Ps. 27.4). All that we have learned so far is given to help us in our quest. In a special way this personal quest for God is concentrated in prayer; and our personal prayer widens out to join with that of our fellowmen in community prayer. When community prayer is the prayer of the living Church itself, gathering people into one in new ways, it becomes liturgy. Liturgy is "the full public worship performed by the Mystical Body of Jesus Christ, that is, by the Head and His members" (SC 7).

In this chapter we discuss the liturgy and Christ's presence therein, the paschal mystery, the meaning of "sacrament," the seven sacraments instituted by Christ, and the use of sacramentals in the Church.

1. Is Christ present to the Church's liturgical prayer and worship?

Yes. Christ is present in many ways to the Church's liturgical prayer and worship.

"Christ is always present in His Church, especially in her liturgical celebrations. He is present in the sacrifice of the Mass, not only in the person of His ministers, 'the same One now offering through the ministry of priests, who formerly offered Himself on the cross,' but especially under the Eucharistic species. By His power He is present in the sacraments, so that when a man baptizes it is really Christ Himself who baptizes. He is present in His word, since it is He Himself who speaks when the holy Scriptures are read in the Church. He is present, finally, when the Church prays and sings, for He promised: 'Where two or three are gathered together in My name, there am I in the midst of them' (Matt. 18.20)" (SC 7).

2. Does the Paschal Mystery of Christ penetrate the liturgy?

Yes. The Paschal Mystery is the mystery of the Lord's "blessed passion, resurrection from the dead, and glorious ascension" (SC 5). Through this mystery Christ redeemed us; and it is this mystery that is constantly celebrated in the liturgy. The liturgy has great power to sanctify because the power of Christ in His mystery penetrates the liturgical acts of the Church.

For this reason faith teaches: "The liturgy is the summit toward which the activity of the Church is directed; at the same time it is the font from which all her power flows" (SC 10), and, "It is the primary and indispensable source from which the faithful are to draw the true Christian spirit" (SC 14).

3. Is the paschal sacrifice of Jesus still offered today?

Yes. Christ's paschal sacrifice is the one sacrifice that brings salvation to the world. This sacrifice has an eternal significance. The risen Lord suffers no more, but He causes this sacrifice to be eternally present before the Father, and through the Eucharistic liturgy He makes that sacrifice present to His people on earth, enabling them to participate in this sacrifice, and to offer this perfect sacrifice with their Lord.

"But when Christ appeared as a high priest of the good things that have come, then through the greater and more perfect tent (not made with hands, that is, not of this creation) He entered once for all into the Holy Place, taking not the blood of goats and calves but His own blood, thus securing an eternal redemption. . . . For Christ has entered, not into a sanctuary made with hands, a copy of the true one, but into heaven itself, now to appear in the presence of God on our behalf" (Heb. 9.11-12, 24). "The liturgy in its turn inspires the faithful to become 'of one heart in love' (Roman Missal) when they have tasted to their full of the paschal mysteries" (SC 10).

4. What is the basic meaning of "sacrament"?

The word "sacrament" comes from the Greek "mysterion," which St. Paul uses for the mystery of God in Christ. In this mystery God redeems mankind through the visible saving act of the Son of God, who was Himself visible in our midst as the saving Lord. A sacrament then is a visible reality through which the Lord accomplishes the saving task which that visible reality signifies and promises.

Jesus further extended this principle when He established His Church, the fundamental sacrament. Through this sacrament all the riches of grace and truth gained through His death and resurrection are made accessible to His faithful. The seven specific sacraments celebrated in the Church are particular ways in which Christ sanctifies His people in the midst of the sacrament of the Church.

5. What are the seven sacraments?

The seven sacraments are visible symbols and signs instituted by Christ for His Church, through which He confers on His people grace and life.

179

The seven sacraments are: Baptism, Confirmation, Holy Eucharist, Penance, the Anointing of the Sick, Holy Orders, and Matrimony.

These seven sacraments are actions of Christ and of His Church. They are symbols and signs that one is blessed by God and saved by Christ's redeeming mercy. They are signs of faith by which we cling in worship to Christ to share the fruits of His paschal gift; they are instruments by which Christ, through the liturgical acts of His Church, in fact confers the graces symbolized by the sacraments.

6. How are visible realities made signs of grace?

Each of the sacraments has a visible, material element or elements, such as bread, wine, water, oil, or visible human actions. This factor is sometimes called the "matter" of the sacrament. Christ chose the most basic human realities; for these realities, like bread and water, have natively a powerful symbolic force which has always been recognized by mankind in its religious acts. These material acts are illumined by sacred words so that they become more clearly signs of faith and instruments of Christ's saving action on mankind. The words assigned to each sacrament are often called the "form" of the sacrament.

Thus in baptism water touches the one to be baptized. Of its nature water tends to make the parched earth teem with life; of its nature water cleanses and makes pure. But the words of Christ used in baptism make clearer the kind of life conferred and the sort of purification accomplished.

7. Does Christ Himself act in the sacraments?

Yes. It is Christ Himself who is the principal Minister in the administration of every sacrament. The sacraments are gifts of Christ through which He confers divine life and divine power through expressive signs adapted to the nature of man.

8. When is a sacrament administered or received validly?

A sacrament is administered or received validly when the full sign is present and the purpose of the sacrament is achieved. For all symbolic actions, secular as well as sacred, concern for validity is basic. When one buys a house, the symbolic act of signing a contract has certain conditions for validity. For example, it may be essential that the signature be witnessed or dated for the contract to be valid, that is, for it in fact to transfer ownership. Similarly a sacrament should always be administered in such a way that it really achieves the sacred purpose intended, and that the special gifts and graces of the sacrament are really received.

9. Are there definite conditions for the valid administration or reception of a sacrament?

Yes. It is clearly of great importance that the sacraments be administered and received validly. It is the task of the Church to state the conditions for the validity of sacraments.

For example, faithful to Scripture, the Church insists that baptism can be validly administered only with water, not with other liquids, and that only bread and wine, not other materials, can be validly used in the Eucharist. It is not that these material signs have any sacramental power in themselves. Their fruitfulness comes from the passion of Christ and His present care. But the sacramental signs are themselves sacred gifts of Christ, and we have a duty to treat them with reverent care.

It is true that God's generosity is not limited to the sacraments. If in good faith a minister should fail to administer a sacrament validly, God is able to supply in other ways the needs of those who seek Him. Still a sacrament itself is simply not administered if the conditions established by Christ personally or through His Church for valid administration are not fulfilled.

10. Should the sacraments always be administered with faith and with love?

Yes. Far more is required in administration and reception of sacraments than observance of minimal demands for validity and lawfulness. Every sacramental act is an act of worship, and should be celebrated with faith, love, and joy.

"Pastors of souls must therefore realize that, when the liturgy is celebrated, more is required than mere observance of the laws governing valid and licit celebration. It is their duty also to insure that the faithful take part knowingly, actively, and fruitfully" (SC 11).

While the ministers have a duty to celebrate the sacraments with faith and charity, the validity of the sacrament does not depend on the worthiness of the human minister. "When Peter baptizes, it is Christ who baptizes; when Paul baptizes, it is Christ who baptizes; when Judas baptizes, it is Christ who baptizes" (St. Augustine).

11. What are sacramentals?

The sacramentals are visible signs instituted by the Church to invoke God's blessing and help. As Christ chose certain visible signs through which He sanctifies His people, the Church selects certain other signs to serve divine worship and to invoke God's blessing. Sacramentals would include the use of holy water and blessed candles, and a multitude of blessings: blessings of children, mothers, the sick, of the bride at her wedding.

Sacraments and sacramentals differ in this: the spiritual efficacy of the sacramentals depends entirely on the faith and devotion of the users, while the sacraments draw their efficacy primarily from the action of the Savior Himself, extending His action through space and time to give life, to heal, to multiply the bread of life.

Many of the sacramentals, or secondary signs, such as the altar, the baptismal font, the sacred vessels, are also drawn directly into worship, supplementing the primary signs.

CHAPTER 27

The Eucharist — Center of Life

The Eucharist is at the very heart of the Church's life. In the Eucharist Christ Himself is present to His people in the paschal mystery. Rich in symbolism and richer in reality, the Eucharist bears within itself the whole reality of Christ, and mediates to us His saving work.

"At the Last Supper, on the night He was betrayed, our Savior instituted the Eucharistic Sacrifices of His Body and Blood. He did this to perpetuate the sacrifice of the cross throughout the centuries until He should come again, and so to entrust to His beloved spouse, the Church, a memorial of His death and resurrection: a sacrament of love, a sign of unity, a bond of charity, a paschal banquet in which Christ is received, the mind is filled with grace, and a pledge of future glory is given to us" (SC 47).

This chapter has two major parts. First it treats of the Eucharist itself and of its central role in Christian life. Then it treats of holy orders, the sacrament in which men are consecrated to serve the Eucharistic ministry.

THE EUCHARIST

1. What is the Holy Eucharist?

The Eucharist is a sacrament, a sacrifice, and a sacred banquet. Under the appearance of bread and wine our Savior Jesus Christ is entirely present in this sacrament, body and blood, soul and divinity. In this sacrament He offers Himself in sacrifice to the Father, and is received as spiritual nourishment.

The word "Eucharist" means thanksgiving. Our Lord in a most special way gave thanks to the Father as He offered it. Moreover, the Eucharistic sacrifice is the most excellent means we have of expressing our thanks to God.

2. Why is the Eucharist the center of Catholic life?

The Eucharist is the center of Catholic life precisely because Christ is the center of all our life. In this sacrament Christ gives Himself totally, that we might share His life and be bound together in His mystical body.

"No Christian community can be built up unless it has its basis and center in the celebration of the Most Holy Eucharist" (PO 6). "For the Most Blessed Eucharist contains the Church's entire spiritual wealth, that is, Christ Himself, our Passover and living bread" (PO 5).

3 Was the Eucharist foreshadowed in the Old Testament?

Yes. In every age God taught mankind to hope for salvation. But in the divine plan salvation was to be achieved only by the sacrifice Christ offered of Himself upon the cross, a sacrifice that is made present now in all places through the sacrifice of the Mass. The sacrifices of the old law could not of themselves bring salvation, but they could and did foreshadow the perfect sacrifice of Jesus Christ.

The Eucharist as sacrifice was symbolized in a special way in the sacrifice of the Paschal lamb, at the time God was about to lead His people from the slavery of Egypt and guide them toward the promised land. The Eucharist was represented by the manna given to sustain the people of God as they wandered through the desert to the homeland that God planned to give them.

4. When did Christ institute the Eucharist?

Jesus Christ instituted the Eucharist at the Last Supper which He celebrated with His apostles the night before He died for us. "He took bread, and blessed, and broke it, and gave it to the disciples and said, 'Take and eat, this is My body' " (Matt. 26.26). Taking a cup of wine, he said: "This cup which is poured out for you is the new covenant in My blood" (Luke 22.20). Finally, he commanded the apostles to do as He had done: that in every place bread might become His body, and wine His blood, and that through His priests He might offer in every place the perfect sacrifice to the Father. "Do this in remembrance of Me" (1 Cor. 11.24).

By offering this first Eucharistic sacrifice at the time of the paschal feast, Jesus indicated the fulfillment of the promises symbolized by the first Passover. Through the sacrifice of the cross, referred to and made symbolically and really present at this sacrificial meal, He redeemed the whole human race from the slavery of sin and made it possible for all to come to the Promised Land of heaven.

5. Was the Eucharist celebrated in the early Church?

Yes. In describing the life of the early Church, Christian writers of that time gave special attention to the Eucharist. For the Eucharist was the community's essential celebration. It signified, and kept most real, the presence of Christ in the community.

St. Luke says of the first Christians in Jerusalem: they "devoted themselves to the apostles' teaching and fellowship, to the breaking of bread and the prayers" (Acts 2.42).

6. Why is the Mass called a true sacrifice?

A sacrifice is the offering of a victim by a priest to God alone, to acknowledge his divine sovereignty and to obtain his mercy. Now the Mass is called a true sacrifice because in it our High Priest, Jesus, truly offers Himself totally to the Father. Jesus does not rise and die again every time the Eucharistic liturgy is enacted, but His one sacrifice is made present to men in every celebration of the Mass. At Mass, as on the cross, Jesus is the chief priest; and the ministerial priest serves as His instrument. It is He who is the Victim, freely offering Himself as He did on the cross, freely offering the suffering and death He endured for us.

But in the Mass His Church joins Him in the sacrifice. With Him, in obedience to Him, the Church also performs the role of priest and victim, making a total offering of itself together with Him.

7. Why do we call the presence of Jesus in the Eucharist a "real presence"?

Jesus is present to the Church in many ways. He is with the Church as she believes, prays, and does works of mercy. He is present in the activity of bishops and priests of the Church when they preach God's word, govern His people, and administer His sacraments. All these presences of Jesus are of course real. But in speaking of the "real presence" in the Eucharist we are recalling that this is the fullest and most rich presence of Jesus. Jesus is present in many ways by his action, care, and power; but the Eucharist *is* Jesus. He is totally present wherever the Eucharist is present. He is present with all his humanity and all his divinity.

Obviously Jesus does not take on a new miniature body to be present in the Eucharist. He has but one body, the body that once hung on the cross and is now at the right hand of the Father. What changes is not Jesus, or His glorious condition, but the number of places in which He is present. When bread is changed into His body, the one body of the Lord begins to be really present where there had been bread.

"Instructed in these matters and certain in faith that what seems to be bread is not bread — though it tastes like it — but rather the Body of Christ, and that what seems to be wine is not wine — though it seems so to the taste — but the Blood of Christ . . . strengthen your heart by receiving this Bread as spiritual food and gladden the countenance of your soul" (St. Cyril of Jerusalem).

8. To whom is the Eucharistic sacrifice offered?

Because the Eucharist, which makes really present the sacrifice of the cross, is the supreme act of worship, it can be offered only to God.

9. For whom is the Eucharistic sacrifice offered?

At every Mass the chief priest is Christ, and His ministerial priest must share Christ's universal saving purpose. Every Mass is offered for the salvation of all, the living and the dead.

Often the faithful ask that a Mass be offered for a special intention; for example, for one who has died, for some spiritual or temporal need, or for giving thanks to the Lord. When Mass is said for a special intention, it is in truth only a plea that part of the fruits of Christ's sacrifice might favor an intention for which one has special concern.

When a financial offering is made with the request that Mass be said for such a special intention, this is to be understood as an expression of a desire to make a sacrifice of their own, joining that small sacrifice to the Eucharistic sacrifice. By this they also contribute in a particular way to the needs of the Church and the sustenance of its ministers.

10. What is meant by Holy Communion?

Holy Communion is a sacrament in which the faithful receive Jesus as the Bread of life, as spiritual food. The Mass is both a sacrifice and a sacred banquet; Jesus is offered to the Father, and He is received as the nourishing strength of His people. Communion unites us more closely with Jesus Himself, and unites us also with all of our brothers and sisters in Christ.

Sometimes Catholics receive Communion under the form of bread alone; sometimes they receive it under the forms of both bread and wine. In either case, one receives the whole Christ.

11. Have we a duty to receive Communion?

Yes. Jesus Himself stressed that we must receive Communion to come to everlasting life. "Unless you eat the flesh of the Son of man and drink His blood, you have no life in you" (John 6.53).

The divine precept does not indicate how often one should receive Communion. The Church commands the faithful to receive Communion at least once a year, ordinarily during the paschal season. The Church also speaks of the duty to receive Communion when one is in danger of death. But one who loves Christ naturally wishes to deepen his friendship with Him by frequent reception of this sacrament.

12. Is Christ's presence in the Eucharist lasting?

Yes. The change that occurs when Christ becomes sacramentally present in the Eucharist is an enduring change. After the consecration Jesus remains bodily present as long as the appearance of bread and wine remains.

13. What are the conditions for lawful reception of Communion?

To receive the sacrament of Communion worthily one must be a bap-

186

tized Catholic in the state of grace and believe what the Church teaches about this sacrament. One conscious of having committed a mortal sin must make a sacramental confession before approaching the sacrament. One must also receive Communion with an upright intention, for example, out of love for Christ or in a desire to grow in grace and in unity with all His Mystical Body. One should not receive Communion simply because others are receiving it. The Church also directs us to abstain from food and drink (except for water and medicine) for at least one hour before Communion.

If one who has sinned gravely has a pressing need to receive the Eucharist and has no opportunity to confess, one should first make an act of perfect contrition, an act which includes in it a promise to confess as soon as possible. One who deliberately received Communion while in a state of mortal sin would commit a grave sin of sacrilege.

"Whoever, therefore, eats the bread or drinks the cup of the Lord in an unworthy manner will be guilty of profaning the body and blood of the Lord" (1 Cor. 11.27).

Reception of the Eucharist together signifies unity in faith and union with one another in the family of faith. Catholics and non-Catholic Christians are regrettably separated in many ways. For this reason non-Catholics could not be admitted to Communion in the Catholic Church except in exceptional circumstances. The local Catholic bishop is to pass judgment in each case.

14. What special gifts of God are symbolized and brought about by the Eucharist?

We receive the Eucharist under the appearance of basic, elemental foods, bread and wine. And the sacrament brings about spiritually the nourishment it symbolizes, for in it Christ provides us richly with all that we need for healing and nourishment in the life of grace. Bread and wine are also symbols of unity: the family of God is to be gathered into one by the power of the Eucharist, as many grains of wheat are gathered to make bread and many grapes are brought together to make wine. Moreover, this basic food is received as food for the pilgrim journey we make toward eternal life, and it gives us the grace and strength to come to that life.

"I am the bread of life; he who comes to Me shall not hunger, and he who believes in Me shall never thirst. . . . For My flesh is food indeed, and My blood is drink indeed" (John 6.34, 55).

"Because there is one bread, we who are many are one body, for we all partake of the one bread" (1 Cor. 10.17).

"I am the living bread that came down from heaven. If a man eats of this bread, he will live forever" (John 6.51).

15. What is the general structure of the Mass?

The Mass contains a liturgy of the Word and a liturgy of the Eucharist.

The liturgy of the Word begins with a greeting, a penitential rite, and prayers, that prepare one to hear the words of God in readings from Holy Scripture. These readings are ordinarily followed by a homily, which explains and applies the word of God to our lives, and on Sundays and great feasts by a communal act of faith.

In the liturgy of the Eucharist gifts of bread and wine (and often other gifts as well) are made; these symbolize the gift of our whole being to the Lord, and our desire to receive Him entirely. In the Eucharist prayer the words of Christ Himself at the Last Supper are spoken in His name by the priest; and Jesus makes present His whole being, and renews the one sacrifice of the cross in the midst of His people. We are called upon to remember God's great saving deeds as these realities are made sacramentally present. All express their inward participation in Christ's sacrifice by the solemn "Amen" at the end of the Eucharistic prayer. Then the Communion rite begins with the Lord's Prayer, and other prayers preparing us to receive the Lord in Communion. Afterwards there is a time for quiet prayer, or a brief prayer in common, and for a solemn blessing, after which the people are dismissed.

Sacred music often adorns the Mass. Some of the prayers of the Mass are often sung, and hymns are frequently offered.

Though the essential elements of the Mass are present wherever Mass is offered, there are a number of "rites" in the Church. In the western, or "Latin," part of the Church the Roman rite is used; in the Eastern Churches united with Rome other rites, rooted in ancient practices, are used.

16. Should Christ be worshipped in the Eucharist?

Yes. At the consecration of the Mass Christ becomes present to us. There He offers Himself to the Father, renewing in our midst the saving sacrifice of the cross. He remains permanently with us in this sacrament. Wherever the sacrament is, there is the Christ who is our Lord and God; hence He is ever to be worshipped in this mystery.

Such worship is expressed in many ways in Catholic devotion: in genuflections, in worship of Him at Benediction of the Blessed Sacrament or in private visits to the Blessed Sacrament, in Eucharistic processions of the Feast of Corpus Christi or at times of the Forty Hours Devotion. In some dioceses and religious communities perpetual adoration is maintained before the Blessed Sacrament. All these forms of worship are appropriate responses to the immense gift of Christ's presence in our midst under the appearances of bread and wine.

188

17. What is the sacrament of Holy Orders?

Holy Orders is a sacrament through which men participate in a special way in the priesthood of Christ, and are empowered by Him to perform the sacred duties of bishops, priests, and deacons.

18. How do the baptized share in the priesthood of Christ?

All the baptized share in a certain way in the priesthood of Christ. "You are a chosen race, a royal priesthood" (1 Peter 2.9-10). All are to worship God fully, consciously, and actively. As members of His Mystical Body the faithful join Him in offering the one sacrifice of the cross in its Eucharistic renewal. But the sacrament of holy orders joins one to the priesthood of Christ in a unique way.

19. Did Christ Himself institute the special office of priesthood in the Church?

Yes. In the New Testament Christ is clearly portrayed as choosing leaders for his flock and giving them powers of teaching, ruling, and sanctifying. Though the apostles had certain special gifts associated with their unique role as first leaders in the Church, they also had other roles which, by the will of Christ, were to be maintained in the Church until the end of time. There was to continue in the Church the Eucharistic sacrifice and the other sacraments. They were to proclaim the word of God with power, in ways that would make personal faith possible. In Christ's name they were to guard and rule the Church with pastoral care, effectively preserving an astonishing unity in the family of faith.

Christ gave men power to do in His name great and saving acts, such as offering the Eucharistic sacrifice and forgiving sins, which no one could do, save by the call and power of Christ.

20. What are some of the requirements for receiving holy orders?

Only a baptized male can be ordained a priest, and the sacrament must be administered by a bishop. To receive holy orders worthily one must be in the state of grace; he must have an excellent character and have the prescribed age and learning; he must intend to devote his life to the sacred ministry; and he must be called to holy orders by a bishop.

The priesthood is conferred by "the laying on of hands," together with the appointed prayers which show that this sacramental action is indeed being performed to confer priesthood.

21. Has a person who judges himself suitable for priesthood a right to receive ordination?

No Catholic ever has a *right* to holy orders. The sacrament of orders exists not for the good of the recipient, but for the good of the Church community. The Church has the right and the duty to call to the priesthood only those whom she judges right to call to this task for the good of the whole Church in accord with the will of Christ.

22. May women be ordained to the priesthood?

No. Over the centuries the Church has believed and taught not only that Jesus never ordained women, but that it was His will that only men be ordained. The Church has believed and taught this constantly as a part of the message of faith. Even the Blessed Virgin, whose role in the Church is more sublime than that of any other human person, was not called to any ministerial priestly office.

Hence the Church does not see the question of the ordination of women as one of policy. She believes she has no right or power to ordain women. She does not believe that women are in some way inferior to men, but that Christ does not call them to this particular office. Moreover, those who enter the ministerial priesthood must not see their postions as roles of power and prestige, but as calls to serve the whole people of God in the special ways Christ calls them to.

23. Have women important roles of service in the Church?

Yes. The service of women in the Church has enriched the Christian community from earliest times. A number of women served Jesus in His ministry, and Mary, His mother, shared (and continues to share) in His saving ministry more intimately than any other human person. The Church has always been blessed with women saints, who have achieved that essential greatness toward which all Church activity aims: eminent love. In the life of the Church, women have been involved in countless indispensable ways: in teaching, in administration, in care of the sick and the poor, and in many other areas.

24. Does Christ Himself act in the distinctive actions of the priest?

Yes. The priest is able to offer the Eucharistic sacrifice, to forgive sins, and the like, not out of any power native to himself as a person, but because Christ chooses to use him as an instrument of His grace. In his specifically priestly acts the priest always acts in the person of Christ; it is the power of Christ that accomplishes the profound effect of priestly acts.

"When you behold the priest offering the consecrated Bread, see in his hand the hand of Christ Himself" (St. John Chrysostom).

25. Is reception of the priesthood a permanent gift and an enduring commitment?

Yes. The priestly consecration is such that it lasts forever. The sacrament of orders touches the very being of the recipient: he belongs to Christ in an enduring way. He remains a priest even if for ecclesial or personal reasons he is dispensed or removed from the exercise of the ministry.

The sacrament of orders confers a character on the very being of the person a permanent sealing by Christ, which endows the priest with certain spiritual powers derived from, and always subject to, the supreme power of Christ.

26. What are the three grades or forms of holy orders?

Holy orders are found in their fullness in bishops, in a secondary manner in priests, and finally in the diaconate.

"Bishops enjoy the fullness of the sacrament of orders, and all priests as well as deacons are dependent on them in the exercise of authority. For the 'presbyters' are prudent fellow workers of the episcopal order and are themselves consecrated as true priests of the New Testament, just as deacons are ordained for service, and minister to the people of God in communion with the bishop and his presbytery" (CD 15).

The words bishop, priest, and deacon are used in the New Testament. However, we are not certain of the precise meaning of each of these words in New Testament passages. There is a legitimate role for historical study to determine how the ministry Christ conferred upon His apostles developed historically: how, under the guidance of the spirit of Christ, the precise relationships of the various orders developed. The Church teaches that these offices are permanent gifts of Christ to the Church.

27. Are bishops successors to the apostles?

Yes. Bishops are indeed successors to the apostles, and by the will of Christ they carry out the essential and enduring tasks of shepherding the flock. They are ministers to unity of faith, and govern the Churches to which they are assigned. They call men to the priesthood, and ordain priests; only bishops can ordain others to become bishops. Collegially they have a care for the whole Church, and in a special way they have responsibility for the local Church over which they have been assigned.

28. What are the chief functions of the priest?

Priests are ordained to continue the saving action of Christ in offering the Eucharistic sacrifice, administering the sacraments, and preaching the word of God. A priest gathers the faithful for the Eucharistic sacrifice which only an ordained priest can offer in the person and name of Christ. He is designated by the bishop to proclaim the faith of the Church and to forgive sins in the sacrament of penance. Other specifically priestly functions are praying for the Church, anointing the sick, and assisting the development within men the divine life received in baptism and by the administration of the other sacraments.

29. Is the priest called to affect the political life of society?

Yes. The priest's proclamation of the Gospel will always touch the political, social, cultural, and economic orders. In his preaching he should make clear the moral imperatives contained in the Gospel message that concern the social order. Like all Christians, the priest has a responsibility to help make the political community just.

Laymen have the more immediate role of sanctifying and ensuring the justice of earthly structures. Priests should not abuse their role in proclaiming the social message of the Church by insisting on particular political, social, or economic options, when there is more than one option in harmony with the Gospel. Because of his sacred calling, the engagement of priests in secular political activity must be limited, and guided by the judgment of their bishops.

30. What is the role of deacons in the Church?

Already in the time of the apostles the richness of the ministry of the diaconate is suggested. Deacons "serve at table," notably at the table of the Eucharistic meal. They are ministers of the charity of the Church. They are witnesses to the faith and defenders of it. They take part also in the Church's task of evangelization.

In the Western Church it became the custom to exercise the office of deacon for only a short time; it was an office filled by one who intended shortly thereafter to become a priest. The Second Vatican Council called for a renewal of the permanent diaconate.

31. What are the signs of a vocation to orders?

Only those who are called by Christ should be ordained. Signs that one may be called by Christ include the following: possession of the health, the intellectual ability, and the strengths of character required for doing priestly work faithfully; and an inner inclination to do priestly work precisely for God's glory and the salvation of all. Yet one may only offer his service to the Church. It is the task of the bishop and those he designates to assist them to comfirm the reality of vocation; and it is in Christ's name that the Church ordains those who are selected. "You did not choose Me, but I chose you" (John 15.16).

Still the whole Church has a responsibility to assist by their prayers and by their support the Church in its effort to find worthy ministers.

A priestly vocation is a call to a state of life requiring one to serve God for the spiritual welfare of others. One who feels he has a vocation should also become aware of the qualities, particularly spiritual, that he must develop and maintain. He must willingly accept the sacrifices necessary to serve well in so important an office.

32.   Why does the Church require those who would become priests to commit themselves to celibate lives?

The Church has excellent reasons for safeguarding the ancient practice of having a celibate clergy. St. Paul noted that celibacy gives one great freedom in the service of Christ and that it can deepen personal attachment to Him (cf. 1 Cor. 7.32-35). Moreover, the Church desires the priests, who preach the duty to bear the cross and to be faithful to God's commands under even the most difficult circumstances, to exhibit in their form of life a willingness to make great personal sacrifices for the Gospel. Priestly celibacy has been called an eschatological sign, a pattern of life by which the priest bears witness to his faith in eternal life. No one's rights are violated by the requirement of celibacy, for while all have a right to marry, no one is required to become a priest.

It is ecclesiastical law, not divine law, that requires celibacy in the priesthood. Hence the Church could change this practice if it found it appropriate to do so. In some eastern rites it is customary to have married men as priests, but in the western Church it became the practice to ordain only those who judged that they were willing and able to live celibate lives in the service of Christ.

CHAPTER 28

Sacraments of Initiation

Three of the sacraments — baptism, confirmation, and the Eucharist — are concerned with Christian initiation: "The three sacraments of Christian initiation closely combine to bring the faithful to the full stature of Christ and to enable them to carry out the mission of the entire people of God in the Church and in the world" (Rite of Baptism for Children).

The Eucharist, which is the center of all sacramental life, has already been treated at length in the preceding chapter. In this chapter we discuss the sacraments of baptism and confirmation.

BAPTISM

1. What is baptism?

Baptism is the first of the seven sacraments. Through this sacrament we are born to a new life; we come to share in the life of the Blessed Trinity, and so become children of God in Christ Jesus, heirs of heaven, and members of the Church. In this sacrament we are cleansed of original sin and all personal sins, endowed with faith, hope, and love, and sealed as members of Christ's kingdom.

2. How is baptism conferred?

Baptism may be administered either by pouring water over the candidate's head or by immersing the candidate in the baptismal water. While the water is applied, the celebrant speaks the baptismal formula: "N., I baptize you in the name of the Father, and of the Son, and of the Holy Spirit."

"And Jesus came and said to them, 'All authority in heaven and on earth has been given to Me. Go therefore and make disciples of all nations, baptizing them in the name of the Father and of the Son and of the Holy Spirit" (Matt. 28.18-19).

The material sign of baptism is the immersion in or pouring of water. Water is both life-giving and cleansing. The formal sign of baptism, the words spoken in baptism, signifies the kind of life given by this water, a share in the life of the Trinity; and it shows that the cleansing is from that which separates us from God, that is, from sin. Because baptism is a sacrament of Christ, it confers the gifts and graces it signifies.

Baptism is conferred most solemnly in the Easter vigil, in which the ceremonies indicate most clearly how the sacrament enables one to share in Christ's saving death and resurrection. Its celebration at other times of the year is adorned with ceremonies that recall the great realities from which it derives its power, the gifts it confers, and the eternal life it promises.

3. What are the effects of baptism?

Through baptism we share in Christ's death and resurrection. We die to sin: original sin and every personal sin is taken away, and we are given a pledge of graces sufficient to guard us from falling again into sin. We come to newness of life: by the sanctifying grace baptism gives us we share in the life of God, become children of God as brothers and sisters of Christ; the theological virtues of faith, hope, and love are infused into our hearts with the gifts of the Holy Spirit. In baptism we are sealed as belonging to Christ forever. Through this we enter the Church, become a priestly people, suited to offer sacrifice to God and to share in the other saving sacraments.

"We were buried therefore with Him by baptism into death, so that as Christ was raised from the dead by the glory of the Father, we too might walk in newness of life" (Rom. 6.4).

4. Was baptism prefigured in the Old Testament?

Yes. This first and basic sacrament was prefigured in many ways in the Old Testament. The words of Genesis that the "Spirit of God was moving over the waters" (Gen. 1.2) at the creation prefigures the baptismal gift of Christ in the "new creation" (2 Cor. 5.17) in which we begin to share Christ's life. The floodwaters in the time of Noah, that destroyed what was hostile to God but saved his elect, suggests the power of the baptismal waters to destroy sin and lead God's people to life. Especially the passage of the chosen people through the Red Sea into freedom foreshadows the gift of this sacrament.

The solemn baptismal ceremonies in the liturgy of the Easter vigil trace the symbols of baptism found in early salvation history and their fulfillment in the paschal mystery and our participation in that mystery through baptism.

5. Is baptism necessary for salvation?

Yes. Baptism is necessary for salvation. Those who are unable to receive sacramental baptism may, however, be saved by the baptism of desire or by the baptism of blood.

"Truly, truly, I say to you, unless one is born of water and the Spirit, he cannot enter the kingdom of God" (John 3.5).

6. What is baptism of desire?

Baptism of desire is an earnest will to receive baptism, a will that can ef-

195

fectively attain the fruits of the actual reception of the sacrament of baptism when one is unable to receive the sacrament itself.

Baptism of desire is most clearly present in those who, moved by grace, explicitly wish to be baptized but die before their intention can be carried out. But the desire for baptism does not always have to be explicit. Baptism of desire can be present in one who, in response to God's grace, comes to faith in God and wishes to do all that God requires. Implicitly this includes a desire to be baptized. Even those who through no fault of their own do not know Christ and His Church may receive baptism of desire if they sincerely wish to do all God wills them to do.

7. What is baptism of blood?

Baptism of blood is the reception of baptismal graces and gifts attained by dying for Christ rather than by the reception of the sacrament.

The Holy Innocents received such a baptism, as did the catechumens in the early Church who were martyred for Christ.

8. Should infants be baptized?

Yes. The Church has solemnly defined the validity of infant baptism. Church law commands Catholics to have their children baptized within the first weeks after birth.

Infant baptism is required because baptism is necessary for salvation, and charity requires that we not neglect so basic a requirement for the salvation of those dependent upon us. Catholic parents rightly wish to bring their children by baptism into the Church, the covenanted people of God. It is right that the children of believing parents should from their first days belong to "a chosen race, a royal priesthood, a holy nation, God's own people" (1 Peter 2.9).

Infant baptism was clearly practiced from the early days of the Church. Origen, writing in the third century, expressly states that the Church's tradition of baptizing infants came from the apostles.

9. Who confers the sacrament of baptism?

Ordinarily baptism is conferred by a bishop, priest, or deacon. In an emergency, however, baptism may be administered by anyone, even by a non-Catholic.

10. How does one administer emergency or private baptism?

To baptize in an emergency, when the one to be baptized is in near danger of death, it is sufficient to pour water over the head of the one to be baptized while saying: "I baptize you in the name of the Father, and of the Son, and of the Holy Spirit."

Baptism is properly a public act, a joyful entrance into the family of faith. One who has received a simple baptism at a time of emergency should be greeted by the Church community with the special ceremonies prepared for the time when they become able to come to the Church.

11. Who may receive baptism?

Any unbaptized person may receive baptism. Those who have not reached the age of discretion do not need any special dispositions to receive baptism validly; but those who are capable of doing so must have faith and a desire to be baptized in order to receive this sacrament.

It is, however, unlawful to baptize an infant without the permission of a parent or guardian.

12. What is meant by the character of baptism?

The Church teaches that baptism, like confirmation and holy orders, imprints a permanent character or sign upon the soul. This character is not a physical or visible sign; rather it bespeaks the permanence of the gifts God confers in these sacraments. The character of baptism is the sign of the permanence of the Christian vocation, and of the enduring nature of God's gift in this sacrament. Those who receive baptism are made suitable to participate all their lives in Christ's royal priesthood. Even if they fail, they can be reconciled to the Church by the sacrament of penance; baptism itself never needs to be repeated.

For this reason one who has been once baptized validly, even if one were not baptized in the Catholic Church, may not receive the sacrament again.

St. Paul speaks of our being sealed in accepting the Gospel: "In Him you also, who have heard the word of truth, the gospel of your salvation, and have believed in Him, were sealed with the promised Holy Spirit" (Eph. 1.13). "It is God who establishes us with you in Christ, and has commissioned us; He has put His seal upon us and given us His Spirit into our hearts as a guarantee" (2 Cor. 1.21-22). That is, God's calling us to Himself in Christ through baptism is a permanent call, with permanent effects.

13. How are Lent and Eastertide related to baptism?

Lent is a time of preparation for baptism. It is a time of instruction for catechumens and a time of formation, of learning conversion of heart through penitential acts, prayer, and works of love, so that one may die with Christ, die to all within oneself that is hostile to new life in Christ, and become ready for rising with Christ. Baptism is solemnly conferred in the Easter vigil liturgy, and the new life in Christ is celebrated throughout

Eastertide, and in every Sunday of the year, since each Sunday is a celebration of the Resurrection.

Lent is for all, not just for those preparing for baptism, a summons to that total conversion that is called for by baptism. Penance and conversion of heart are never completed in this life: we never reach that entire inner renewal leading us to think, judge, and arrange our entire life under the impulse of the charity revealed to us in Christ. The witness of Scripture and the life of the Church will not let us abandon corporal penances. Specific regulations for fasting and absence vary in different countries. In the United States of America all Fridays of Lent are days of abstinence, that is, days on which meat is not to be eaten. Ash Wednesday and Good Friday are days of fast as well as of abstinence. On fast days one is to abstain from solid foods except at the one full meal and the two smaller meals permitted. Fasting binds those between the ages of 21 and 59; those who have reached the age of 14 are bound by abstinence. For sufficient reasons, the faithful may judge themselves excused or seek a dispensation from these particular regulations. But we can never be excused from the duty of doing penance. Fasting and abstinence are not the only forms of penance; almsgiving and many other forms of merciful care for the unfortunate and a more intense exercise of prayer also serve conversion of heart.

14. What is a godparent?

A godparent is one chosen from the family of faith to show special care for the person to be baptized. Godparents for infants and children accept the duty to help their godchildren receive a sound formation in faith if their parents are unable or fail to do so. Every godparent is called to be a support to the faith of their godchildren through their prayer and example.

A godparent chosen by or for the one baptized should be a Catholic living the faith, of mature years (ordinarily at least sixteen years of age), and one who is able and willing to fulfill a role of spiritual concern for the one baptized. Each baptismal candidate should have at least one godparent, but may have a godfather and godmother. In special circumstances, as in the case of children of mixed marriages, a baptized and believing Christian of a separated community may serve as an additional witness to the baptism.

15. What are the baptismal promises?

The baptismal promises are pledges to remain faithful to the Gospel teaching and way of life that one is committed to in the reception of baptism. To receive baptism is to take one's place in the new and everlasting covenant. God promises us life everlasting and the means to come to that life; and we freely promise to live in faith, hope, and love.

Adults to be baptized make these promises personally; Catholic parents speak the baptismal promises for their children. But the children are themselves called to confirm these promises freely when they come to the age of discretion; they make these promises personally when they make their First Communion and at their confirmation. Every Catholic is invited to renew the baptismal promises joyfully every Easter, which is celebrated as the anniversary of baptism for every Catholic.

The name to be given at baptism should not be out of harmony with the Christian calling of the person. The name of a saint is ordinarily given. Ideally, the saint whose name is chosen should become well known to the one baptized, as a patron and friend.

CONFIRMATION

16. What is confirmation?

Confirmation is a sacrament in which, by the laying on of hands and the anointing with chrism, a baptized person receives in a special way the gift of the Holy Spirit, to enable him or her to come to Christian maturity and to be a courageous and faithful witness to faith.

"Peter and John . . . came down and prayed for them that they might receive the Holy Spirit; for it had not yet fallen on any of them, but they had only been baptized in the name of the Lord Jesus. Then they laid their hands on them and they received the Holy Spirit" (Acts 8.14-17).

17. Who administers the sacrament of confirmation?

Ordinarily the sacrament of confirmation is administered by the bishop. However, a priest may be authorized to confer the sacrament also.

"Ordinarily the sacrament is administered by the bishop so that there will be a more evident relationship to the first pouring forth of the Holy Spirit on the day of Pentecost. . . . In this way the reception of the Spirit through the ministry of the bishop shows the close bond which joins the confirmed to the Church and the mandate of Christ to be witnesses among men" (Rite of Confirmation).

18. How is confirmation administered?

In administering this sacrament the bishop (or priest) lays his hands on the one to be confirmed; he then anoints the forehead with chrism, olive oil perfumed with balsam, saying: "Be sealed with the gift of the Holy Spirit."

The laying of the hands of the bishop upon the head of the person expresses an invocation of the power and strength of the Holy Spirit. In

199

Scripture kings, prophets, and priests were anointed with oil; and this prayerful anointing occasioned the coming of the Spirit of God upon them. Oil itself was rich in significance: it was a food condiment, a beauty preparation, a medicine, an unguent for athletes, mixed with perfume it was a refreshment after bathing, and it was a sign of joy. The words spoken as the oil is placed on the forehead make clear the kind of strength, healing, and joy this sacrament is to signify; and by the power of Christ the sacrament confers what it signifies.

Other prayers, readings, and ceremonies accompany the essential sign of the sacrament. The celebrant prays that the recipient may receive the "fullness of royal, priestly, and prophetic power," and be filled with the gifts of the Holy Spirit.

19. Why is confirmation called the sacrament of the Holy Spirit?

Confirmation exists to extend to the Church of every time and place the gift of the Holy Spirit sent to the apostles on Pentecost. Many signs accompanied the coming of the Spirit. But the most notable effect was the transformation of this frightened, cowardly group of men into inspired and fearless witnesses to their Lord's resurrection and to His saving power. In confirmation we too receive the Holy Spirit, with His gift of courage and His other saving gifts.

Christ had promised to send the Holy Spirit as His most distinctive gift. "I will pray the Father, and He will give you another Counselor, to be with you for ever, even the Spirit of truth, . . . He will teach you all things, and bring to your remembrance all that I have said to you" (John 14.16-17, 26). This promise was fulfilled for the apostles at Pentecost: "And they were filled with the Holy Spirit and began to speak in other tongues, as the Spirit gave them utterance" (Acts 2.4). The promise is fulfilled for us too in the sacramental gifts of Christ.

20. How is confirmation a sacrament of Christian maturity?

Those who have been baptized are indeed transformed and given a new life; but in the life of grace, as in our natural life, there is a need for growth and maturing. The baptized still need the special gift of the Spirit as a further pledge of guidance, inspiration, courage, and growth.

"The sharing in the divine nature which is granted to men through the grace of Christ has a certain likeness to the origin, development, and nourishing of natural life. The faithful are born anew by baptism, strengthened by the sacrament of confirmation, and finally are sustained by the food of eternal life in the Eucharist" (Pope Paul VI).

Different customs have arisen concerning the time for the administration of confirmation. Some, perceiving confirmation precisely as a sacra-

200

ment of Christian maturity, and as a time for a more mature commitment to Christ, choose to have confirmation at a somewhat later age, in adolescence. Others prefer to stress that confirmation is a sacrament of initiation, and urge that it be received at an earlier age, before first Communion, since the Eucharist is the climax of initiation. The Rite of Confirmation states that for children of the Latin Church "the administration of confirmation is generally postponed until about the seventh year," yet allows that it may, for pastoral reasons, be postponed to "a more mature age." If we see the Christian life as a whole, progressing from rebirth to mature manhood in Christ, there is no difficulty in regarding confirmation, even when administered in adolescence or later, as a sacrament of initiation. On the other hand, Catholics of eastern rites confirm even infants immediately after baptism.

The sponsor for confirmation should have the traits required in godparents at baptism. In fact, it is appropriate for the baptismal godparent to be the sponsor at confirmation.

21. What are the effects of the sacrament of confirmation?

Confirmation, one of the sacraments that may be received only once, confers a permanent character: it makes a lasting difference in the life of the person who receives it. God's gift of His Holy Spirit is an unrepented gift; the power of the Spirit is made ever accessible to the one who is confirmed. The special presence of the Spirit made real in us by confirmation is a constant call to growth in Christian life. Confirmation does not bring one to maturity at once. But it is a pressing divine call toward, and a promise of divine assistance in, living our Christian vocation maturely. This gift calls us to be witnesses to Christ in the world and defenders of the faith. Those who have been strengthened by the Holy Spirit in this sacrament "are more strictly obliged to spread and defend the faith both by word and by deed as true witnesses of Christ" (LG 11). They are also more urgently called to labor to make the kingdom of God more richly present in our midst: they "are assigned to the apostolate by the Lord Himself" (AA 3).

God "has put His seal upon us and given His spirit in our hearts as a guarantee" (2 Cor. 1.22). "You shall receive power when the Holy Spirit comes upon you; and you shall be My witnesses . . . to the end of the earth" (Acts 1.8).

22. How is confirmation related to the paschal mystery?

Confirmation, like all the other sacraments, derives its effectiveness from the paschal mystery of the Lord's death and resurrection. But the chrism also signifies our sharing in the destiny of the Lord's anointed, the Christ. No Christian can grow to maturity in Christ without accepting His invitation: "If any man would come after Me, let him deny himself and take up his cross daily and follow Me" (Luke 9.23). Through bearing the cross we become able to possess also the strength of the Lord's risen life: "It is no longer I who live, but Christ who lives in me" (Gal. 2.20).

Through sharing the paschal mystery with Christ we come to possess the gifts of the spirit that were most intensely present in Christ: the gifts of wisdom, understanding, counsel, fortitude, knowledge, piety, and fear of the Lord. The indwelling spirit completes the saving work of Christ by producing in those responsive to His grace the fruits of the Holy Spirit: charity, joy, peace, patience, benignity, goodness, long-suffering, mildness, faith, continence, and chastity.

CHAPTER 29

Sacraments of Healing

"Those who approach the sacrament of penance obtain pardon from the mercy of God for offenses committed against Him, and at the same time are reconciled with the Church, which they have wounded by their sin, and which by charity, example, and prayer seeks their conversion. By the sacred anointing of the sick and the prayer of her priests, the whole Church commends those who are ill to the suffering and glorified Lord, asking that he may lighten their suffering and save them (cf. James 5.14-16)" (LG 11).

In this chapter we discuss the sacraments of penance and anointing of the sick, each of them a sacrament of healing instituted by Christ our Physician.

PENANCE

1. Did Christ in His earthly ministry forgive sins?

Yes. Christ's mission on earth was to save us from our sins, and from the many evils that flow from sin. Though He cured bodily ailments, and though His compassion for every kind of suffering was real, He used such cures as signs of a more radical moral and spiritual therapy which He desired to extend to all. The Gospels portray Him as specially declaring that He healed the body "that you may know that the Son of man has authority on earth to forgive sins" (Mark 2.10).

2. Does Christ still forgive the sins of His people?

Yes. Through the ministry of His Church He still forgives the sins of those who, moved by His grace, come to Him with contrite hearts seeking forgiveness and a renewal of the life of grace.

3. What is the sacrament of penance?

Penance is a sacrament in which sins committed after baptism are forgiven by Christ through the ministry of His priests. It is also called the sacrament of reconciliation; for in it we are restored to friendship with God, to greater peace with our brothers and sisters, and to a more profound peace within our hearts.

"Jesus said to them again, 'Peace be with you. As the Father has sent Me, even so I send you.' And when He had said this He breathed on them, and said to them, 'Receive the Holy Spirit. If you forgive the sins of any, they are forgiven; if you retain the sins of any, they are retained' " (John 20.19-23).

". . . Our Savior, Jesus Christ, when He gave to His apostles and their successors power to forgive sins, instituted in His Church the sacrament of penance. Thus the faithful who fall into sin after baptism may be reconciled with God and renewed in grace" (Rite of Penance).

4. What is the external sign of the sacrament of penance?

The external sign of the sacrament of penance is made up of those acts which exhibit it as a saving tribunal, a judgment of mercy. In this tribunal the sinner is called to confess his or her sins and to give outward expression to the inner sorrow felt for them; and the priest, in the name of Christ, pronounces his decision by the act of absolving the penitent, that is, forgiving the sins that have been confessed.

If it is necessary, the priest judges rather that the sins cannot be forgiven until the penitent is more disposed for forgiveness.

It is as Christ's minister that the priest hears the confession of guilt; the words spoken to him there are therefore guarded by the most solemn obligation of complete secrecy.

5. What are the principal acts of the penitent?

The principal acts by which the penitent expresses his repentance are: contrition, confession of sins, and satisfaction for them.

6. What is contrition?

Contrition is sincere sorrow for having offended God, and hatred for the sins which have been committed, with a firm purpose of sinning no more. Contrition must be interior, supernatural, supreme, and universal.

Contrition is interior when it comes from our heart and not merely from our lips. It is supernatural when it is grounded on motives of faith, and not merely on a natural regret for evil deeds and their unhappy consequences. It is supreme when we have such sorrow for our sins that we would suffer anything rather than separate ourselves from the love of God again by mortal sin. It is universal when we have such sorrow for every mortal sin that we have committed.

7. What is "perfect contrition"?

Contrition is called "perfect contrition" if the motive for our sorrow is true love of God, if we are sorry because we have offended the God whom we choose to love above all things. It is called "perfect," not because the quality of the penitent's act of sorrow is itself perfect, but because charity is the perfect motive for contrition. Contrition is called "imperfect" if it is based on some other motive of faith, for example, if one is sorry because one believes God, knows God is just and faithful to His word, and knows that one will be rightly punished by God if one does not turn away from sin to serve Him.

An act of perfect contrition can at once restore to the friendship of God one who has fallen into mortal sin. But one would still have the duty to confess the sin and receive absolution when it is possible to do so. Even one who has so received grace again may not, except in extraordinary circumstances, receive the Eucharist until the grave sin has been confessed and absolved.

One who has committed mortal sin must come to true repentance ("metanoia" in Greek signifies a complete change of mind, of thinking). Repentance will be sincere if it is interior, supernatural, supreme, and universal. For then one will be resolutely turning away from sinning, and turning again toward God.

Sorrow for sin implies a firm will to avoid all mortal sin in the future. This firm will is called a "purpose of amendment." If one has sincerely turned from sin to the Lord, he or she will be determined to remain in grace, and, by the strength of His grace, never to turn from Him again. The intention not to sin again does not imply certainty that our weakness will never betray us in the future; but it involves an honest intention to sin gravely no more, and a will to use the means necessary to remain in the state of grace.

8. Must we confess our sins?

The Church teaches that it is necessary by divine law to confess to a priest each and every mortal sin — and also the circumstances which make a sin a more serious kind of mortal sin — that one can remember after a careful examination of conscience. Neither sins committed before baptism nor sins that have already been confessed and absolved need to be confessed. It is not necessary to confess all venial sins. But it is wise to confess the venial sins that most impede our love of Christ and charity to our neighbors.

"Individual and integral confession and absolution constitute the only ordinary way by which the faithful person who is aware of serious sin is reconciled with God and with the Church; only physical or moral impossibility excuses the person from confession of this type, in which case reconciliation can take place in other ways" (Canon 960).

The words of Christ instituting the sacrament of penance imply that the minister of His forgiveness must discriminate wisely: "If you forgive the sins of any. . ." (John 20.23). Hence the Church judges that the minister of the sacrament must know the sins and be able to assess in some way the spirit of repentance of the penitent. It would be a sacrilege, a grave sin of abusing a sacrament of Christ, to deliberately refuse to confess a serious sin in this sacrament.

An examination of conscience is a sincere effort to call to mind any and all grave sins that we have committed since our last worthy confession, and to remember venial sins that it would be most helpful to confess. It should be undertaken prayerfully and thoughtfully, with trust in the great mercy of God.

9. Should confession be received only by those who have committed mortal sins?

No. Devout penitents frequently are guilty of no grave sins. But they fruitfully bring before Christ in this sacrament the venial sins that mar and limit their charity, taking care to be sorry for the sins they do confess.

Forgiveness for venial sins can also be obtained in other ways: by acts of contrition, by works of charity, and the like. But the sacrament does give us special graces to make possible a deeper loyalty to Christ and to strengthen us in times of trial.

There are other great advantages that confession makes possible, even when it is not obligatory. Not only do we receive that special sacramental grace of the sacrament of penance; but the time of confession becomes a time also for receiving advice and encouragement from the confessor. Often it is wise to choose a confessor with great care and regularly confess to the same person, so that the guidance we receive can be more penetrating and helpful.

10. What is meant by satisfaction for our sins?

Forgiveness for sin is an act of divine mercy which we cannot merit. But even when our sins are forgiven a certain measure of temporal punishment is due for them. That is, the commission of sin calls for doing works of penance as well as for conversion of heart. One who has committed sins will receive punishment for them in this life or in the next, unless by making satisfaction, by doing deeds of penance willingly, one imposes the punishment on oneself.

11. What is the element of satisfaction in the sacrament of penance?

The penitent must complete the penitential act by making some satisfaction for his or her sins. For this reason the priest will impose a "penance" that is to be carried out. In the early days of the Church these penances were often very severe. Today the penance is usually the saying of certain prayers that the priest judges appropriate for a particular person, although other kinds of penitential acts may be assigned.

"The kind and extent of the satisfaction should be suited to the personal condition of each penitent so that each one may restore the order which he disturbed and through the corresponding remedy be cured of the sickness from which he suffered. Therefore, it is necessary that the act of penance really be a remedy for sin and a help for renewal of life" (Pope Paul VI).

It is important that we do suitable penance for our sins. But aware of the seriousness of sin, and of the imperfection with which we do penance, it is appropriate for us also to seek some remission of the temporal punishment due to sin by gaining indulgences.

12. What is an indulgence?

An indulgence is a remission before God of all (plenary indulgence) or part (partial indulgence) of the temporal punishment due to sins that have already been forgiven. The Church has the authority given it by Christ to grant to sinners who have already repented and been forgiven their sins a share in the merits of Christ and the saints, so that the burden of temporal punishment due to sin may be removed or lightened.

The principle underlying indulgence is as old as the Church. It is based on the doctrine of the Mystical Body of Christ. All members of this Body, St. Paul wrote, should contribute to the well-being of an ailing member. Paul rejoiced that his own sufferings could benefit the Christians of Colossae, and he added: "In my flesh I complete what is lacking in Christ's afflictions for the sake of His body, that is, the church" (Col. 1.24).

To gain an indulgence, one must say the prayer or do the good deed to which the Church attaches the indulgence, be in the state of grace, and have the proper intention.

13. What is sacramental absolution?

Absolution is the act of the priest, speaking in the name of Christ, declaring and imparting the forgiveness of the Lord for our sins.

"God, the Father of mercies, through the death and resurrection of his Son has reconciled the world to himself and sent the Holy Spirit among us for the forgiveness of sins; through the ministry of the Church may God give you pardon and peace, and I absolve you from your sins in the name of the Father, and of the Son, and of the Holy Spirit" (Rite of Penance).

14. What are the effects of the worthy reception of penance?

The effects of the worthy reception of penance are: forgiveness of our sins; restoration to grace and the friendship of Christ, if we have been in the state of mortal sin; freedom from the debt of eternal punishment, if one had been in mortal sin, and freedom in part at least from the temporal punishment due to sin; assistance in avoiding sin in the future; and recovery of the merits of past good works, if by mortal sin we had lost these.

15. What would make reception of the sacrament of penance invalid and sinful?

One would receive confession invalidly if one did not have true sorrow for one's sins, if one did not intend to avoid grave sin in the future, if one culpably neglected to confess all of one's grave sins, or if one refuses to do the assigned penance for one's sins.

One who has made an invalid and sinful confession has the duty to confess this fact, to confess all the sins committed since the last worthy confession, and to seek to make the new confession with a devout will to have the sorrow and purpose of amendment required for recovering grace.

16. When should one receive the sacrament of penance?

One who has committed mortal sin should seek to receive this sacrament of reconciliation as promptly as possible. A serious Catholic will always be unwilling to live without the grace of Christ. Canon law requires that those who have committed mortal sin confess the sin and receive absolution before receiving Communion, and that those who have committed mortal sin receive this sacrament at least within a year. But it is useful and good to receive the sacrament frequently, even if one has committed no mortal sins. "This is not a mere ritual repetition or psychological exercise, but a serious striving to perfect the grace of baptism so that, as we bear in our body the death of Jesus Christ, his life may be seen in us ever more clearly" (Rite of Penance).

17. When should children receive the sacrament of penance?

The proper time for children to begin receiving the sacrament of penance is at about the age of seven years, before they receive their first Communion.

A child's introduction to penance is not to be long delayed. The first confession can be an early help in enabling children to ratify their baptismal turning to Christ in a more free and personal way. When they are well prepared, confession is no burden to children; and it provides them with precious helps in learning to acquire peace and gladness in walking in the ways of Christ before the more turbulent years of adolescence.

18. In what ways may the sacrament of penance be celebrated?

The sacrament of penance may be received either within a communal ceremony or in an individual form. Even the communal ceremony guards the important personal elements of the sacrament: the individual confesses his or her sins in private, with personal sorrow and purpose of amendment. And even the individual form guards certain community elements: it is an act in which one confesses to a priest who has been given by the bishop public authority to absolve, and it is an act of the Church's liturgy.

Communal celebration of penance involves joining other penitents in shared prayer, listening to the word of God calling us as individuals and as a community to penance, in expression of a shared spirit of repentance and of a resolve to avoid the personal and social aspects of sin. The social context helps the individual toward a more sincere personal sorrow and conversion, and prepares one for personal confession and amendment.

The individual ceremony for confession also has significant advantages. It enjoys considerable flexibility, and provides the opportunity for combining spiritual direction and pastoral guidance with the administration of the sacrament.

ANOINTING OF THE SICK

19. Did Jesus show special concern for the ill and suffering?

Yes. The Gospels regularly portray Christ ministering to the sick, and curing them. He cared for them out of compassion and love, and pointed out that such concern is a sign of the presence of the kingdom. He taught that all are called to share such concern.

20. Does Jesus still minister to those who are ill?

Yes. Christ cares for the ill and the suffering through those who out of love care for them in His name; and He personally ministers to those who are gravely ill in the sacrament of the anointing of the sick.

21. What is the sacrament of the anointing of the sick?

The anointing of the sick is the sacrament in which, through the anointing with blessed oil by the priest and through his prayers, Christ gives health and strength to the soul and sometimes to the body when we are in danger of death from sickness, accident, or old age.

Christ cared for the sick out of compassion for them in their distress. But He always saw physical healing as secondary to spiritual healing and the forgiveness of sins.

Already in the Gospels the disciples exercised a ministry to the sick. They "anointed with oil many who were sick and healed them" (Mark 6.13). The Epistle of St. James shows that this was a permanent ministry in the Church. "Is any among you sick? Let him call for the elders of the

Church, and let them pray over him, anointing him with oil in the name of the Lord; and the prayer of faith will save the sick man, and the Lord will raise him up; and if he has committed sins, he will be forgiven" (James 5.13). "This sacred anointing of the sick was instituted by Christ our Lord as truly and properly a sacrament of the New Testament" (Council of Trent).

22. Who may receive the sacrament of the sick?

All the faithful who are in danger of death from illness, accident, or old age may receive this sacrament. Reception of it should not be delayed until one is at the point of death.

Old people who are in a weak condition may be anointed even if they have no specific serious illness. Sick children may be anointed if they have sufficient use of reason to be comforted by it. A sick person should be anointed before surgery when a dangerous illness is the reason for the surgery. The sacrament may be repeated if the sick person recovers after anointing or if, during the same illness, the danger becomes more serious.

The faithful should be encouraged to ask for the sacrament as soon as they are aware of a dangerous illness, and to "receive it with faith and devotion, not misusing the sacrament by putting it off" (Rite of Anointing).

Relatives and friends of the sick have a responsibility in charity to assist them in calling the priest, or to help get them ready to receive the sacrament worthily, especially in the case of graver illnesses.

23. What is the outward sign of this sacrament?

First, there is a laying on of hands. The minister of the sacrament and any other priests who are present impart this characteristic scriptural gesture of blessing. Then the minister anoints the forehead and hands of the recipient with blessed oil saying: "Through this holy anointing may the Lord in his love and mercy help you with the grace of the Holy Spirit. (Amen.) May the Lord who frees you from sin save you and raise you up. (Amen.)" (Pastoral Care of the Sick).

The oil used for this sacrament is olive oil that has been blessed by the bishop at the Chrism Mass on Holy Thursday. It is blessed during these sacred days recalling the Lord's death and resurrection, to signify that this sacrament receives its power from the paschal mystery.

The liturgical rite for this sacrament helps to reveal the community dimensions of concern for the sick. The sacrament is administered by the priest, a leader in the community; relatives and friends of the sick person are invited to participate. After the greeting, introduction, and penitential rite, there is a Liturgy of the Word. The readings may be followed by a homily. Then the sacrament itself is administered. This is followed by a prayer for the sick person or persons. After this the Lord's prayer is recited; the sick may receive Communion, and a blessing is given.

24. What are the effects of this sacrament?

This sacrament gives the grace of the Holy Spirit to those who are sick. By this grace the whole person is helped, sustained by trust in God, and strengthened against the temptations of the Evil One and against anxiety over death. Thus the sick person is enabled not only to bear suffering bravely, but also to fight against it. A return to physical health may follow the reception of this sacrament if it will be beneficial to the sick person's salvation. If necessary, this sacrament also provides the sick person with the forgiveness of sins and the completion of Christian penance.

25. Should one be in the state of grace to receive this sacrament?

Yes. The anointing of the sick is not intended to replace the sacrament of penance. The sacrament of penance should precede the anointing, and it would be gravely wrong to receive the sacrament of anointing while one is knowingly guilty of grave sin. Still, in certain circumstances the anointing of the sick can replace penance. If the person is in grave sin and unable to receive the sacrament of penance, but is disposed to receive the gift of a sacrament because of prior acts of faith and hope and right fear of God, the sacrament of the sick brings forgiveness of even serious sin.

26. Should the sick also receive the Eucharist?

Yes. Those who are seriously ill may and should receive the Eucharist frequently.

27. What is meant by Viaticum?

Viaticum, "food for the journey," is the sacrament of the Eucharist brought to those who are not simply sick but are very near to death. The Eucharist is always the sacrament promising eternal life and resurrection from the dead. "He who feeds on My flesh and drinks My blood has life eternal, and I will raise him up on the last day" (John 6.54).

"Communion received as Viaticum should be considered a special sign of participation in the mystery of the death of the Lord and His passage to the Father" (Pastoral Care of the Sick).

CHAPTER 30

Christian Marriage: Christ and Human Love

We have found that the sacramental signs, whereby Jesus has chosen to act on us through His Church, for the most part make use of material elements — water, bread, wine, and oil. Marriage has a more sublime sign, one taken from human love. The sacramental sign is expressed in a pledge of enduring commitment. The love of a husband and wife for each other signifies God's eternal love for mankind and the love that binds together Christ and His Church.

The Church honors the married vocation, and recognizes the supreme compliment Christ has paid to marriage in giving it sacramental status. The Church proclaims marriage a sacred sign, a sacrament, an act of worship, a reminder of Christ's love, an effective means by which He acts to make human love capable of being lasting, faithful, fruitful, like His own love of the Church.

In this chapter we discuss covenant love in marriage, the relation of virginity and marriage, and the threefold good of marriage: offspring, fidelity, and the sacrament. Also treated here are the problem of broken marriages, the actions taken by the Church to guard the marriage state, and the vocation of married persons to holiness.

1. Is God Himself the Author of marriage?

Yes. "God Himself is the Author of marriage" (GS 48). He ordained that marriage should serve precious human purposes and bring great benefits to spouses.

The two accounts of creation each also contains an account of the institution of marriage by God. In the first account the blessing of procreation is stressed: "So God created man in His own image, in the image of God He created him; male and female He created them. And God blessed them, and God said to them. 'Be fruitful and multiply, and fill the earth and subdue it' " (Gen. 1.27-28). The second account stresses the goodness of conjugal love that remedies the loneliness of human persons and creates an enduring union: "Therefore a man leaves his father and his mother and cleaves to his wife, and they become one flesh" (Gen. 2.20-24).

2. Does the Old Testament prize exclusive and enduring love between spouses?

Yes. In many ways the Old Testament expresses a realization of high ideals of exclusive and enduring love. "So take heed to yourselves, and let none be faithless to the wife of his youth. For I hate divorce, says the LORD the God of Israel" (Mal. 2.15-16). Frequently the Old Testament compares the union of spouses with the covenant between God and His people, suggesting that spouses should have the faithful love God had for Israel, and that Israel owed to the Lord.

Jesus tells the Jewish people of His time that it was because of the "hardness of your hearts" (Matt. 19.8) that they were not faithful to the expectations of faithful love that God willed for spouses from the beginning. Yet many passages of the Old Testament show that this ideal was not forgotten: the portrait of the ideal wife in Proverbs, the spouses in the Song of Songs, and the picture of marriage in Tobit.

3. How does Christ's love for His Church illumine marriage?

A marriage is meant to be a covenant of generous love. The most generous and unselfish love ever seen has been that of Christ Himself, who gladly endured the cross to save His spouse, the Church. The love between Christ and His Church is the source of the grace that enables Christian marriage to imitate the Lord's love for the Church, in its indissoluble fidelity and in its loving fruitfulness.

"Husbands, love your wives as Christ loved the church and gave Himself up for her, that He might sanctify her, having cleansed her by the washing of water and with the word, that He might present the church to Himself in splendor, without spot or wrinkle or any such thing, that she might be holy and without blemish. Even so husbands should love their wives as they do their own bodies. He who loves his wife loves himself. For no man ever hates his own flesh, but nourishes and cherishes it, as Christ does the church, because we are members of His body. 'For this reason a man shall leave his father and mother and be joined to his wife, and the two small become one.' This is a great mystery, and I mean in reference to Christ and the church" (Eph. 5.25-32).

4. Is marriage a sacrament?

Yes. The marriage of two baptized persons is a sacrament. Their commitment to one another to live in a union of marital love whose charter was established by God is a sign and reminder of the love that Christ has for His Church. It is a sign that confers the grace it signifies. That is, Christian marriage is an encounter with Christ that makes effective the graces it signifies, the graces needed to make human love enduring, faithful, and fruitful, and so a suitable image of the love between Christ and the Church.

5. Does Catholic faith also honor virginity?

Yes. Catholic faith does honor virginity, or celibacy, when it is accepted

213

precisely to further God's kingdom and to bear a striking witness to faith in eternal life. Christian virginity by no means looks down on marriage, which is holy and a sacrament; but those who choose to live in virginity willingly forgo the blessings of marriage to give themselves more exclusively and with greater freedom to the Lord.

The Church salutes virginity as a more excellent vocation, although it requires a special calling by grace. A life of virginity may be lived in a religious community or in the midst of secular pursuits.

The Church sees both virginity and marriage as ways of living Christian love. Married persons are a visible sign of Christ's love for His Church and of God's love for His people. They remind of all of God's love, and of the fact that all love comes from God and should lead back to Him, for "God is love" (1 John 4.16).

Celibates for their part may forgo marriage, but they do not renounce love; they are rather witnesses in a special way to that greater love of Christ, of which marriage itself is a sign. They are reminders to all that married love, sacred as it is, is transitory and a means to that perfect love of God and one another.

6. What is meant by the "threefold good" of marriage?

The Church often speaks of the "threefold good" of marriage as a reminder that marriage is not a trivial reality, but one that serves most precious and enduring human goods. By God's design marriage is intended to promote conjugal love, to provide in a fitting way for offspring, and to serve the sacramental good.

7. What is the good of conjugal love?

Conjugal love is the love distinctive of spouses, a generous and self-giving love by which each commits himself or herself to the other until death. It is a distinctive kind of friendship, a free covenant between the spouses which pledges a mutual self-giving that is exclusive and permanent, so that each can confidently entrust all his or her life to the other. Through this love each spouse finds a remedy for the loneliness the human person can experience and helps to enrich and bring to fulfillment the life of the other. Such enduring and faithful love is made possible by the sacrament of matrimony, which draws from the power of Christ's saving love to give strength to the love of those who marry in Christ.

"Christian couples, therefore, nourish and develop their marriage by undivided affection, which wells up from the fountain of divine love, while in a merging of divine and human love, they remain faithful in body and mind, in good times and bad" (Pope John Paul II). Thus conjugal love "far exceeds erotic inclination, which, selfishly pursued, soon enough fades wretchedly away" (GS 49).

8. Does Christian faith recognize equality between spouses?

Yes. The generous and faithful love required in marriage presupposes the fundamental equality of the partners in marriage. "Firmly established in the Lord, the unity of marriage will radiate from the equal personal dignity of wife and husband, a dignity acknowledged by equal and total love" (GS 48).

Acknowledgment of such equality cannot be taken for granted even today. Christ laid the foundation for this teaching by insisting that the duties of husbands to their wives are as demanding as the duties of wives to their husbands. "Whoever divorces his wife and marries another, commits adultery against her; and if she divorces her husband and marries another, she commits adultery" (Mark 10.11-12). St. Paul adds: "For the wife does not rule over her own body, but the husband does; likewise the husband does not rule over his own body, but the wife does" (1 Cor. 7.4-5). This equality acknowledges a complementarity between husbands and wives, and a need for each to serve the other in diverse ways, so that the enduring unity of marriage, which is essential for the happiness of the spouses and the security of their children, may be guarded.

9. Why is the procreative good a great blessing to marriage?

The love of spouses rejoices in the goodness of life; it is a great joy to them when a child whose reality flows from their being and their love comes to be. "Marriage and conjugal love are by their nature ordained toward the begetting and educating of children. Children are really the supreme gift of marriage. . ." (GS 50).

"God is love" (1 John 4.8). He not only summons us into being by His love, but He also shares with us the creative power of love. This He does by making us capable of conjugal love, which is procreative. Parents "should realize that they are cooperators with the love of God the Creator, and are, so to speak, the interpreters of that love" (GS 50). Their mutual love too bursts its bonds into creativity. For this, all the living can be grateful.

This does not mean that parents should bring children into the world irresponsibly. As we have noted in an earlier chapter, Christian couples may indeed rightly reflect on the number of children they can wisely bring into this world, taking into account all relevant factors. At the same time, however, they will rule out any and all forms of artificial birth control.

10. What is the sacramental good?

Sacramentality is a gift by which marriage is made sacred; as a sign of the perpetual love between Christ and the Church, it becomes itself a covenant that is entirely indissoluble. It arises from the free consent of the spouses, who themselves minister this sacrament to each other. This free act is sealed by God's gift which makes it possible and necessary for this marriage to endure until death.

"Marriage arises in the covenant of marriage, or irrevocable consent, which each partner freely bestows on and accepts from the other. This intimate union and the good of the children impose total fidelity on each of them and argue for an unbreakable oneness between them. Christ the Lord raised this union to the divinity of a sacrament so that it might more clearly recall and more easily reflect his own unbreakable union with his Church" (Rite of Marriage).

11. Can a Christian marriage ever be dissolved?

No. The Church has firmly proclaimed and always taught that a sacramental marriage between Christians in which there has been true matrimonial consent and consummation is absolutely indissoluble except by the death of one of the partners. As a sacrament which recalls and is sanctified by Christ's undying love for the Church, Christian marriage creates a tie that endures for life, no matter what happens between the spouses.

This is the teaching of Christ in the Gospels. "So they are no longer two, but one. What therefore God has joined together, let no man put asunder" (Matt. 19.6). "Everyone who divorces his wife and marries another commits adultery, and he who marries a woman divorced from her husband commits adultery" (Luke 16.18).

The Church teaches that even nonsacramental marriages, marriages in which one or both of the partners is not baptized, cannot be dissolved by the will of the partners or by any human authority. However, God does permit in some cases the dissolution of nonsacramental marriages. In the case of married unbelievers, one of whom becomes a Christian, the Church may permit the Christian to remarry, if the unbelieving spouse refuses to live peacefully with him or her. The Church has so understood the words of St. Paul (cf. 1 Cor. 7.12-16), and has judged that in such cases God gives the Church the right to dissolve a nonsacramental marriage. This right is called the Pauline privilege.

12. Why does the Church not permit divorce and remarriage in extremely difficult cases?

It is true that marriage is often subjected to severe pressures, and that the number of those divorced and perhaps remarried outside the Church presents a grave and urgent pastoral problem. Still, the Church, faithful to the word of Christ, does not and cannot permit divorce and remarriage as a solution to these problems. This by no means implies insensitivity to the pain of persons in difficult circumstances. But the good of all husbands and wives, and the good of children generally, demands that the indissolubility of marriage be safeguarded. Precisely because they know that their marriages cannot be dissolved, married couples are supported in their efforts to triumph over the grave obstacles that can threaten every married life.

The Church as a family of faith has the duty to assist married people in problems that threaten their marriages. The Church owes strong support to those who wish to heed Christ's teaching about the indissolubility of marriage although they find this very difficult, perhaps because the human and visible reality of their marriage has been shattered.

The Church also has a duty to surround the entrance into marriage with safeguards and with pastoral helps that ensure as much as possible the lasting character of the marriage. Before a marriage the priest who is to assist at the marriage has the responsibility to see that the couple is in fact free to marry, that they receive sufficient instruction to realize the importance and dignity of the sacrament they are about to receive, and that they are aware of the purposes and the meaning of marriage, and are entering into a genuine marriage covenant. To assist in providing such pastoral care, Church law insists that a Catholic can be married validly only in the presence of a priest and witnesses.

While the Church can never permit divorce and remarriage, it does, when there are grave reasons for this, permit the separation of married partners from common life together. For in some extreme circumstances it can be imprudent for a couple to try to continue to live together. Moreover, the Church may at times judge that an apparent marriage was never a true marriage. No real marriage covenant was established if one of the partners failed to give, or was incapable of giving, free consent; or if one or both did not intend a real marriage, a bond of faithful love at least in principle open to offspring. If for any reason an apparent marriage was not a genuine marriage from the start, it may be possible to obtain from the Church an official acknowledgment of that fact in a decree of nullity. Each diocese has a matrimonial tribunal or court to hear and judge matrimonial cases. Should it be determined that one had not been validly married, genuine marriage with another partner would of course not be excluded.

13. What are "impediments" to marriage?
To guard the married state, the Church has also the right to proclaim the existence of, or to establish, impediments to marriage. An impediment is a circumstance which because of divine or Church law would cause an attempted marriage to be invalid, not to be a true marriage at all.

217

As a teacher, the Church proclaims the existence of certain barriers. For example, it teaches that impotence, when it precedes the marriage and is permanent, makes a marriage invalid by the very law of nature, and that the same natural law excludes the possibility of a valid marriage between certain very close relatives. There are other impediments the Church establishes to guard the faithful and to protect the sacredness of marriage. From these latter impediments the Church can, of course, dispense in appropriate circumstances.

14. What are the duties of one who knows that he or she is living in an invalid marriage?

A Catholic who is knowingly a partner in an invalid marriage is in reality and before God not married to his or her apparent spouse. Hence the performance of the marriage act within that union is not a sacred and holy seal of married love, but really a wrongful use of sex. Those who have seriously disobeyed divine or ecclesiastical law by entering into an invalid marriage have a duty to return to the state of grace as quickly as possible, and certainly to abstain from Holy Communion until they do so. Some solution is always possible, even in the most difficult cases. At times one must accept a considerable amount of self-denial and bear the cross generously, but God's grace is able to make even difficult burdens bearable.

Even if individuals feel that they do not now have the moral strength to do what the law of God demands of them, they ought not despair. In prayer, in faithful attendance at Mass, in doing the works of Christian love, they can with God's grace gradually acquire the courage to do with peace whatever is necessary. Pastors and diocesan marriage tribunals will try to be of assistance to those in invalid marriages. Every solution must, of course, be one compatible with Catholic teaching. It must be entirely faithful to the teaching of Christ that sacramental and consummated marriages can in no way be dissolved, or treated as though they could be dissolved.

15. Should marriage promote the holiness of the spouses and their families?

Yes. Marriage is intended above all to increase that love which is the essential meaning of holiness. "This outward expression of love in married life not only embraces mutual help, but should also extend to this, and should have this as its primary purpose, that the married partners help each other in forming and perfecting themselves daily more fully in the interior life, so that through their partnership in life they may advance ever more and more in virtue, and especially that they may grow in true love toward God and their neighbors, on which indeed 'depends the whole law and the prophets' (Matt. 22.40)" (Pope Pius XI).

"Married couples should follow their own proper path to holiness by faithful love, sustaining one another in grace throughout the entire length of their lives. They should imbue their offspring, lovingly welcomed from God, with Christian truth and evangelical virtues. . . . By such lives, they signify and share in that very love with which Christ loved His Bride and because of which He delivered Himself up on her behalf" (LG 41).

Part Four

In Christ: Fulfillment of All

CHAPTER 31

The Death of a Christian

"It is appointed for men to die once, and after that comes judgment" (Heb. 9.27).

Earthly life can be made rich with Christ's presence. Through faith and sacraments and works of love our lives are penetrated by Christ's life. Still, though Christ is present to us, with the Father and the Holy Spirit, the divine presence remains veiled. For in this life "we walk by faith, not by sight" (2 Cor. 5.7). The gifts of grace give joy and energy, but also a thirst for fulfillment in ways not now possible.

At the end of time, when Christ will come to pass judgment on all, and when those who have died will rise again, the redemption of mankind will be brought to its total fullness. But this world, and the time of trial, ends for each person with death. In this chapter we speak of death, of the judgment which follows it, and of purgatory, hell, and heaven.

1. What is death?

Death is the end of our natural life in the flesh, the separation of soul and body. At death our time of pilgrimage and trial is over, and we come to God to be judged.

> "The dust returns to the earth as it was, and the spirit returns to God who gave it" (Eccle. 12.7).

2. Is death natural or is it a punishment for sin?

Death is both natural and a punishment for sin. On the one hand death is natural for human nature. Our lives are measured by time; we grow old, and death seems even appropriate after a full life. There is "a time to be born, and a time to die" (Eccle. 3.2). The natural reality of death gives urgency to our lives, and reminds us that we have but a limited time in which to shape good and meaningful lives.

But death is also a penalty for sin. Because of sin we suffer "bodily death, from which man would have been immune had he not sinned" (GS 18). God would have caused our time of trial to end in other ways; "but death spread to all men because all men sinned" (Rom. 5.12). Death as we now experience it is not merely a liberator from the burdens and limitations of earthly life, but as something we fear, the "last enemy" (1 Cor. 15.26) that will be destroyed by the all-embracing redemption of Christ. Though our souls survive death, death is more than a passing to another land or another manner of living. We are not merely souls; we are beings of flesh and blood. To die is to lose the fullness of our being, which we naturally love.

3. What do we mean by saying the soul survives bodily death?

To say that the soul survives bodily death is to say that something of our very nature, most proper to us, continues to live when our flesh is dissolved in death. The soul of a human person is not the whole person. Rather the soul is the living principle of a human being, created to give life to his body. After bodily death, this living principle continues to exist. Because of this, one can continue to live and love God, and share God's life most richly in the beatific vision, even when one's mortal flesh is dissolved.

Still, to be away from the body is not to be a full person. The departed in Christ look forward to "the resurrection of the body" (Apostles' Creed).

4. What did the Old Testament teach about death?

The Old Testament taught that there is a close relationship between sin and death. There is a general assurance that life and death are in the hands of God. But in much of the Old Testament there is not yet a clear recognition that significant personal life continued after our years on earth. A long life on earth seemed a special divine favor.

Later Old Testament writings, however, speak with a much fuller hope. "Many of those who sleep in the dust of the earth shall awake; some to everlasting life, and some to shame and everlasting contempt" (Dan. 12.2). Wisdom literature gives an even brighter picture of human immortality: "But the souls of the righteous are in the hands of God, and no torment will ever touch them. In the eyes of the foolish they seemed to have died . . . but they are at peace. For though in the sight of men they were punished, their hope is full of immortality" (Wisd. 3.1-4).

5. What does the New Testament teach about death?

The New Testament teaches that we do not perish entirely at death. Rather, we come to Christ, our Savior and Judge, when we die. This is implied by Christ's words to the Good Thief and by the words of St. Paul that express his longing to be "away from the body and at home with the Lord" (2 Cor. 5.8).

6. What is meant by the particular judgment?

The particular judgment is the judgment that takes place immediately after death. Each person appears before the Lord to receive judgment, and then enters into eternal life and the blessed vision of God, or begins to suffer eternal separation from God. However, those who have died in the state of grace, but in venial sin or in need of further satisfaction for sin will be purified in purgatory for a while before entering heaven.

Thus the Second Vatican Council recalls that of those who have died, "some . . . are being purified" and "others are in glory" (LG 49). The divine judgment is far from arbitrary. Before death each one chooses life eternal or rejects it by the free acceptance or free rejection of the divine call and gifts. God's judgment clearly indicates to us what we have made ourselves to be.

7. What is purgatory?

Purgatory is the place or state of those who have died in grace, but burdened by venial sins and imperfections, or before they have done suitable penance for their sins. In purgatory they are cleansed of these last hindrances to their entry into the vision of God.

Although the doctrine of purgatory is not explicitly taught in Scripture, Catholic teaching on purgatory is grounded on what Scripture explicitly teaches about divine judgment, on the need for holiness to enter into the vision of God, and on the reality of divine temporal punishment for sin. What was implicit in Scripture was made explicit in the teaching of the Fathers and in the early practices of the Church. From early centuries prayers for the faithful departed were encouraged and Mass was offered for them. Aware of the bonds that link us with those who have died in Christ, the Church never ceases to remember and pray for the departed.

8. What kind of suffering does the soul endure in purgatory?

Certainly the greatest pain is that of separation from God. The soul then realizes far more than it could before the infinite goodness of God, and it suffers from knowing that it is for a while impeded from the beatific vision by obstacles of its own making. The Church has no decisive teaching on the precise nature of other punishments intended to purify the souls in purgatory.

St. Augustine says that the suffering of purgatory is more severe than any earthly suffering. Yet those in purgatory have also a radical peace, for they are now sure of salvation, and know that God wills this "purgation" out of His great love for them.

9. Do those who die in infancy enter heaven?

Infants that have been baptized enter promptly into eternal life; infants who have not been baptized will certainly be treated mercifully by God. However, no one who dies without the state of grace can enter heaven.

Nonbaptized infants have not received grace by the sacrament of baptism, and seem unable to achieve grace by a baptism of desire. Hence we are not certain that they will enter the blessed vision of God.

Many theologians have taught that unbaptized infants enter limbo, a state where those who are unbaptized but who have committed no personal sins would enjoy natural happiness but not the beatific vision. God could by extraordinary mercies provide means for them to acquire grace before death. But revelation does not give us certainty on this. For this reason the Church insists that the faithful take care to have their children baptized promptly.

10. Does Catholic faith teach that there is a hell?

Yes. Following the example of Christ, the Church has always warned the faithful of the fearful reality of hell. Scripture speaks plainly of eternal punishment for grave and unrepented sin, and warns against the deliberate malice which corrupts the person from within and leads to eternal death.

A refusal to believe in hell is a refusal to take God and the moral life seriously.

When Christ spoke of hell, He spoke in compassion, to warn us away from this ultimate tragedy, this "second death" (Rev. 21.8) with its permanent separation from the everlasting life in God.

11. Is the punishment of hell unending?

Yes. The New Testament frequently refers to the punishment of hell as unending. The faith of the Church decisively teaches this.

"And they will go away into eternal punishment, but the righteous into eternal life" (Matt. 25.46).

12. What is the nature of the punishment of hell?

The most severe element of the punishment is eternal separation from God. Scripture speaks also of "the eternal fire" (Matt. 25.41) of hell. The Church does not define the nature of that fire, but it does teach that the punishment of the damned involves also a suffering caused by created realities. This too is appropriate, since they have turned toward created things in evil ways. With these there is also the pain of remorse, the self-hatred that burns sadly in those who have not loved God or neighbor.

13. Is the punishment of hell unjust?

No. Faith teaches that God is just and merciful, that no one is punished more than he or she deserves. Moreover, no one goes to hell as one predestined there by God, or accidentally, but only by deliberately and knowingly doing grave evil and persisting in that to the end. Deeds done without real freedom, or without sufficient understanding of their malice, do not merit eternal damnation.

The mystery of hell remains disturbing. We ought to dread the thought that persons created for eternal life could shape their wills to unending rejection of God. But it is human malice, not divine harshness, that makes hell necessary. And it is our comfort that the Son of God chose to die on the cross to save from such punishment all who would be willing to choose everlasting life.

14. Do those who die in grace enter promptly into heaven?
Yes. The Church teaches that those who die in grace will enter promptly into the presence of Jesus and the beatific vision of the Blessed Trinity. Those who die in grace, but with venial sins, or who have not done sufficient penance for their sins, will first need a time of purifying. But those who die in grace may die in peace. They are entering into life.

Many gifts of Christ help the faithful to be prepared te enter heaven promptly after death. All should see to it that the dying have access to the sacrament of penance (reconciliation), and that of anointing; and that they are given Communion as Viaticum, that is, as food for the journey. The dying should be surrounded by the strengthening prayers of the Church.
Go forth, Christian soul.
May you live in peace this day. . . .
May holy Mary, the angels, and all the saints
come to meet you as you go forth from this life.
May Christ who was crucified for you
bring you freedom and peace. . . .
May you see your Redeemer face to face
and enjoy the sight of God for ever
(Pastoral Care of the Sick).

15. Is entrance into eternal life at death the final state of those who are saved?
Entrance into the eternal life of the Father, the Son, and the Holy Spirit, and into the company of the angels and saints brings one to an essentially perfect happiness. Yet the blessedness of those who have thus come to life is still not totally fulfilled. They await the resurrection of their bodies, the glorification of Jesus in his glorious last coming, and the gathering into total newness of life of the full number of all the redeemed.

16. What is the communion of saints?
The communion of saints is the union of love and spiritual help that

227

binds together all those who belong to Christ: the faithful living on earth, the blessed in heaven, and those suffering in purgatory. Our union with those we love "who have gone to sleep in the peace of Christ is not in the least interrupted" (LG 49). The saints in heaven intercede for us; we pray for those in purgatory; the ties of love bind together all the members of Christ until the final resurrection and the final judgment when all will be made perfect in God.

CHAPTER 32

The Fulfillment of All

"Here we have no lasting city, but we seek the city which is to come" (Heb. 13.14). Salvation history aims at a final fulfillment. Even now the work of Christ goes on in the world. Already the kingdom of God has begun to appear; already it grows. But it awaits a decisive act of God, a deed of Christ, to bring to completion the work He has begun in us. Christian faith is not waiting for a final catastrophe to mark the end of time; rather, it looks forward with confidence to God's total deliverance of His people into perfect freedom and complete fullness of life.

In this chapter we discuss the elements that enter into this crowning of God's glory in Christ: the end of history as it now is, and the transformation of the world by God; Christ's second coming, the resurrection of the body, the final judgment, and the life to come.

1. Will this world come to an end?

Yes. This world as we know it, and the course of history as it has been experienced, will come to an end.

> "This gospel of the kingdom will be preached throughout the whole world, as a testimony to all nations; and then the end will come" (Matt. 24.14).

2. Will the end of the world be destructive and frightening?

To say that the world will end is not to say that the earth and all the good fruits of nature and of our own work will be destroyed. "As deformed by sin, the shape of this world will pass away" (GS 39). All that is unworthy of the final glory of God's loved ones will be destroyed, but all that is good and precious will be brought to full flowering.

> "After we have obeyed the Lord, and in His Spirit nurtured on earth the values of human dignity, brotherhood, and freedom, and indeed all the good fruits of nature and of our enterprise, we will find them again, but freed of stain, burnished, transfigured" (GS 39).

The last days will indeed be terrible for those who have fixed their hearts in the pursuit of evil ways and placed their hopes on what cannot possibly endure, who have refused to love God and love their brothers and sisters on earth. For these the last days will bring despair: "men fainting with fear and with foreboding of what is coming on the world; for the powers of heaven will be shaken" (Luke 21.26). But for those who have loved Christ, who have loved justice and mercy, it will be altogether different. "Now when these things begin to take place, look up and raise your heads, because your redemption is drawing near" (Luke 21.28).

The material world will itself in a certain sense participate in the paschal mystery. It too will pass through a death to a rich renewal. Some passages of Scripture stress the dying aspect: "The earth and the works that are upon it shall be burned up" (2 Peter 3.10); some stress the newness of life: "But according to His promise we wait for new heavens and a new earth" (2 Peter 3.13).

3. Are human efforts to improve a world that is passing away futile?

No. God's transformation of the world at the end of time is the completion of the merciful plan that began with the creation of the world. We were created in an imperfect world in which we could decide whether, in response to his call and grace, we wished to become worthy of eternal life in the perfect kingdom that was to come. God's mercy willed that our free acts in this life, and specifically our efforts to make this world more like the kingdom, should contribute to the building of the final kingdom.

This is one reason why our work in this world has such importance and dignity. Human efforts to put intelligence and care into the service of divine love, and into the remaking of this world, are elements in the building up of God's kingdom. Here on earth God's kingdom "is already present in mystery" (GS 39); human labor can serve the growth of that kingdom, and then "when the Lord comes, it will be brought to full flower" (GS 39).

4. How will this world be transformed?

In the transformation of the world all that is precious, all that God's love has created and human love moved by grace has nourished, will be preserved. But all that is flawed and defective, all that sin has wounded, will be removed or healed and brought to fulfillment. We shall understand God's love when we see the richness of the life that He has planned for us "from the foundation of the world" (Matt. 25.34).

Here we find the fulfillment of the Old Testament promises. All of man's ancient enemies, death, pain, sorrow will be removed. Our deepest longings, our thirst for an infinite good, will be satisfied. "Face to face" (1 Cor. 13.12) we shall see God "as He is" (1 John 3.2) in the midst of a transformed world. "God Himself will be with them; He will wipe away every tear from their eyes, and death shall be no more, neither shall there be crying nor pain any more, for the former things have passed away. . . . To the thirsty I will give water without price from the fountain of the water of life" (Rev. 21.3-4, 6).

5. Will Christ appear in glory at the end of time?

Yes. Christ Himself promised that He will come in glory as Lord and Judge. By His cross and resurrection He saved us, and the transformation of the world, the resurrection of the dead, and the beginning of a new life for redeemed mankind are the completion of His saving work.

> Catholic faith has always looked forward with confident hope to the final coming of Christ in glory. The early Christians' prayer "Marana tha," Aramaic for "Our Lord, come!" (1 Cor. 16.22), was an expression of their eager desire to see the final triumph of Christ's saving work.

> The coming of Christ in glory is called the "Parousia." The word literally means presence or arrival. The ceremonial entry of a king or triumphant conqueror into a city was called a "parousia." In this final coming Christ will be recognized as Lord of all. Those who believed in Him will be proved right; His glorification will be for all mankind the beginning of the "life of the world to come" (Roman Missal).

6. When will Christ come again?

We do not know the exact time when Jesus will come in glory. The time is known only to God, but we have been told that it will come unexpectedly, "like a thief" (2 Peter 3.10).

7. How should we interpret scriptural accounts of the last days?

We should understand these accounts, as we understand all Scripture, in accord with the teaching of the Church. The last days are often described in a vivid, imaginative language that is sometimes called "apocalyptic." Some, misunderstanding isolated texts of Scripture, have come to view the times that early Christians looked forward to with great joy as though they were bitter days of cruel destruction. Similarly, some have mistakenly come to expect a Messianic kingdom in which Christ would rule a temporal kingdom on earth for a thousand years (hence the term "millenarianism") before the final entrance into heaven. But such views are alien to faith. The Church teaches that Christ's final kingdom is associated proximately with the resurrection of the dead, with final judgment, and with the glory of His eternal kingdom.

8. What is meant by the "resurrection of the body"?

Catholic faith teaches that all who have died will rise again when Christ comes in glory. Our rising will be patterned on the resurrection of Jesus: "He who raised the Lord Jesus will raise us also with Jesus and bring us with you into His presence" (2 Cor. 4.14). In His kingdom we are called not to be simply souls or spirits, but to be fully alive, in body and in soul.

> The resurrection will be a universal resurrection. All the dead will rise again. The just will rise to glory, and the unjust shall rise to judgment.

231

9. Will we rise with the same bodies we now have?

Yes. Each will rise as the same person he or she was, in the same flesh made living by the same spirit.

> Christ's resurrection is the pattern for ours. Two points need to be stressed. One is that the body is to be the same body. The Gospels stress this element of identity: "See My hands and My feet, that it is I Myself" (Luke 24.39). The second is that the body will be transformed and penetrated with new and unending life. "Christ being raised from the dead will never die again' (Rom. 6.9); He "became a life-giving spirit" (1 Cor. 15.45).

10. What is the general judgment?

The general judgment is the final judgment of all. In the final judgment Christ vindicates God's justice and mercy, judges all human persons rightly on the basis of the love that they have shown, and initiates the new life of the everlasting kingdom.

> This will be the crowning act of Christ as Savior. Through it He will complete His works as Redeemer, because through it He will accomplish His Father's will that all might be made one, that all who are willing to come to life might be gathered into the final kingdom.

> Christ's goodness will shine even in the condemnation of those who have refused to come to life. His just sentence will recognize and confirm their own deliberate and definitive rejection of God. Love had earnestly called them to eternal life, a life that could be grasped only freely; and they chose not to accept it.

11. What does it mean to enter heaven?

To enter heaven is to come to the fullness of life. The richest graces of this life are but a seed, a promise, that points toward the richness of life there. We shall have faith no more, for now we shall see God as He is; we shall hope no more, for the promises of God will be completely fulfilled. And we shall love with a freedom and a fullness that exceeds our present comprehension.

> Faith then does not inquire into where heaven is. Jesus has risen bodily, and where His living humanity is it is good for those who love Him to be. The scriptural expectation of "new heavens and a new earth" (2 Peter 3.13) suggest that in the age to come the whole renewed universe will be heaven to those who have loved God and dwell in His light.

12. What is the greatest joy of heaven?

The greatest joy of heaven is the possession of God Himself, in whom we find every good and the fullness of peace. Those who enter heaven do

.ot merely see God. God brings those who come to eternal life to share intensely in His inner life: "Enter into the joy of your Master" (Matt. 25.21). We enter into the life of the true God, the Blessed Trinity, the pattern of all love. We shall taste the joy of the divine Persons when we give ourselves to the Father and the Son and the Holy Spirit, when God has strengthened and transformed our love.

> "Nevertheless I am continually with You; You hold my right hand. You guide me with Your counsel, and afterward You will receive me to glory. Whom have I in heaven but You? And there is nothing upon earth that I desire besides You. . . . But God is the strength of my heart and my portion forever" (Ps. 73.23-26).

13. What are the other joys of eternal life?

Though it is beyond our power to grasp or speak adequately of the life that is to come, divine revelation suggests some of the elements of this life. It will be a life of interpersonal love. We shall remain persons, personally sharing the intense love of the personal God, enabled by Him to love one another intensely. Heaven is not the dissolution of our personal individuality into some vast divine substance. Rather, Scripture speaks of heaven under the image of the joyful personal celebration of a banquet and often of a wedding meal, at which Christ is Bridegroom. Persons and personal love endure forever.

The life of heaven will be a full, free, dynamic life. When we enter into the joy of the Lord we begin to live with a vital gladness and freshness that can never become weary.

Then our life will be filled with every kind of goodness. It will be a life purified from all the sorrows that we have experienced on earth.

> "What no eye has seen, nor ear heard, nor the heart of man has conceived, what God has prepared for those who love Him" (1 Cor. 2.9).

14. Will heaven seem strange and alien to us?

No. Heaven is our native land. We are "strangers and exiles" (Heb. 11.13) until we come to that land and that Life to which our whole heart can give itself in gladness. Then in the light of God we shall know ourselves fully; only then shall we begin to know one another entirely, and be able to love one another with full hearts. We shall remember and understand all the experiences and trials of this life without regret, infinitely grateful that God has enabled us to serve Him freely and has crowned His first gifts with the second life.

> Nothing will be lost of all the precious realities we have known. In the resurrection of the flesh all whom we have loved will be restored.

233

15. Will all in heaven be perfectly happy?

In heaven each will be perfectly happy, and have all the joy that he or she can bear. But the gladness of the blessed will differ according to the measure of each one's love. "For star differs from star in glory. So it is with the resurrection of the dead" (1 Cor. 15.41-42). This difference is known and rejoiced in without jealousy.

"They feast on the abundance of Your house, and You give them drink from the river of Your delights. For with You is the fountain of life; in Your light do we see light" (Ps. 36.8-9). To this joy Christ calls every person through the promptings of His Spirit and the voice of His Bride, the Church. "The Spirit and the Bride say, 'Come.' And let him who hears say, 'Come.' And let him who is thirsty come, let him who desires take the water of life without price" (Rev. 22.17).

Appendixes

APPENDIX • I

The Bible

Throughout this catechism we have referred to the Bible and to particular sections within it. Even though it is now commonly published as a single volume, the Bible actually consists of a collection of sacred writings, or scriptures, composed over the course of many centuries. They are entirely exceptional writings, which the Church recognizes in faith as God's special message to those whom He calls. All of the Church's teaching and preaching must be nourished and regulated by Holy Scripture. "For in the sacred books, the Father who is in heaven meets His children with great love and speaks with them; and the force and power in the word of God is so great that it stands as the support and energy of the Church, the strength of faith for her sons, the food of the soul, the pure and perennial source of spiritual life. Consequently, these words are perfectly applicable to Sacred Scripture: 'For the word of God is living and efficient' (Heb. 4.12) and it is 'able to build up and give the inheritance among all the sanctified' (Acts 20.32; cf. 1 Thess. 2.13)" (DV 21).

INSPIRATIONS AND INERRANCY

Other groups besides Christians possess and revere collections of religious literature, but the distinguishing characteristic of the Bible is its divine inspiration. Acting as the principal Author, God moved ("inspired") the human authors of the Scriptures to understand and freely will to write precisely what He wished them to write. Being God's word in this unique fashion did not keep the Scriptures from being cast in a rich variety of literary forms ranging from intricate and mystical psalm prayers to highly interpretative and often poetically formulated styles of religious historical narratives. Though common in the ancient Near East and as accurate as our contemporary equivalents, these literary forms can at times be very enigmatic to modern readers. Yet, because it is divine as well as human, the Bible achieves the varieties of communication peculiar to each of these forms free from any error regarding that which the divine Author wished specifically to express.

THE CANON OF SCRIPTURE

The dual traits of inspiration and inerrancy have been recognized and taught by the People of God since even before the Bible was completed.

237

Corresponding to these qualities of the text of Scripture, the Church possessed the ability in faith to distinguish and then to preserve and use the various parts or "books" of what came to be called the Bible. These divinely inspired works were produced over a period of more than a thousand years.

The official or standard list of these inspired writings is still referred to by the Greek word "canon," a word used among the early Christians and meaning a measuring standard or rule. The Canon of Scripture is divided into two main sections, called the Old Testament and the New Testament, and these contain the books written before and after the life of Jesus respectively. This terminology derives from the testaments or contractual agreements dominating the relationship between God and His people ratified at Sinai (the Mosaic Covenant) and at the Last Supper (the New Covenant).

CONTENT AND ARRANGEMENT

There is no universally accepted sequence which the Old Testament canon follows, although the most frequent pattern places historical materials first (within this class the first five books of the Old Testament form a special set, often called the Pentateuch, or the Mosaic books, or the *Torah*, the Law), followed by so-called wisdom or sapiential literature, and then prophetic or exhortational writings. When this division is used, the books of the Old Testament (some of which have alternative names) are typically listed in the following order:

The Pentateuch
  Genesis
  Exodus
  Leviticus
  Numbers
  Deuteronomy

The Historical Books
  Joshua (Josue)
  Judges
  Ruth
  1 Samuel (1 Kings)
  2 Samuel (2 Kings)
  1 Kings (3 Kings)
  2 Kings (4 Kings)
  1 Chronicle (1 Paralipomenon)
  2 Chronicles (2 Paralipomenon)
  Ezra (1 Esdras)

Nehemiah (2 Esdras)
Tobit (Tobias)
Judith
Esther
1 Maccabees (1 Machabees)
2 Maccabees (2 Machabees)

The Wisdom Books
Job
Psalms
Proverbs
Ecclesiastes (Qoheleth)
Song of Songs
Wisdom
Sirach (Ecclesiasticus)

The Prophets
Isaiah (Isaias)
Jeremiah (Jeremias)
Lamentations
Baruch
Ezekiel (Ezechiel)
Daniel
Hosea (Osee)
Joel
Amos
Obadiah (Abdias)
Jonah (Jonas)
Micah (Michaeas)
Nahum
Habakkuk (Habacuc)
Zephaniah (Sophonias)
Haggai (Aggeus)
Zechariah (Zecharias)
Malachi (Malachias)

A standardized order of the New Testament books is more commonly found. It begins with the four accounts of events in the life of Jesus called Gospels. The word "gospel" means "good news," a term Christianity has applied from earliest times to its Founder's presence and deeds and their saving effects. All four canonical Gospels present the "good news" in this basic sense. Differences in the evangelists' choice of material and manner of retelling it (vocabulary, sequence, inclusion of details, and the like) evidence the different readerships for which the Gospels were originally designed as well as the theological emphases of their human composers. The fifth book in the New Testament canon is the Acts of the Apostles, in which we have a historical record of the first decades of the Church. Next are the Epistles, letters of instruction and correction written to the first Christian communities by their apostolic pastors. Varying in length from the sixteen chapters of the Epistle to the Romans down to the few sentences of the Second and Third Epistles of St. John, they preserve a treasure of details about the joys and problems of the first-century Church. The last book of the New Testament, and hence of the Bible, is Revelation, known also as the Apocalypse. This is a highly symbolic depiction of the final triumph of Christ, the punishment of His adversaries, and the establishment of the just in heaven to praise and share the divine glory. The New Testament canon, then, is as follows:

Gospels: Matthew
               Mark
               Luke
               John
The Acts of the Apostles
Epistles: Romans
               1 Corinthians
               2 Corinthians
               Galatians
               Ephesians
               Philippians
               Colossians
               1 Thessalonians
               2 Thessalonians
               1 Timothy
               2 Timothy
               Titus
               Philemon
               Hebrews
               James
               1 Peter
               2 Peter
               1 John
               2 John
               3 John
               Jude
Revelation (Apocalypse)

For a period of time shortly before the rise of Protestantism in the sixteenth century certain critics questioned the canonical authenticity or divine inspiration of some parts of the Bible. To some extent at least this was a revival of questions raised in some quarters centuries earlier. The Council of Trent (Session 4, April 8, 1546) resolved any doubts in this area for Catholics by declaring that all the books of the Old and New Testaments (as listed above) were equally inspired in their entirety, a declaration reaffirmed by both the First and Second Vatican Councils. One surviving residue of the historical disagreement is reflected in Catholic authors' references to the sections that had been called into question as "deuterocanonical," while some or all of the same material is usually labeled "apocryphal" by other church groups which exclude some or all of it from their Bibles or include the parts they consider noncanonical in separate appendixes. The word "deuterocanonical" means literally "of or pertaining to a second canon." The Council of Trent did not establish a new list of the books of the Bible, but rather it formally confirmed the canonicity of all parts of the list fixed in tradition more than a thousand years earlier. The deuterocanonical parts of the Bible are Tobit, Judith, 1 Maccabees, 2 Maccabees, Wisdom, Sirach, Baruch, and parts of Esther and Daniel, and, in the New Testament, Hebrews, James, 2 Peter, 2 John, 3 John, Jude, and Revelation.

INTERPRETATION AND USE

Just as it has the exclusive ability to distinguish which writings constitute the Bible, the Church alone possesses the means to understand and interpret Scripture infallibly. Since God chose a literature and culture already separated from us by more than nineteen centuries, continual research into the world of the human authors and their contemporaries is the indispensable cost of further insight into the sacred text. To help those without special training to read this literature, the Catholic Church has long insisted on the tradition that editions of the Bible include notes explaining unusual or disputed passages.

Moreover, because God and His Self-revelation infinitely transcend and surpass us, His help is an absolute necessity if we are to expand our horizons, so limited by sin, apathy, and human nature itself. The use of the Bible by groups or individuals remains an occasion for God's continuous grace and enlightenment to those who avail themselves of its riches. This is why the Church so strongly urges that studying and praying from the Bible be the lifelong project of every Christian. The Catholic reads and studies the Scriptures always within the Family and Spirit of the Church. "Sacred tradition and Sacred Scripture form one sacred deposit of the word of God, which is committed to the Church. . . . The task of authentically interpreting the word of God, whether written or handed on, has been entrusted exclusively to the living teaching office (magisterium) of the Church, whose authority is exercised in the name of Jesus Christ. This teaching office is not above the word of God, but serves it, teaching only what has been handed on, listening to it devoutly, guarding it scrupulously, and explaining it faithfully in accord with a divine commission and with the help of the Holy Spirit; it draws from this one deposit of faith everything which it presents for belief as divinely revealed. It is clear, therefore, that sacred tradition, Sacred Scripture, and the teaching authority (magisterium) of the Church, in accord with God's most wise design, are so linked and joined together that one cannot stand without the others, and that all together and each in its own way under the action of the one Holy Spirit contribute effectively to the salvation of souls" (DV 10).

The General Councils of the Church

A general, or ecumenical, council is an assembly of the bishops of the Church gathered together to consider and make decisions on ecclesiastical matters: on the doctrine, discipline, liturgy, and life of the Church. Decisions of a general council are binding on all members of the faithful. Church law, reflecting the teaching on the role of Peter in the Church, requires that a general council be called by and be approved by the Holy Spirit. No assembly of bishops can be a general council unless it is convoked by, or its convocation is approved by, the Roman Pontiff; no decrees or actions of a general council are effective and binding unless they are approved by the Roman Pontiff.

There have been twenty-one general councils. These are listed below with their dates. The first eight general councils were held in the Greek-speaking East; all subsequent ones have been held in the West. The first general council was held in Nicaea in the year 325; the most recent was held at the Vatican in 1962-1965. The spacing of the general councils in the history of the Church has varied widely. There were two general councils in the fourth century, two in the fifth, one in the sixth, one in the seventh, one in the eighth, one in the ninth, none in the tenth or eleventh, three in the twelfth, three in the thirteenth, one in the fourteenth, two in the fifteenth, two in the sixteenth, and then none until the latter half of the nineteenth century. A mere sixteen years separated the ninth and tenth general councils; more than three centuries elapsed between the nineteenth and twentieth.

1. First General Council of Nicaea, 325.
2. First General Council of Constantinople, 381.
3. General Council of Ephesus, 431.
4. General Council of Chalcedon, 451.
5. Second General Council of Constantinople, 553.
6. Third General Council of Constantinople, 680-681.
7. Second General Council of Nicaea, 787.
8. Fourth General Council of Constantinople, 869-870.
9. First General Council of the Lateran, 1123.
10. Second General Council of the Lateran, 1139.
11. Third General Council of the Lateran, 1179.
12. Fourth General Council of the Lateran, 1215.

13. First General Council of Lyons, 1245.
14. Second General Council of Lyons, 1274.
15. General Council of Vienne, 1311-1312.
16. General Council of Constance, 1414-1418.
17. General Council of Basel-Ferrara-Florence, 1431-1445.
18. Fifth General Council of the Lateran, 1512-1517.
19. General Council of Trent, 1545-1563.
20. First General Council of the Vatican, 1869-1870.
21. Second General Council of the Vatican, 1962-1965.

Catholic Prayers

In this appendix we include some of the most cherished prayers of the Church that are found often on the lips of Catholics.

Our Father

Our Father, who art in Heaven,
hallowed be Thy name;
Thy kingdom come;
Thy will be done on earth as it is in heaven.
Give us this day our daily bread;
and forgive us our trespasses
as we forgive those who trespass against us;
and lead us not into temptation,
but deliver us from evil. Amen.

Sign of the Cross

The Sign of the Cross is a simple and profound prayer. In part it is an action or gesture. One marks oneself with the cross to show faith in Christ's saving work. A cross is described on the body by the right hand moving from the forehead to the breast, and then from shoulder to shoulder. In the Western Church the cross stroke is made from left to right; in the Eastern Church from right to left. While tracing the sign of the cross, one says: "In the name of the Father, and of the Son, and of the Holy Spirit." This formula, which recalls the words of Christ sending His apostles to teach and baptize (cf. Matt. 28.19), expresses here an act of faith in the Blessed Trinity.

Glory Be to the Father

Glory be to the Father,
and to the Son, and to the Holy Spirit.
As it was in the beginning,
is now, and ever shall be,
world without end. Amen.

Hail Mary

Hail Mary, full of grace,
the Lord is with you;

blessed are you among women,
and blessed is the fruit of your womb, Jesus.
Holy Mary, Mother of God,
pray for us sinners,
now and at the hour of our death. Amen.

The Rosary

The Rosary is a popular form of prayer that combines meditation on the mysteries of faith with the recitation of vocal prayers. A "decade" of the rosary corresponds to each of the fifteen mysteries commemorated in the rosary. Ten Hail Marys are said for each decade; they are preceded by an Our Father and followed by a Glory Be to the Father. While reciting a decade of the rosary, one is to meditate on the particular mystery for that decade and on its meaning for our life. The entire rosary is divided into three chaplets: the joyful, the sorrowful, and the glorious mysteries. To "say a rosary" commonly means to pray one such chaplet of five mysteries. Commonly a chaplet is preceded by the recitation of the Apostles' Creed and of an Our Father and three Hail Marys, offered as a petition for an increase of faith, hope, and love. The Church has long recommended this form of prayer as a convenient and effective way of meditating on the great mysteries of our salvation.

The Joyful Mysteries
1. The Annunciation.
2. The Visitation of Mary to Elizabeth.
3. The Nativity.
4. The Presentation of Jesus in the Temple.
5. The Finding of Jesus in the Temple.

The Sorrowful Mysteries
1. The Agony of Jesus in the Garden.
2. The Scourging at the Pillar.
3. The Crowning with Thorns.
4. The Carrying of the Cross.
5. The Crucifixion.

The Glorious Mysteries
1. The Resurrection of Jesus.
2. The Ascension of Jesus into Heaven.
3. The Descent of the Holy Spirit upon the Apostles.
4. The Assumption of Mary into Heaven.
5. The Coronation of Mary as Queen of Heaven.

The Apostles' Creed

I believe in God, the Father almighty, Creator of heaven and earth.

And in Jesus Christ, His only Son, our Lord; who was conceived by the Holy Spirit, born of the Virgin Mary, suffered under Pontius Pilate, was crucified, died, and was buried. He descended into hell; the third day He arose again from the dead; He ascended into heaven, sits at the right hand of God the Father almighty; from thence He shall come to judge the living and the dead.

I believe in the Holy Spirit, the Holy Catholic Church, the communion of saints, the forgiveness of sins, the resurrection of the Body, and life everlasting. Amen.

Acts of Faith, Hope, and Love

Faith

O my God, I firmly believe that You are one God in three Divine Persons, the Father, the Son, and the Holy Spirit. I believe in Jesus Christ, Your Son, who became man and died for our sins, and who will come to judge the living and the dead. I believe these and all the truths which the Holy Catholic Church teaches, because You have revealed them, who can neither deceive nor be deceived. Amen.

Hope

O my God, trusting in Your infinite goodness and promises, I hope to obtain pardon of my sins, the help of Your grace, and life everlasting, through the merits of Jesus Christ, my Lord and Redeemer. Amen.

Love

O my God, I love You above all things, with my whole heart and soul, because You are all-good and worthy of all my love. I love my neighbor as myself for love of You. I forgive all who have injured me, and I ask pardon of all whom I have injured. Amen.

Act of Contrition

O my God, I am heartily sorry for having offended You, and I detest all my sins, because I dread the loss of heaven and the pains of hell, but most of all because they offend You, my God, who are all-good and deserving of all my love. I firmly resolve, with the help of your grace, to confess my sins, to do penance, and to amend my life. Amen.

Morning and Evening Prayers
Morning Offering
O my God, I adore You, and I love You with all my heart. I thank You for having created me and saved me by Your grace, and for having preserved me during this night. I offer You all my prayers, works, joys, and sufferings of this day. Grant that they may be all according to Your will and for Your greater glory. Keep me from all sin and evil, and may Your grace be with me always. Amen.

Evening Prayer
O my God, I adore You, and I love you with all my heart. I thank You for having created me and saved me by Your grace, and for having preserved me during this day. I pray that You will take for Yourself whatever good I might have done this day, and that You will forgive me whatever evil I have done. Protect me this night, and may Your grace be with me always. Amen.

Grace at Meals
Before Meals
Bless us, O Lord, and these Your gifts, which we are about to receive from Your bounty. Through Christ our Lord. Amen.

After Meals
We give You thanks, almighty God, for these and all the gifts which we have received from Your bounty. Through Christ our Lord. Amen.

Prayers for the Dead
Sacred Scripture reminds us that it is good to pray for the dead (cf. 2 Macc. 12.39-45). We have a special obligation to ask God's mercy on those of our parents, family members, relatives, friends, and benefactors who have gone from this world and await the final judgment of God. The Book of Psalms has a beautiful prayer (cf. Ps. 130) that the Church has long used in prayers for the departed. Christian prayers for the dead usually end with the Eternal Rest, a plea for God's mercy.

> Eternal rest grant unto them, O Lord,
> and let perpetual light shine upon them.
> May they rest in peace. Amen.

Index

cross, 66
Cyprian, St., 91
Cyril of Jerusalem, St., 185

deacon, 191, 192
death, not complete ceasing to be, 33; of a Christian, 223-228
Divine Office, 176
divisions, principal, within Christendom, 112
divorce and remarriage, 216-217

ecumenical movement, 111
envy, 166
equality, of men and women, 34
Eucharist, 64, 66, 176, 180; center of life, 183-188; instituted by Christ, 184-185; is a sacrament, a sacrifice, and a sacred banquet, 183
evil, mystery of, 37-39
existence, God's, by reason, 23

faith, what is, 93; pray for, 16, 24; gift of God, 21, 22; proclaim and defend, 131; act of, 172, 247
fasting, 198
Fatima, 107
fornication, 143
freedom, makes us like God, 33; religious, 114
fruits of the Holy Spirit, 102
Fulgentius, St., 130
fundamental option, 135, 136

Gabriel, 52
general judgment, 232
genocide, 140
gifts, of the Holy Spirit, 165, 202
Glory Be to the Father, 245
gluttony, 166
God, is Teacher of life, 15; reveals Himself as a personal God, 24; knows all things, 25; all-powerful, 25; creates all things, 27; is only One, 26; is holy, 26; is transcendent, 25; present everywhere, 25
godparents, 198
gospel counsels, 161
grace, 33, 35, 63, 120, 121, 128, 163, 218, 227; sanctifying, 164-165; actual, 166; at meals, 248
Guadalupe, 107

Hail Mary, 172, 245-246
heaven, 17; the greatest joy of, 232-233; perfectly happy in, 234
hell, 226
heresy, sin of, 111
Herod, 64
Hinduism, 113
homosexual acts, 143
hope, 132; act of, 172

Ignatius of Antioch, St., 62
Immaculate Conception, 55
impediments to marriage, 217-218
incest, 143
indissolubility, of marriage, 216
indulgence, 207
infallibility, of the pope, 101; in ordinary teaching, 99; the Christian community in, 98-99
infancy narratives, 52
infants, should be baptized, 196

Islam, 113

James, St., apostle, son of Alphaeus, 58
James, St., apostle, son of Zebedee, 58
Jesus Christ, 45; birth of, 53; public life of, 57-61; was entirely without sin, 49; is only one Person, 47; by dying He destroyed our death, 62-66; by rising He restored our life, 67-71; our Mediator, 63
Job, 38
John, St., apostle, brother of James, the son of Zebedee, 58
John Chrysostom, St., 190
John the Baptist, 53, 57, 58, 59
Joseph, St., 52, 104, 107, 108-109
Judaism, 110
Judas Iscariot, 58, 64
justice, 156
justification, 163

knowledge, of God by reason, 23; human, of Jesus, 48

Law, Code of Canon, 102
Leo, St., the Great, pope, 92
lie, 147
liturgy, 175, 176; of the hours, 176; the paschal mystery and sacramental life, 178-182
Lourdes, 107
love, of God, 133; act of, 172; conjugal, 214
lust, 143, 166

magisterium, 96, 99
Magnificat, 53, 55
marks, of the Church, 87
marriage, Christian, 212-219
Mary, mother of Jesus, 51-56; mother and model of Church, 104-109
Mass, 176, 188
masturbation, 143
matrimony, 180, 212-219
Matthew, St., apostle, 58
mediatrix, Mary, 106
meditation, 173, 174
miracles, 59
missions, historical, of the Trinity, 60
Moses, 59, 110, 120
Moslems, 113
murder, 140
mystery, 78; of Christ, 120

natural law, 126; government leaders must obey, 157
natural family planning, 143, 144, 145
Nestorius, Nestorians, 51, 54
Newman, Cardinal, 51

orders, holy, 180, 181-193
Our Father, 172, 245

parents, first, created in holiness, 35
particular judgment, 224-225
Parousia, 231
Pauline privilege, 216
peace, 157-158
Penance, 180, 203-209; rite of, 204, 207, 208
Person, only One, Jesus, 47
persons, human, are basically equal, 149, 150
Peter, St., apostle, 16, 89, 90, 100, 101, 102, 113